Bullying Scars

BULLYING SCARS

The Impact on Adult Life and Relationships

Ellen Walser deLara, PhD

OXFORD
UNIVERSITY PRESS

OXFORD
UNIVERSITY PRESS

Oxford University Press is a department of the University of Oxford. It furthers
the University's objective of excellence in research, scholarship, and education
by publishing worldwide. Oxford is a registered trade mark of Oxford University
Press in the UK and certain other countries.

Published in the United States of America by Oxford University Press
198 Madison Avenue, New York, NY 10016, United States of America.

© Ellen Walser deLara 2016

First Edition published in 2016

Library of Congress Cataloging-in-Publication Data
Names: DeLara, Ellen, author.
Title: Bullying scars : the impact on adult life and relationships / by Ellen W. deLara.
Description: Oxford; New York : Oxford University Press, [2016]
Identifiers: LCCN 2015037104 | ISBN 9780190233679 (alk. paper)
Subjects: LCSH: Victims of bullying. | Bullying—Psychological aspects.
Classification: LCC BF637.B85 D445 2016 | DDC 302.34/3—dc23
LC record available at http://lccn.loc.gov/2015037104

9 8 7 6 5 4
Printed by Integrated Books International, United States of America

To Thom, with loving appreciation.

CONTENTS

CONTENTS

PREFACE

"If sharing my struggle can help even one person, then suffering through the 8th grade will feel worthwhile."

Vincenza, age 27

When people hear that my research is about bullying, everyone has a story to tell. There is a sense of urgency to convey the distress that they or their child has experienced. From the many, many accounts told to me, I know there are aftereffects of bullying in childhood lasting into adult life. This book is based on my original research with over 800 adults, and I wrote it to bring to light this important phenomenon. Most often, we would like to believe that the torment children undergo from peers, parents, and even school personnel is left behind at graduation day or when kids move out on their own. This is not the case for many. Bullying leaves its unique imprint on a person's development, and it can be felt for life. This book is a natural extension of my research with children and adolescents on the issue of peer bullying and school violence. My previous books and articles have addressed these problems that plague our schools. Over 1,200 children and teens have shared their ideas and opinions with me on how to solve the challenge of peer bullying. *And Words Can Hurt Forever: How to Protect Adolescents from Bullying, Harassment, and Emotional Violence* (2002, 2003) written with James Garbarino, highlights their concerns. Over the years, I have been privileged to be taken into their confidence. For this new book, 836 adults communicated to me the impact of bullying on their lives. Similarly, I am honored that they were willing to do so. For many, revisiting and recounting memories was an act of bravery. Remembering was not a problem; the incidents were readily available. *Bullying Scars: The Impact on Adult Life and Relationships* is the result of my research study with adults from all over the United States and from other countries.

As a result of conversations with friends, family members, and even casual acquaintances at social gatherings, I became aware of the continuing damage from bullying people take with them into adult relationships, the workplace, all of adult life. I wanted to know about the long-term association between being involved in bullying during school years and various aspects of functioning in adult life. In particular, the book explores the connections between bullying and adult relationships.

There are three defining moments in my research, writing, and teaching about bullying and its impact on children and adults. The first was when my son, then 16 years old and an excellent student and athlete, let me know that there was considerable physical bullying and violence in his very well regarded public high school. A school that the community would not have suspected contained problems of this magnitude. As a social worker and a mother I knew I had to do something to try to change the situation. So I made it my mission to do so. The second occurred after experiencing workplace intimidation and bullying myself, which eventually resulted in leaving my teaching position at a prestigious Ivy League university to pursue a PhD. The third occurred while I was working on my doctoral dissertation topic. Jerome Ziegler, who served as a mentor throughout my doctoral work, told me that whatever it was I chose to do, it should be something that would make a real difference for people at a national policy level. My own children had been bullied at school, I had been bullied in the workplace, and my mentor challenged me to take those experiences and do something that would make a difference for others who might face the same obstacles.

As the last decade has unfolded I have watched the public discourse on bullying change from trying to understand who is involved in bullying, to a focus that puts the responsibility on children to assume responsibility for changing a culture of bullying and intimidation at school, to a systems-based approach that recognizes the absolute necessity for adults, schools, and communities to take the lead in effecting change. I emphasized in my book *And Words Can Hurt Forever* that parents are often well served by finding others to share their concerns and by forming coalitions to affect change in their local schools and communities.

I have been a researcher in the area of bullying and school violence for almost 20 years. As a social worker and psychologist, I have had a private practice for over 35 years helping children, adults, couples, families, and groups. I have presented to innumerable groups of school personnel and community members on the topic of bullying and its impact on children. To write this book, I drew on my collective knowledge and experiences interviewing children, teenagers, and adults who suffered through various forms of bullying. Though I have to this point written exclusively about the consequences of bullying on children, I saw that it is time to address the impact of childhood bullying on adults. To understand their distress I listened intently to the stories of adults and relied on my education in both child and adult development to assist me in making sense of what was shared with me. I am deeply indebted to the generosity of those who volunteered to make themselves a part of this study. Mistrust of others becomes a tragic byproduct of bullying; consequently it took a great deal of courage for some people to participate. It is time to expand the conversation about bullying in childhood and adolescence to consider the long-term effects into adulthood. The trauma of bullying and harassment can leave serious and painful scars on the lives of adults. The anxiety, depression, stress, and relationship dysfunction that can come as a result of childhood bullying are serious at the individual and family level. The consequences are a national health issue and warrant our concern and attention. *Bullying Scars: The Impact on Adult Life and Relationships* addresses this widespread, yet little discussed, problem for adults.

This book is written for anyone who is interested in this phenomenon but most specifically for adults who have seen or endured bullying as a child or as an adolescent. It sets into context what happened and why adults may still experience repercussions. Anyone who has experienced bullying in any form and in any capacity—as a victim, a bystander, or a bully—will not feel alone after reading this book. Feeling alone in the experience contributes in a profound way to sad and often traumatic life-long memories. *Bullying Scars: The Impact on Adult Life and Relationships* is meant for parents, educators, anyone who has experienced bullying, and for therapists as well. They need the information to help those dealing with bullying. The book provides a critical view into the actual lived events of those involved in this childhood phenomenon. As adults, we are likely to forget or to be in denial about childhood incidents. We like to believe that these incidents are isolated and, after powerful childhood events are over, they carry no weight. Most importantly, the book is written in the hopes that with the understanding that the consequences of bullying last into adult lives, readers will help to prevent it.

ACKNOWLEDGMENTS

I owe a great debt of gratitude to all who participated in this research study. Without their willingness to volunteer, there would be no book at all. All very busy people, they gave generously of their time to this project because they considered it a worthy effort. Their stories are the heart of the book. I would like to thank graduate assistants Kristina Fangmann, Kristin Rabbia, Danielle Hayes, Liz Wood Leonard, and especially Anthony Dimitrion, whose help in data entry and preliminary analysis was invaluable. I also thank graduate students from the Department of Marriage and Family Therapy at Syracuse University for their aid in data collection. Thank you to Dr. Peter Vanable, chair of the Psychology Department, for his cooperation in the research project. Special thanks to Dr. Rachel Razza, Syracuse University, for invaluable collaboration and support in analyzing aspects of the data.

My thanks to Stan Wakefield, my agent, who skillfully guided the manuscript to Oxford University Press and who patiently answered my numerous questions.

I want to express much appreciation to my editor, Dana Bliss, at Oxford University Press, who was enormously helpful and understood the project from the very beginning. I want to thank him for his excellent feedback and comments—all offered in the most encouraging and palatable form, a true gift.

To Dean Diane Murphy and Syracuse University: I extend my thanks for the research leave that supported the writing of the book.

Friends and loved ones are critical to the undergirding and completion of any project like this. I thank my dear friends:

Connie Shapiro, who provided loving support and encouragement every step of the way and even directed me to her agent. She was as constant as her name.

Susan Murphy, who was interested in the research from the beginning.

Christopher Griffith, former student and now friend and colleague, for teaching me about trauma-informed cognitive-behavioral therapy.

And in memoriam:

Gerry Thomas, who was always interested in my work and wanted to hear the fullest explanation on every topic.

Jerry Ziegler, Dean Emeritus, Cornell University, for serving as mentor, colleague, and dear friend for many, many years.

My family are the most important people in my life and carried me through from the beginning. So individual thanks is required for each of them. I am truly grateful to my children:

My son, JR, for sending thoughtful blogs and other commentaries my way, for offering constant support, and for listening to every single update on the book's progress.

My son, Eric, for starting the ball rolling on this topic and for his involvement in numerous discussions on the book.

My daughter, Lynne, for everyday understanding and encouragement and for providing current examples.

My sister, Lynne Nonni, for her interest and suggestions.

My nephew, Bryan Nonni, for his perspective on this subject.

My mother-in-law, Barbara Freeman, for weekly inquiries without fail.

My Dad, Jerry Walser.

Most of all, my gratitude to my husband, Thom, without whom the work would not be started or finished. He sustained me, provided endless support, read and reread the manuscript, and provided insight and helpful comments. Importantly, he reminded me to laugh even while I was pursuing such a serious project.

I would like to acknowledge dedicated teachers everywhere who make a difference in the lives of children and especially to those who make their schools safe and secure spaces for children.

The names of those who participated in the research for this book have been changed. I am very grateful for the generosity of spirit exhibited by those who shared their experiences with me. Together, we hope that their contribution to this important endeavor will spare others from experiencing similar suffering or, at the least, allow others to know they are not alone.

INTRODUCTION

Millions of children are affected by bullying every day. We are beginning to understand the anxiety and depression that it produces for them. Now it is time to turn our attention to another aspect of this pernicious phenomenon—the impact on adults of the bullying they experienced as children. While some people seem to escape childhood bullying relatively unscathed, this is not true for many, many others. Bullying leaves behind a variety of consequences. *Bullying Scars: The Impact on Adult Life and Relationships* investigates the numerous outcomes of childhood bullying. It does this through an intensive research study I engaged in with adults of all ages who were involved with bullying or harassment in their own growing-up years.

This book is an eye-opening look at the consequences adults are still dealing with from the bullying they endured as children and adolescents. Firsthand accounts from people of all ages reveal their innermost secrets about insecurities in friendships and marriages. Feelings of mistrust in others remain intact from childhood torment while people struggle to figure out how to overcome all they went through. The book is distinctive because it conveys the voices of adults recounting their childhood experiences. Their stories paint a clear picture of those who are victimized, a clear picture of the problem of childhood bullying as it lasts for many years into adult life. The stories are insightful and they lend us wisdom we would not otherwise have. The long-term association between being involved in bullying during school years and various aspects of functioning in adult life are discussed as they were shared with me. In particular, the book explores the connections between bullying and adult relationships.

The news is replete with stories about bullying that end tragically with suicide. This makes us wonder about the other impacts of the phenomenon of bullying. The general public is beginning to have an awareness that bullying is not something that should be tolerated and that it can have disastrous effects at the time it occurs. However, most people have no knowledge about the burdens that adults who have lived through this are carrying. *Bullying Scars: The Impact on Adult Life and Relationships* brings this understanding into clear focus with numerous case studies and vignettes. In general, adult well-being is strongly correlated with childhood experiences. This trend tends to hold true in numerous studies. Children experiencing adverse occurrences show adverse adult outcomes in terms of everything from pervasive unhappiness to undesirable health outcomes including suicide (Bellis, Hughes, Jones, Perkins, & McHale, 2013; Biebl, DiLalla, Davis, Lynch, & Shinn, 2011; Meltzer, Vostanis, Ford, Bebbington, & Dennis, 2011; Ttofi, Farrington, Lösel, & Loeber, 2011). There are data trends with regard to the incidence of childhood bullying, but data trends for impact on other aspects of adult development, impact on adult relationships, and potentially "positive" consequences, as discussed in this book, are not readily available. This is due to the fact that, although researchers are beginning to study the adult impact of childhood bullying, data that reflect long-range consequences exist in only a few specific categories. Those categories are health and mental health outcomes for adults involved in bullying as children, for example. Among other issues, my data do demonstrate health and mental health issues for the participants in the research study. However, my research goes further. It explains the mistrust that adults contend with in their current relationships and how it stems from childhood bullying. It looks at some of the questionable decisions adults make based on bullying and peer mistreatment. I have found a collection of variables that illustrate the effects of bullying on adults that I call adult post-bullying syndrome. Significantly, participants in the book describe growth-producing and ultimately highly meaningful outcomes.

AN ECOSYSTEMIC PERSPECTIVE

The book takes an ecosystemic perspective because bullying is not two-dimensional. There are bullies, victims, bully/victims, and witnesses. Bullying can be circular. Over the course of a day or a week a person can be a victim, a witness, or a bully. Bullying takes place within ecosystemic contexts. It can occur in families, neighborhoods, schools, communities, or in the workplace. Systems strive for homeostasis, to stay the same. The bigger the system, the greater this is felt as an imperative. Homeostasis lends the predictability that systems require to operate and that players in the system come to count on (Von Bertalanffy, 1973). In thinking about bullying from a systemic perspective, it is important to remember that all members of any system contribute to the functioning of that system.

Some contribute actively; some contribute by being passive. Consequently, systems can allow bullying to take place either with full knowledge or inadvertently. Shunning and shaming techniques are often used or tolerated in systems to preserve their values and rules (Scott, 2000).

WHY DID PEOPLE PARTICIPATE IN THE STUDY?

Hundreds of adults were interviewed during the research for this book. People wanted to participate because they felt they had an important story to tell. Recurrent comments were: "I want to share my experience; I want the information out there so people won't feel alone" and "I want to help others." After participating, people remarked that just the opportunity to put their experiences into words was cathartic. *Bullying Scars: The Impact on Adult Life and Relationships* discusses issues of shame, trust, and feelings of revenge. It relies on trauma theory, systems theory, and attachment theory in explaining the reasons for the outcomes the participants continue to experience. These theories are intertwined throughout in a highly readable fashion.

WHAT WERE THE METHODS USED FOR THE STUDY?

During the course of several years I had the privilege to interview over 800 people at various stages of life. They ranged in age from 18 to 65. Males constituted about a quarter of all participants; females the other three-quarters. Approximately 70% were Caucasian and 30% were minority. They came from all over the United States, and some were international. I gathered the information for the book through individual interviews, focus groups, and a retrospective bullying questionnaire that I designed. Consequently, this is considered a mixed-methods study. Using a mixed-methods approach to the questions in any inquiry gives us a clearer picture of the phenomenon under investigation than a single-method approach provides. The questionnaire for the study consisted of 31 questions asking about bullying from kindergarten through to graduation from high school. Twelve of the questions were "yes–no," and 13 asked for a brief example if a "yes" was given to the preceding question. The other questions concerned demographic information. The survey instrument has a very high (.913) overall reliability rating for the impact of bullying as determined by Cronbach's alpha. All quantitative data were subjected to descriptive analysis. A computer program, SPSS 21, was used to store and manipulate the quantitative data. Descriptive statistics, cross-tabulation, and independent t-tests were used to analyze the quantitative data. The questionnaire includes queries about current functioning as well as questions about past events of bullying and sexual harassment. All the participants were asked if they thought bullying had an impact on them and if so, what it was. They were asked to explain any consequences they experience now in relationships, any impact they noticed on decisions they have made in their lives, and, importantly, if they could see any positive benefit in their lives as a result of their experiences with bullying. Time and space were provided for participants to add additional information.

Similar questions were asked using an open-ended inquiry format during the focus groups and individual interviews. The qualitative data were stored and analyzed using NVivo 10. Grounded theory was used to examine the data and search for thematic responses. Member checks and triangulation were employed to further substantiate credibility, authenticity, and coherence of the data (Greene & Caracelli, 1997; Lincoln & Guba, 1988). Following a grounded theory approach, qualitative data were classified and categorized using a constant comparative strategy (Corbin & Strauss, 2014; Glaser & Strauss, 1967; Strauss & Corbin, 1998). The data were sorted using open coding. After transcription of the focus groups and individual interviews, themes were categorized by both categorical analysis strategies and analysis of content. Categories were reduced as they moved to saturation. Axial coding was utilized to relate the original categories to subcategories. The themes that emerged in the surveys, the focus groups, and the individual interviews were similar, lending credibility to the findings. The delimited categories became the major themes presented in the book.

A word here about quantitative and qualitative data. Researchers and the public are partial to what is called "hard data." This implies data related to numbers—how many of this and how many of that. While sheer numbers do tell us something, they do not facilitate discovering the multiple meanings behind the data. Further, they do not account for particular kinds of bias in data collection. For example, numbers can seem purely rational and logical, devoid of human prejudice. However, numbers collected via any kind of survey or other research instrument cannot escape human bias simply based on what questions are asked, how questions are phrased, definitions that are given, and the sample size and population. It is one of the fallacies of quantitative data investigation that it is without certain types of bias. Qualitative research, too, has its limitations in terms of investigator bias. It is for this reason that mixed-methods research can be viewed as useful. It attempts to overcome investigator bias by hearing from the participants of any study in multiple ways. Interestingly, the thoughts of one participant in a qualitative research study are thought to capture the thoughts of numerous other people (Templeton, 1994). Templeton (1994) argues that the "truth" exists in each response, that it is available and can be discerned by a creative and savvy interviewer. She contends that all responses are valid, so the question asked of the data should not be "Which one is true? But what is the truth that contains all of these expressions?" (p. 110). Having conducted individual as well as group interviews for over 35 years, I felt prepared to establish a good working rapport with each participant and to collect data successfully using this methodology. I want to emphasize that the names of all of the participants have been changed to protect their anonymity.

As this was a retrospective mixed-methods study, participants were asked to describe events that happened to them in the past. For some, the past was not far removed. They described incidents that occurred in high school and they were college students or newly in the workforce at the time of the interviews. For others, the bullying they experienced was farther back. One of the disadvantages of retrospective studies is that there is a threat to the validity of the data in terms of recall bias. However most researchers believe the threat to bias is reduced when interview subjects are asked to remember distinct events. Of note, all who remembered bullying events could and did recall them instantly and often with a great deal of emotion. I attempted to control for recall bias by asking numerous questions about the incident cited to look for inconsistencies in the story or in its reported impact. Also, the number of participants in the study, over 800, helps to reduce any validity threat to generalizations that may be made. In this study, people were asked to report not only on bullying experiences from their past but also to assign meaning to those experiences for their current adult lives.

WHY IS THE BOOK IMPORTANT NOW?

A good deal is known at this point about the psychological impact and consequences of bullying on children. We have less information about the long-term effects on adults. Little is known about the impact of childhood bullying on adults and their relationships. *Bullying Scars: The Impact on Adult Life and Relationships* focuses on the consequences adults experience as a result of childhood bullying. The results of the study are often startling. Results indicate lifelong negative consequences for adults in terms of self-esteem. The participants also indicated that their current relationships with friends and intimate partners are affected adversely.

Of particular interest is the finding that some adults reported growth-producing outcomes in their lives from painful bullying interactions.

CHAPTER SUMMARIES

Bullying: The Parameters of the Problem into Adulthood

This chapter describes the problem of bullying and harassment and identifies the various shapes that bullying can take, for example physical, emotional, and sexual harassment. There is something of a dilemma in the field at the moment. Researchers use several different definitions of bullying, and their definitions are often different from those that children, adolescents, and adults employ. This chapter provides some definitions used by researchers as well as those used by "real people" and discusses the problem endemic to the difference. This may be called the "definition debate." The chapter also contains some statistics on the challenge of bullying and harassment at this point. It points out which theories are used to inform and shape the discussion. There is a description of systems theory as it pertains to schools and the workplace. Also, there is a brief discussion on why kids bully.

Adult Post-Bullying Syndrome

There is a great deal of discussion in the public domain about trauma—what causes it and the ensuing consequences. We are used to thinking about trauma as it relates to war, other horrific events, or physical injury to the brain. We are not used to the idea that trauma can be incurred through the everyday experiences of bullying that children face. This chapter discusses trauma, post-traumatic stress disorder (PTSD), and some of the biological changes that the brain undergoes. But it also focuses on something new. From my research, I have discovered that there is an "adult post-bullying syndrome"—not named anywhere until now, when I am identifying it in this book. There are numerous symptoms but they may include trust issues, relationship problems, people-pleasing, low self-esteem, rage, and what can be considered positive effects.

"I Was Different": The Traces That Difference Leaves Behind

One of the major reasons, if not the major reason, that someone faces bullying is due to being different. The difference may be of any kind from race to gender to income to something as inconsequential as wearing the wrong clothing on a particular day. The effects of being held out as different from others are profound. Body image problems still haunt those who were victimized. This chapter details some ways that the effects continue to impede people as well as motivate them. It elucidates the shame that people still feel regarding their difference through the vehicle of case studies and vignettes.

People-Pleasing Versus Revenge: Impact on Development

People have a variety of responses to bullying. For children, revenge is one response and might be seen in acts of school violence. Adults have their ways of exacting revenge against those who bullied them also. Some of those means are discussed in this chapter. At the other end of the continuum is "people-pleasing." Once the victim of childhood bullying, some adults try to ingratiate themselves to others, hoping this will be enough to prevent bullying and harassment now in adult life. Sometimes people-pleasing and seeking revenge reside in the same person.

Consequences in Relationships

Bullying in childhood can be responsible for negative consequences in adult friendships and intimate relationships. Issues of trust are paramount. The lack of trust starts with being bullied by peers and adults; it can move into dating violence and from there to domestic violence. Various case studies depict how people struggle to overcome their mistrust of others engendered by incidents they lived through as children. As humans we are particularly sensitive to acceptance or rejection by others. It forms the basis of trust and therefore the basis of the ability to form relationships. Discussions of trust, acceptance, rejection, and attachment and their impact on adults in their relationships are featured prominently in this chapter.

"Angry Words Echo in My Brain": Health and Mental Health Impacts

We are beginning to know something of the consequences on health and mental health for children as they are being bullied, though this information is not widely disseminated to the general public as yet. The chapter discusses the concept of adverse childhood experiences. It also deals with some of the consequences for adults on their health, mental health, and general well-being from involvement with childhood bullying. The impacts are long-term. The focus in this chapter includes both adults who were bullied and those who were the bullies.

"I Am So Self-Conscious": The Impact of Sexual Harassment

Sexual harassment is an ordinary part of the day in elementary and secondary schools. Adults have difficulty seeing how this can be a long-lasting problem for children once they grow up. Indeed, most adults think kids are not paying much attention to the phenomenon of sexual harassment at all except for when it results in a tragic outcome. This chapter provides case studies and vignettes describing, in detail, the impact of sexual harassment that has lasted well into adulthood. It also provides for discussion on sexual harassment of lesbian, gay, bisexual, transgender, and queer or questioning young people.

Does Bullying Affect Decisions?

As adults we attempt to make rational decisions. We take all kinds of factors into account, especially for anything we consider to be serious. In the interviews I did for the book, it became obvious that having been the target of bullying, or being involved in any way, led to some decisions that people were both happy about and regretted. Employment decisions can be affected by childhood bullying. This chapter talks about a variety of decisions, how they were arrived at, and the impact on people's lives today.

It Comes Home to Roost: Bullying and the Family

Bullying affects the family in a variety of ways. This chapter takes a look at some instances of bullying within the family, for example parental and sibling bullying. However it focuses primarily on the effects on parenting. Those who were bullied or involved in bullying as children have some unique responses now as they take on the role of parent in their own families. Their outlook and behaviors have been shaped by their early bullying experiences.

Is There Anything Positive?: The Unexpected Outcomes of Bullying and Harassment

Ordinary people as well as the iconic—such as Tom Cruise or President Obama—have all been the victims of bullying. What do people do with this? Are any able to turn it around for their benefit? What contributes to a positive outcome as an adult? This chapter discusses the trauma and post-traumatic stress that can result from bullying experiences, but it also discusses the concept of post-traumatic growth, a little known phenomenon. This is supported by several case examples of how people who were bullied turned their experiences into something positive for themselves once they achieved adult status.

Conclusion

This chapter sums up the most significant points of what has been presented in the book through a review of some of the subcategories of each chapter. It helps the reader to see that victims, bullies, bully/victims, and witnesses are part of a greater system such as the family, school, or community. It describes some of the actions people can take to turn the effects around in their own lives. In addition, specific therapeutic approaches are described for the treatment of lasting influences and trauma.

SUMMARY

This book brings into unobstructed focus the vestiges of childhood bullying. It features how adults cope with residual damage. Aspects of the book are unique based on compelling stories people shared. The research establishes a precedent for future research to investigate trends about the impact on adults in their relationships, on their development, on their sense of self, and on any outcomes that can be turned around for growth.

It is time to expand the conversation about bullying in childhood and adolescence to consider the long-term effects into adulthood. The trauma of bullying and harassment can leave serious and painful scars on the lives of adults. The anxiety, depression, stress, and relationship dysfunction that can result due to the effects of childhood bullying are serious at the individual and family level. The consequences are a national health issue and warrant our concern and attention. *Bullying Scars: The Impact on*

Adult Life and Relationships addresses this widespread, yet little discussed, problem for adults.

It is critical that we begin to recognize that the effects of so-called typical childhood teasing and bullying do not just go away; instead they shape development and last a lifetime. After reading this book, I would like people to understand that childhood bullying is detrimental. It cannot be considered lightly, as in "Kids will be kids." If you stop to ask and then truly listen, you will hear the accounts of many for whom childhood was a time to be endured, not enjoyed. For many, the memories of bullying are indelible. The shadows of their experiences are the basis of this book.

CHAPTER 1

Bullying

The Parameters of the Problem into Adulthood

"It takes a really mentally strong person to forget it; and I don't think most people do."

Warren, age 15

When Glenn was a little boy, he was repeatedly physically bullied by his classmates. He was thrown to the ground, and as he recounted, "The kids stepped on my chest." How terrifying this must have been for a little boy in elementary school. His recollection is that no one interrupted it; he just had to suffer through. He remembers feeling completely helpless. The abuse continued in middle school, where he was constantly called derogatory names. He had no friends and ate alone in the bathroom during lunchtime. By the time he was in high school, the bullying had pretty much stopped, because "I was already labeled a loser by then so people left me alone." He never told his parents about the ongoing peer abuse, thinking there was nothing they could do about it. Unlike many kids who are treated so poorly by their peers, Glenn did not take out his anger by bullying anyone else. What he did instead was retreat inside himself. Now at age 32, he says he likes to be alone and not having any friends is fine with him. He sees the impact on him evident in the fact that he does not trust people and he has no relationships. In terms of adult decisions, Glenn chooses work and recreational activities in which he can be alone.

Memories can be ephemeral and unreliable. However, the memories associated with bullying seem to be readily available to most of us, as if the bullying happened yesterday. These memories appear to be in a very different category of recall than other, less emotionally charged, recollections.

We may not be able to depend on our memory for the name of a movie we saw once or for directions to a restaurant we enjoyed, but even a single incident of bullying can be seared into our memories.

Bullying exists on a continuum ranging from "psychological intimidation (e.g., group exclusion, starting rumors, sexual gestures) to verbal abuse (name-calling) to physical abuse (hitting, kicking, inappropriate touching, sexual abuse) to life-threatening violence (threatening with a weapon . . .)" (deLara, 2008, p. 335). Virtually everyone has exposure to bullying. Children participate every day as witnesses, victims, or bullies or in all categories. Adults can instantaneously recall their own bullying experiences. By the time we leave high school, most everyone has witnessed some form of bullying by peers or adults. It is naïve to think that the impact of bullying is left behind us at the doors of the school. Instead we carry aftereffects. Exploring what these are and how they affect us is the premise of this book.

Most of us would like to believe that the consequences of bullying stop at high school or college graduation. That people just pick up and move on with their lives. While this may be true for a segment of the population, it is not true for everyone. There are lifelong consequences for many, many adults. What are these consequences? How do they affect adult development? What are the impacts on adult mental health? What can be seen in adult relationships? Are there *any* positive outcomes that result from the bullying that was experienced during childhood?

Think for a moment about a bullying incident that happened when you were a child. Were you bullied? You may have been a victim, a witness, a bully yourself, or all of these. Can you remember the feelings you experienced? What was your reaction then? Now, consider how incredible it is that you can remember that incident so vividly years later. Most adults can call that to mind easily, too easily for comfort.

STATISTICS

The statistics on bullying and harassment run a broad range. Early national studies concluded that 33% of children were involved in bullying (Nansel et al., 2001) while more recent studies indicate that approximately half of all students are involved (AAUW, 2011; Hinduja & Patchin, 2014; Wang, Iannotti, & Nansel, 2009). In a National Institute of Health study of students in 6th through 10th grade, 21% said they were bullied physically, 54% said they were bullied verbally, and 51% indicated they were bullied socially by being purposely excluded or ostracized (Wang et al., 2009). For gay, lesbian, bisexual, and transgender students, the statistics are even worse, as 92% report being verbally bullied and harassed at school (Kosciw, Greytak, Bartkiewicz, Boesen, & Palmer, 2012). Some researchers highlight the differences in types of bullying engaged in by boys and girls. Typically, relational violence is thought to be the province of girls while physical violence is more often seen among boys. However, both genders engage in relational and physical aggression as forms of bullying (Daniels, Quigley, Menard, & Spence, 2010; Garbarino & deLara, 2002; Pronk & Zimmer-Gembeck, 2010; Wang et al., 2009). At this time, we have a great deal of data describing the poor effects of being the target of bullying and even of being a bully. However, most studies fail to include children who witness bullying and harassment. Being a witness or bystander brings with it many adverse effects. We are only at the beginning of our understanding of the long-term outcomes for adults who were involved in bullying or sexual harassment in any way.

Cyberbullying is a relatively new means to bully, harass, and torment someone. Studies on cyberbullying also show a wide range of victimization from a low of 5% to a high of over 70% of all children and teens who spend time on any form of social media. One study of secondary school students in Canada found the majority identified another student at school as cyberbullying them, 36% said they had been cyberbullied by a friend, 13% had been cyberbullied by a sister or brother, and 48% did not know who had cyberbullied them. Further, one-third indicated that they bullied others online and that they felt funny, popular, and powerful as a result (Mishna, Cook, Gadalla, Daciuk, & Solomon, 2010). The consensus, at the time of this writing, is that somewhere between 6% and 30% of teenagers in the United States have experienced some type of cyberbullying (DeVoe & Murphy, 2011; Hinduja & Patchin, 2014; Kowalski, Limber, & Agatston, 2008; Kowalski, Morgan, & Limber, 2012; Shetgiri, Espelage, & Carroll, 2015).

We do know that educators are usually unaware of the extent of cyberbullying. This is true even for younger teachers who are more tech-savvy. Sadly, some teachers are not interested in knowing about cyberbullying from the students' perspective and prefer that it remain "under the radar" (Cassidy, Brown, & Jackson, 2012). This is hopefully something that will change, because educators play an important role in preventing cyberbullying and encouraging positive online behavior.

The vast majority of adults included in this book were not adversely affected by cyberbullying while they were growing up because this form of bullying was not yet prevalent when they were in school. A few vignettes of online bullying are included. However, the impact of cyberbullying on adult development will be the topic for many future studies.

THE DEFINITION DEBATE

It is important to consider some definitions of bullying. What is *your* definition of bullying? Does the image of someone trying to extract lunch money come to your mind? Or do you see an image of physical assault? Is your definition based on your own lived experience or on something you have read? The definitions of bullying vary among adults, even among researchers on this subject. How we define bullying is important for interrupting and curtailing it. The technical definition used by educators and most researchers on bullying and school violence was first suggested by Dan Olweus in 1978 in his book *Aggression in the Schools: Bullies and Whipping Boys*. Olweus defined bullying as when a boy or girl is exposed, repeatedly and over time, to intentional aggressive actions by one or more others who have more power than the victim.

It is very significant to note that this definition is not typically the definition that teens, or even most adults, use. When I have investigated this phenomenon with children and adolescents, they say bullying is "anytime someone is mean to you." They are quite clear about this and can distinguish between what is meant for fun and what is mean-spirited (deLara, 2012; Garbarino & deLara, 2002). Another broad definition is provided by McWilliams, Goodman, Raskauskas, and Cordon (2014), who conclude bullying is, "direct or indirect aggressive behaviors by one child . . . against another child who is unable to defend himself or herself effectively" (p. 301). The definition provided by researchers Smith and Sharp (1994) is closest to what I have found in my own research: "A student is being bullied or picked on when another student says nasty and unpleasant things to him or her. It is also bullying when a student is hit, kicked, threatened, locked inside a room, sent nasty notes, and when no one ever talks to him" (p. 1). Researchers understand that in many instances, bullies and victims are not distinctly defined roles. They are often the same person (Centers for Disease Control and Prevention [CDC], 2011; deLara, 2012; Faris & Felmlee, 2011).

Though the Olweus definition is used by most researchers, bullying from a child's perspective is understandably subjective and will not bend to fit the constraints imposed by adult definitions. For children and adolescents, the bully does not necessarily have more power and the bullying is not necessarily behavior that occurs over time, but may be a one-time traumatic experience (deLara, 2012; see Vaillancourt et al., 2008). When asked about sexual harassment, kids do not mention anything about power or chronicity. They say sexual harassment is "When someone starts a rumor about you." "When someone follows you." "When someone touches you."

The hundreds of adults I have interviewed, too, use a very different definition of bullying than most researchers have adopted. The vast majority say, "Bullying is when someone is picking on you or being mean."

What do you consider sexual harassment, hazing, bullying, and teasing? How we think about these actions is important in how we go about trying to curtail them for children and how we try to understand adults who are left with the aftereffects. It's essential to remember that sometimes children and adolescents are bullied or harassed by their friends, so the element of power or chronicity may be absent (Daniels et al., 2010, Wei & Jonson-Reid, 2011).

A new definition of bullying has been adopted by the CDC and the US Department of Education in an attempt to standardize how researchers and educators conceive of this phenomenon:

> Bullying is any unwanted aggressive behavior(s) by another youth or group
> of youths who are not siblings or current dating partners that involves an
> observed or perceived power imbalance and is repeated multiple times or is
> highly likely to be repeated. Bullying may inflict harm or distress on the tar-
> geted youth including physical, psychological, social, or educational harm.
>
> Gladden, Vivolo-Kantor, Hamburger, & Lumpkin, 2014, p. 7

There are some aspects of the definition to consider. Of critical importance is that it does not reflect the lived experience of children. Over many years of interviewing hundreds of people, over 90% gave a very different definition based on their experience and perspective. Another issue with the new definition is that due to its restrictive nature, it will potentially result in reflecting a lower proportion of children involved with bullying. Children are literal beings. They will respond to the constraints of this definition accordingly and not report instances where they feel they have been bullied if those instances fall outside the guidelines of the definition.

The definition describes bullying as embodying "an observed or perceived power imbalance" between the bully and the victim (p. 7). You must read further to discover that it elucidates this point by saying that a power imbalance can shift even when it involves the same people. This clarification points to the idea that power between peers is not static. However, as with most things, adults will gravitate to the brief two sentence definition and not pursue additional nuances. The idea of excluding siblings and dating partners from the definition may be short-sighted. Siblings do bully one another (Bowes, Wolke, Joinson, Lereya, & Lewis, 2014; Hoetger, Hazen, & Brank, 2015; Menesini, Camodeca, & Nocentini, 2010), and they very often attend the same school. Omitting this form of behavior from the bullying definition creates intervention dilemmas for school personnel. Are they to overlook sibling bullying when they see it? Current dating partners are typically peers within the same school, and though it may be difficult for school personnel to be up-to-date on the frequent changes in dating partners, it is important for school staff to make an effort. The reason for this is the fact that dating violence and peer bullying are often interwoven (Connolly et al., 2015; Connolly, Pepler, Craig, & Taradash, 2000; Debnam, Johnson, & Bradshaw, 2014). There is another reason to pay attention to what may appear to be dating behavior. According to adolescents I have interviewed, there are many actions adolescents take in the hallways that adults mistake for acceptable public displays of affection when in fact they are crude attempts at bullying (deLara, 2008; Garbarino & deLara, 2002).

Lastly, the proposed subtypes in the new definition for bullying do not include sexual bullying except as "inappropriate sexual comments" (p. 7). This does not take into account such things as being grabbed in a sexual manner by a peer. Again, this is a common enough event during the course of a school day (deLara, 2008), so it should not be excluded. The new definition is considered "a starting point that will need to be revised periodically as more becomes known about bullying" (Gladden et al., 2014, p. 7). This is an important qualification and I am glad that it has been added. While the attempt to standardize a definition of bullying is commendable, at this point it is adult-driven and will function as a convenience for those who adopt it. Antibullying programming will still suffer without employing a definition used by the primary stakeholders, children and adolescents.

While researchers continue to use the standard Olweus (1993) definition for what constitutes bullying, people who have lived through the experience offer something different for us to consider. When I asked adults how they would define bullying, they gave the following kinds of responses:

"Bullying is when someone is being mean or demeaning toward you."
"Bullying is physical or emotional taunting and isolation."
"Bullying is physical or psychological abuse by peers."
"Bullying is trying to intimidate someone."

"Bullying is when people are forced to feel inferior or dominated by an individual or group."

"Any act done to make someone feel out of place, unwanted or unimportant."

"Bullying is anything that makes you feel bad about you."

These are representative of what I heard over and over from people ages 18 to 65. One thing these real-people definitions have in common is they do not talk about chronicity. That is not a factor. Also, they do not say that someone has to have more power. That is not seen as a factor necessary for an action to be considered bullying.

One young woman, age 24, described bullying as "aggression used to manipulate another person, physically or emotionally." She was born and grew up in Guyana. She attended religion-based private schools from elementary through high school, where bullying was strictly prohibited by anti-bullying policies that were taken seriously by the staff and teachers. Peter, age 29, offered an interesting perspective. He concludes that a bully may not be bigger but bullies are typically more opinionated than others. This makes them attractive to other kids because as a teenager "you don't know anything then" and bullies seem to. So some kids will gravitate to them.

Others participating in the study said bullying is:

"A conscious decision of an individual to inflict pain on another person that they deem inferior to themselves or a threat to themselves." (Male, 33)

"The putting down and pushing away of someone, often because they are somehow 'different' from you." (Female, 24)

"Hurting others, physically or psychologically, for your own pleasure or to avoid your own pain." (Male, 36)

"Any affront to a person that makes them uncomfortable or violates their well-being." (Female, 26)

None of the definitions cited above conform to the standard definition used by the majority of researchers in the field. This dissonance between the definition used by "real people" and that used by researchers is a problem. It is problematic because by insisting that repetition and power imbalance must be criteria for bullying, researchers and educators may miss out on reaching thousands of kids. Surveys are distributed to children using the standard research definition. Consequently, children are responding about bullying using the definition provided to them, not with the definition they use for themselves. As a result, the numbers reflecting victims, bullies, and bystanders from these surveys are misleading. Programs aimed at curtailing bullying offer information and advice that is not commensurate with children's lived experience. This leaves programs lacking and children without the support and intervention they need.

WHY DO KIDS BULLY?

In 2012, actress and child advocate Marlo Thomas wrote a piece called "When the Bullied Strike Back" for the *Huffington Post*. She was asking the question Why do kids bully? These were some of the responses:

> "Yes, I have been a bully. I bullied a girl on the school bus every day in sixth grade because that was my way of dealing with problems I had at home. Just a few weeks ago, I saw her Facebook status, saying how she wanted to kill herself. And I felt awful knowing that I was one of the causes of her considering suicide. So I messaged her and apologized for everything I've done. She didn't commit suicide and I am so thankful."
>
> Tabitha, 15

> "In elementary school, I was pretty ruthless, always jockeying for position. After this one girl had been in a car accident, I drew a picture of a dog and wrote: "This is YOU!" My intent was not to be a bully or hurt someone deeply. I was just trying to get a laugh. I didn't realize it could have a long-term impact on her. I was just a loudmouth trying to be cool, wanting to be part of a group."
>
> Noel, 12

> "In elementary school, kids put you down so they can be popular. It's all about "Who You Are." I had trouble pronouncing some words and my teeth were not straight, so kids called me "horse" or "donkey." I got angrier and angrier. And so I started bullying. One girl ended up getting home-schooled and moving away."
>
> Kaylie, 15

Kids bully others for all kinds of reasons including factors based on personality, family, and community issues. One of the most prominent reasons is that they have learned that this is an acceptable means of interpersonal interaction, much to the consternation of those who would like to convince them otherwise. Some children are bullied at home by parents or siblings. On a regular basis, kids see their peers engage in bullying at school that goes unnoticed and unpunished. They see their teachers and other school personnel bully and torment students (Davis & Nixon, 2013; Garbarino & deLara, 2002). And they see that no one intervenes. In the last quote by Kaylie, we see a good example of the victim-and-bully cycle that takes place endlessly in many schools. Those who are victimized turn to bullying to contend with their own rage or to protect themselves. This raises the questions: What are the consequences in adult life when someone learns to lash out in anger as a result of bullying in childhood? What are the consequences as an adult when bullying was a "normal" part of life as a child?

BULLYING TAKES PLACE IN A SYSTEM

Schools as Systems

General systems theory (von Bertalanffy, 1968) is useful in understanding how bullying occurs and is perpetuated in systems. Schools operate as systems, and all systems strive for homeostasis, to stay the same. The bigger the system, the greater this is experienced as an imperative especially by those in charge. Homeostasis lends the predictability that systems require to operate and that players in the system come to count on. W. Richard Scott (2000), an organizational expert, noted that systems will use diverse forms of shunning and shaming techniques to preserve the rules and values of the organization. Systems will go to great lengths to maintain the status quo by explicitly or implicitly designating some actors within the group to shun and shame others into "acceptable" behavior. Systems tolerate abusive environments and climates. After the shooting at Columbine High School in 1999, reporters Adams and Russakoff from the *Washington Post* wrote that while the community and nation at large wanted to blame mental illness and guns for the shootings at the high school, the perpetrators and their friends, along with other kids at the school, gave clear indication that the school tolerated a culture of emotional and physical abuse of peers toward one another (Adams & Russakoff, 1999). Systems that are dysfunctional will produce scapegoats for someone to blame when things go wrong (Posner & Schmidt, 1993). Troubled kids or anyone who is considered "other" are typical scapegoats in school systems. In any system or organization that is dysfunctional, people are scapegoated by others as the ones who are *causing the problems* in the system. This serves to divert attention away from everyone except the one who is scapegoated. It also serves the function of letting everyone else in the system off the hook; no one has to take a look at his or her behavior or contribution to why things are going wrong. This is a way not only of escaping any responsibility of one's own but also of keeping things the same in the system. In this way, it is a homeostatic mechanism (see deLara, 2006). Unfortunately, in many school systems, kids are given "permission" to bully others. This sense of permission comes in several varieties. The most pernicious is when school personnel bully students. This is a form of social modeling that kids learn from and feel free to copy (Shakeshaft, 2004). Adults are the obvious role-models for children at school. If they are harassing students, some children will see this as despicable, while others will view it as the opportunity for their own bad behavior. Another variety of "permission" occurs when adults look the other way during incidents of bullying. In many schools and school districts, there is a true hierarchy among the students that not only the students recognize but also the adults adhere to. The athletes are often at the top of the pyramid. While I have seen the athletes in some schools act as the defenders of students who are being picked on by their peers, in many others, the athletes are acting as the bullies themselves (see Volk & Lagzdins, 2009). Unfortunately, if this is not outright sanctioned by adults at school, it is often overlooked. Athletes occupy a special place at school and represent the pride the district attributes to itself. Notice the next time you drive by a high school. You are likely to see signs that read for example: "Home of the Championship Wildcats" indicating the district's sports teams. There will rarely, if ever, be a sign indicating the winning debate or science teams from the district.

The sanctioning of athletes as the elite of the school is not only a school phenomenon but also exists more widely at the community level as well. Most of us are aware of communities where the biggest social event of the week is the Friday night high school football game. This kind of accolade cannot help but bestow a special kind of power on youngsters endowed with the community's responsibility and honor. It can go awry in many ways, however. One example is when adults fail to recognize and refuse to accept their own responsibility for bullying at school. Shortly after the tragedy at Columbine High School, the principal issued a statement that the two boys who committed the act never approached him to let him know that they were being harassed for four years by the school athletes. He professed that had he known he would have done something (Gibbs & Roche, 1999). In a climate where athletes are at the top of the social hierarchy, it would be most improbable that two teenage boys would go to the principal in this way.

Another variety of permission-giving is the failure to intervene by adults. The teens and adults I have had the chance to interview over the years commented repeatedly on this common phenomenon during their school years. One young man from a large suburban school reported the following incident to me:

> "When I was a freshman, I was on my way to English and I saw a fight break out in the hallway. I hurried in to tell my teacher so she could do something. She just said: 'Oh that happens all the time. Just walk around it when you see it.' She didn't even call the office. She didn't do a thing."

This not only signals the apathy of adults to the students but also is another implicit form of permission from the system to engage in peer-on-peer violence. Students rightfully come to some conclusions: Adults will not protect them, they can get away with bullying others, and they will most likely have to stand up for themselves in bullying episodes.

These various ways of ignoring or permitting bullying are all ways in which the school as a system is enabling bullying. It is the way that the system operates. When there are kids at the top (e.g., the athletes) and kids at the bottom (e.g., those on the autistic spectrum, those with disabilities, kids with any kind of "difference") there is always the chance of bullying unless a school takes an active, preventive approach.

Another ingrained systemic issue is represented in the relative hierarchical status of first-year students (in middle school and in high school) compared with upper-class students. Older students feel free to intimidate, haze, and otherwise bully incoming boys and girls on virtually any basis—age, size, weight, any difference (Leland, 2001). Because this hierarchy, and its accompanying status perks, is so much a part of our established culture, it becomes difficult for anyone to interrupt it. And thus the system continues to enable bullying.

Systems perpetuate dysfunction in active and passive ways. School personnel can preserve the culture of bullying by "not seeing" it, by not intervening, or by actively participating themselves. One school social worker shared this sad account of her school: "I work at a city middle school and this is what I see. Staff have low regard for the students and treat them inappropriately and disrespectfully. The kids are provoked by this and retaliate by disrespecting the teachers or taking it out on other students. Then they get in trouble for it." Children look to the adults in their lives for direction and guidance. Just at the age when kids need adults to show them respect so that they can learn to show it to others, adults let them down. To add to this, when adults "pick on" or otherwise treat students poorly, children feel entitled to do the same thing.

Workplace Systems

Workplace systems, too, attempt to maintain homeostasis. Adults are creatures of habit and like things to stay the same even when this may mean that some interactional patterns in the work place are dysfunctional. All of us have heard of a bully at work, and many have been subjected to one. Workplace bullying has been defined as "repeated, health-harming mistreatment of one of more persons (the targets) by one or more perpetrators that takes one or more of the following forms: verbal abuse; offensive conduct/behaviors (including nonverbal) which are threatening, humiliating or intimidating; or work interference-sabotage which prevents work from getting done" (Pomeroy, 2013, p. 4). Research indicates that workplace bullying affects job performance and job turnover and increases intentions to quit a job (Deery, Walsh, & Guest, 2011). As a result, the impacts are felt not only at the individual level but also in terms of costs to the organization. Of workers in the United States, 70%–80% say they deal with rudeness at work, and many go out of their way to avoid their boss or coworkers (Ghosh, Jacobs, & Reio, 2011; Sypher, 2004).

Victims of workplace bullying and harassment "are often silenced into believing there must be something wrong with them, that they are not good enough or that if they just try harder they will win their supervisors' approval" (Pomeroy, 2013, p. 5). Targets in the workplace suffer threats, intimidation, humiliation, disparaging remarks about the quality of their work, verbal abuse, rumors, and other forms of aggression. Women, minorities, and employees lower on the hierarchy are the most likely victims of this kind of bullying. Some studies indicate that women are more likely than men to engage in bullying at work (Pomeroy, 2013), while in a representative sample of the Norwegian workplace, being male was predictive of being a bully (Hauge, Skogstad, & Einarsen, 2009).

The problem of workplace bullying is common in the hospitality industry and in the health, education, and social services fields. Victims report experiencing significant physical and psychological health consequences (van Heugten, 2013). Data from a diverse sample of employees and coworkers indicate that individuals who measure low in agreeableness along with those who measure high in neuroticism are much more likely to engage in incivility at work than others (Milam, Spitzmueller, & Penney, 2009). Some of the more malicious bullying behaviors include false accusations of mistakes at work, discounted ideas, vicious rumors or gossip, harsh criticism, screaming and tantrums, retaliation against complaints made by the victim, lying about performance, and other demeaning and aggressive tactics. It is important to note that large-scale studies show workplace bullying results in both anxiety and depression for those who are the targets (Hauge, Skogstad, & Einarsen, 2010; Lahelma, Lallukka, Laaksonen, Saastamoinen, & Rahkonen, 2012) as well as sleep difficulties (Lallukka, Rahkonen, & Lahelma, 2011).

Where do workplace bullies come from? One answer can be found in the research of Hauge et al. (2009; Hauge, Skogstad, & Einarsen, 2011), which indicates that bullying will thrive in stressful, dysfunctional environments. Further, being male and once being a target of bullying, regardless of the frequency, strongly predict involvement in the bullying of others. An ecosystemic model and an individual developmental model are both useful in trying to understand the phenomenon of bullying at work. From a developmental perspective, it can be easily understood that children and adolescents who have traversed their entire childhood as bullies will attempt to bring that form of behavior to work with them, especially if it has worked "well" and particularly if they find themselves in positions of some authority or power. From an ecosystemic perspective, elements from the societal, corporation, and management levels may all serve as antecedents to bullying behavior in an organization (Johnson, 2011; Salin & Hoel, 2011). Heinz Leymann, highly regarded for his work on bullying in European organizations, believed that workplace bullying is a result of organizational difficulties that include deficiencies in leadership behavior, low department morale, and that the victim has a "socially exposed position" (Einarsen, Hoel, Zapf, & Cooper 2011, p. 23). Someone who could be considered "socially exposed" might be someone others think of as "different," someone who is isolated in the system, someone considered a threat in some way, or someone who does not conform to the norms and mores of the organization. Jonathan Martin might have been that person. Martin and Richie Incognito are both professional football players in the National Football League (NFL). Martin accused Incognito of bullying and harassment that included racial epithets and death threats. Unfortunately, Martin had been the target of bullying in his early years and here it was again. As a result of his very poor treatment by Incognito and what looked to be the encouragement of the coaches who wanted him "toughened up," Jonathan Martin left the team. Incognito was put on unpaid leave. All of this represents an organizational problem, has cost the organization in terms of real dollars and bad publicity, and may be representative of a wider cultural problem in the NFL. Other leagues, such as the National Basketball Association, have sent out warnings to the teams in their jurisdiction to avoid these kinds of behaviors (Boren, 2014). Bullying at work causes damage for individuals as well as untold damage to organizations.

One woman, age 34, provided an example of typical verbal bullying behavior at her place of employment:

> "There are mostly woman at my place of work. I am always on guard because I saw what happened in my high school. I was bullied and sexually harassed because of my family's money and my clothes. Girls can be treacherous and I've witnessed some of these women at work tear another co-worker apart. Sometimes right to her face; other times just in rumors. But that can be bad enough. Once I started to join in just to be accepted then I thought: 'What am I doing?' and stopped. I don't want to be like that. You wonder if you're going to have to, to survive the place."

Even academic settings, where camaraderie and civility might be expected, are replete with bullying and incivility in interpersonal interactions (see Twale & De Luca, 2008).

Adult bullies at work create a toxic environment where confidence and self-esteem are lost, talents are sacrificed, and productivity is impaired. Victims experience shame at their inability to control their own lives against intrusions by the bully.

IS BULLYING SO TERRIBLE?

"Everybody gets teased and bullied in school, don't they? It's not so terrible and you outgrow it. After all, bullying is just a 'rite of passage,' isn't it?" These sentiments are expressed frequently in our culture. It is indicative of what most adults believe, even some mental health professionals, researchers, and others who should know better. But problematically many people never "outgrow" the effects of being bullied and tormented as children. It impacts the decisions they make, the relationships they form, and their very sense of self-worth. Being bullied carries a lifelong message. That message is: "You are inadequate, you are 'less than' everyone else." Your outlook about yourself and about relationships is often forged in the fires of bullying and harassment and carries over into adulthood. In the interviews for this book, approximately three-quarters of the participants reported experiencing one or more negative consequences in their adult lives as a result of childhood bullying. These included a lack of trust in relationships, difficulty making or maintaining friendships, poor self-image, generalized feelings of helplessness, anxiety, and depression. These consequences are discussed more fully throughout the book in vignettes and case examples.

A typical reflection was shared by a 33-year-old woman: "The bullying and harassment I experienced were some of the worse things that have ever happened to me. That's why I wanted to be part of this study. I want people to know that bullying is terrible and that I still carry it all with me today." Bullying scars. It is not benign. It leaves a profound, soul-deep imprint and it leaves consequences to be dealt with over a lifetime.

Some survivors of childhood bullying and harassment may experience adult post-bullying syndrome, an entity distinct from PTSD. The specifics of this phenomenon are discussed in the upcoming chapter, and people who suffer with it are noticeable throughout the book.

CHAPTER 2

Adult Post-Bullying Syndrome

In my investigations of the effects of childhood bullying on adults, I have seen various impacts on development and on adult relationships. While some people seem to have managed the effects well, others are left with a complex set of symptoms I have called adult post-bullying syndrome (APBS). This syndrome is based on the trauma of bullying episodes and shares some things in common with post-traumatic stress disorder (PTSD). However, it is a separate entity. As such it needs to be recognized so that people can understand what it is they are up against. Naming is the first step to any recovery. In this way, mental health practitioners can be useful to those seeking help with its effects, such as the depression and anxiety that are inherent. Otherwise, like the proverbial blind men trying to identify the elephant, we are left naming only parts and confusing adult post-bullying syndrome with other traumas. I address the components of APBS later in the chapter. First, what constitutes trauma and post-traumatic stress disorder?

WHAT IS TRAUMA?

There is a great deal of discussion in the public domain about trauma—what causes it and what the consequences are. We are used to thinking about trauma as it relates to war, other horrific events, or physical injury to the brain. We are not used to the idea that trauma can be incurred through the everyday experiences of bullying that children face. Trauma has been described as "overwhelming sensory arousal combined with negative cognitions," which basically leads to "blowing the intellectual circuits of the brain" (Garbarino, 2013). One dictionary defines trauma as an experience that produces psychological injury or pain. Behavioral responses to trauma can include "fight, flight, or freeze" reactions (Gilbert, 2009; Van der Kolk, 1988). Though we think of children as resilient, they are subject to many forms of physical and psychological trauma. Bullying is among them. Trauma affects what children anticipate, what they think about, and how they process information. It influences how they behave and how they regulate their biological system. The age at which children are subjected to trauma and the frequency of trauma play a role in brain development. Repeated traumatic events have a pervasive effect on a child's neurobiological development. This pervasive consequence "is expressed in problems with self-regulation, aggression against self or others, problems with attention and dissociation, physical problems, difficulties in self-concept, and trouble negotiating interpersonal relationships" (van der Kolk, 2003, pp. 293–294).

BULLYING, THE BRAIN, AND TRAUMA

The effect of trauma on brain development is dependent on age and other factors. Trauma affects children differently at different stages of brain growth, and it is sensitive to the child's own ability to perceive danger. Fear of danger is experienced in various areas of the brain. Two prominent areas are the amygdala, which is alert for threat even in the brain of a newborn, and the hippocampus, which places our risks to safety in context for us. This capability does not fully develop until about 5 years of age (van der Kolk, 2003). When a child experiences trauma that leads to PTSD, neurobiological development is impacted in several ways. Certain brain structures may be delayed in development, neuroendocrine responses are affected, and we can see issues with ability to think, process emotions, and control behavior (Anda et al., 2006; van der Kolk, 2003). "Prolonged alarm reactions," such as might be the case for children who are abused at home or by peers at school, "alter the limbic, mid-brain and brain stem functioning" and "alter the capacity to integrate sensory input" (van der Kolk, 2003, p. 294). Interestingly, research indicates that children who have a secure attachment to their primary caregiver are better able to soothe themselves after encounters with bullying and violence. This is because as infants their parent or caretaker was attuned to their needs and helped calm their central nervous system when they were stressed (van der Kolk, 2003). This may point the way toward helping parents provide therapeutic interventions for their children and it is indicative of the need for stress-reduction measures in adults bullied as children. Adults react to stress based on childhood experiences as these become embedded in stress management systems of the brain (Hostinar & Gunnar, 2013).

Verbal abuse by peers conveys its own imprint on the brain. Teicher and colleagues (2010) found that verbal bullying by peers is associated with significant alterations in brain structure for those who are victimized. In particular they found damage to the corpus callosum, which connects the left and right hemispheres of the brain and carries most of the neural traffic to and from the cerebral cortex. They studied young adults ages 18 to 25, none of whom had a history of domestic violence, parental abuse, sexual abuse, or physical abuse by peers. They made these exclusions so they could look at the effects of verbal abuse exclusively. The Verbal Abuse Questionnaire, consisting of various types of verbal bullying, was given to over 700 participants. The majority of abuse occurred between ages 11 and 14 for this group. The findings were that the greater the exposure to peer verbal abuse, the greater the likelihood these young adults were experiencing anxiety, depression, and other psychiatric symptoms along with drug use. Verbal abuse during the middle-school years appeared to be particularly toxic for the participants in this study. Further, the researchers looked for any connection between peer verbal abuse and corpus callosum damage by doing neuroimaging scans. Evidence of this link was discovered; damage to the corpus callosum increases the risk that a person will have psychological problems. It appears from this research and other studies that once substantial brain changes have taken place due to abuse, neural pathways and disrupted hormones act as trip wires for still other changes in the brain and endocrine system eventuating in psychological and behavioral issues (Knack, Jensen-Campbell, & Baum, 2011; Teicher, Samson, Sheu, Polcari, & McGreenery, 2010).

The Bully's Brain

Most of us are able to reign in our negative feelings and any inclination to act violently based on our moral stance and cues around us. Research indicates that people who act aggressively may have an abnormality in brain regions responsible for emotion regulation (Edmiston et al., 2011). Further, they show problems with glucose metabolism. The prefrontal cortex, orbital cortex, anterior cingulate cortex, and amygdala may not be functioning properly. As a result, serotonin levels and other hormones are affected. When serotonin levels are low, there is a greater likelihood of retaliation and aggression to a perceived slight or unfairness (Crockett et al., 2013). The orbital cortex is important in decision-making, and the amygdala helps us process emotions. Most individuals are able to contain their behavior when these brain areas are aroused by anger. Impulse control is not a problem. However, when there are problems in the emotion regulation circuits of the brain, impulsive aggression can be the result. Those with damage to the frontal lobes, which act as mediators for impulses, are at particular risk. For anyone displaying impulsive aggressive behavior, a medical professional needs to be consulted to provide an adequate evaluation (Fallon, 2013). Without a neurological work-up most people will assume that a child's or adult's problems are strictly behavioral and voluntary.

Is Bullying Traumatic?

Is bullying traumatic? How is bullying related to PTSD? These two phenomena are not frequently explored together. One research team decided to look at national data involving students in 8th and 9th grades for their exposure to bullying and any PTSD symptoms they were showing. They found that while boys were twice as likely as girls to be repeatedly bullied, girls were more likely to have symptoms of PTSD than boys. Further, more than 25% of the boys and 40% of the girls demonstrated signs of PTSD that were within the clinical range. This means that these children, in particular, should be receiving treatment for the effects of bullying. The study also pointed out a clear association between frequency of bullying and PTSD symptoms. Exposure to bullying as either a bully or a victim is a positive risk factor for developing PTSD (Idsoe, Dyregrov, & Idsoe, 2012).

What Is Post-Traumatic Stress Disorder?

Post-traumatic stress disorder is characterized as a mental disorder that occurs after experiencing "an event outside the range of usual human experience [that] would be markedly distressing to almost anyone" (Burstow, 2005, p. 430). Approximately 55% of the population will experience at least one traumatic event in their lifetime, however only 5%–10% go on to develop PTSD (Kubiak, 2005). Post-traumatic stress disorder symptoms are placed in four general groups. They include intrusive memories or re-experiencing, avoidance, negative changes in thinking and mood, and changes in a person's typical emotional reactions to any given situation. This is sometimes called arousal. It is important to note that symptoms can begin immediately after a traumatic event or in some cases they do not surface until years later (American Psychiatric Association, 2013).

Intrusive memories or re-experiencing:

- Recurrent, unwanted distressing memories of the traumatic event
- Reliving the traumatic event as if it were happening again (flashbacks)
- Upsetting dreams about the traumatic event
- Intense or prolonged psychological distress or physical reactions to something that reminds you of the event

Avoidance:

- Trying to avoid thinking or talking about the traumatic event
- Avoiding places, activities, or people that remind you of the traumatic event

Negative changes in thinking and mood:

- Negative feelings about yourself or other people
- Blaming yourself or other people
- Emotional numbness
- Lack of interest in activities you once enjoyed
- Hopelessness about the future
- Memory problems, including not remembering important aspects of the traumatic event
- Difficulty maintaining close relationships

Changes in emotional reactions:

- Irritability, angry outbursts, or aggressive behavior
- Hyperarousal, or being on guard for danger
- Overwhelming guilt or shame
- Self-destructive behavior
- Trouble concentrating
- Sleeping difficulties
- Being easily startled or frightened (American Psychiatric Association, 2013)

ADULT POST-BULLYING SYNDROME

In interviewing the people in my research study, I began to notice something unusual. While many of the participants spoke of the bullying episodes they experienced as traumatic and described the impact they felt at the time and what they are left with now in terms of traumatic memories, no one explicitly said they felt like they had PTSD. However, collectively, they listed many symptoms that did fit the PTSD diagnosis. Still others clearly experience what I call adult post-bullying syndrome, or APBS. I have named it this to distinguish it from PTSD.

While APBS can share some symptoms with PTSD, there are distinct differences. One is that there can be both negative and positive aspects to APBS, whereas there are no positive aspects in the research literature associated with PTSD. The negative symptoms of APBS can mimic those of PTSD or the effects seen from child abuse. These effects, similar for child abuse (Carlisle & Rofes, 2007), APBS, and PTSD, and lasting into adulthood, can include shame, anxiety, and relational difficulties. Further, negative cognitions about the self often occur after a trauma. This trauma-related thinking is often inaccurate and serves to support and maintain PTSD (Kolts, Robinson, & Tracy, 2004; Lemos-Miller & Kearney, 2006; Moser, Hajcak, Simons, & Foa, 2007). The changes in emotional reactions that characterize PTSD can lead to unexpected and often unpredictable outbursts of anger and aggression. Something can happen to which the person with PTSD just reacts. There does not appear to be an intermediary step of thinking. There is the event, then the reaction. This is a critical difference between PTSD and APBS, where adults do not tend to show this kind of event/reaction immediacy but rather seem more inclined to take no action and instead ruminate on past and present events.

While there are negative aspects of adult post-bullying syndrome, there are some unexpected positives that seem to accompany it also. In interviewing people who appear to experience APBS, I noticed that they have a tendency to exhibit some, if not all, of the following issues:

1. Self-esteem issues and shame
2. Problems trusting others
3. Problems in relationships
4. People-pleasing tendencies
5. Substance misuse
6. Emotional problems and disorders
7. Feelings of anger, rage, and revenge

8. Body issues
9. Positive or unexpected outcomes

Self-Esteem Issues and Shame

"I have low self-esteem, a poor self-image, and virtually no confidence in myself."

"Unfortunately, I took right to heart, literally, the hurtful things that were said to me. Now that I am grown up I try to see things differently, but in my core I still believe they are true."

Self-doubt and harsh self-judgment are byproducts of childhood bullying. They leave an indelible mark on self-esteem for those who suffer with APBS. Children take to heart relentless torment through name-calling and castigation of their character and looks. Years later, as adults, people can still easily recall what they were bullied about: their weight, their height, their clothes, having acne, the people to whom they were attracted. People with APBS typically report having low self-esteem. They feel a sense of shame connected to the core of their being. People who feel a great deal of shame or who are shame-based can manifest this in arrogant behavior. This can be seen in vacillations in thinking between: "I'm a loser" and "I'm better than all of you."

Problems Trusting Others

"I find it hard to trust other men at work."

"My worry that people are judging me is constant."

Problems trusting others can take a generalized state form (as in "I don't trust anybody") or can be very specific to certain groups. People suffering with APBS tend not to trust others. They are particularly cautious in intimate relationships such as friendship and marriage, always expecting that they will be betrayed. Further, they do not trust people who look, act, or even dress like those who bullied them. This lack of trust is problematic for establishing relationships in the first place and for managing them.

Problems in Relationships

"You begin to think you don't deserve anything. You don't deserve a good relationship."

"At the first sign someone is not nice, I distance myself."

The problem of mistrusting others significantly impairs a person's ability to connect with other people and then to stay connected. People who trust easily establish relationships readily and maintain them. They do not have attachment problems. Children who have been bullied and then end up with adult post-bullying syndrome often appear to either run from relationships or manage to get into abusive ones. After all, they have learned as children that their peers or siblings will treat them badly. For the most part, they never learned how to stop bullying as children. Consequently, they do not know how to and often do not even want to extricate themselves from physically or emotionally abusive relationships as adults. This is all they know. At the other end of the continuum are adults so scarred from their bullying experiences that they are willing to end even their marriages based on what, to others, might seem reparable. But to some adults suffering with APBS any hint of disrespect or bullying is intolerable.

People-Pleasing

"My strategy in relationships is to be a people-pleaser."

A majority of those with adult post-bullying syndrome declared that they were "people-pleasers." Never feeling quite good about themselves, never being good enough, based on the maltreatment they endured through bullying, they have determined that pleasing others is their best defense. It makes a kind of emotional sense. Having experienced numerous forms of bullying from verbal to emotional to sexual to physical, becoming someone that no one could object to seems like a good strategy. However, in the process authenticity of self can be lost. This is a high price to pay.

Food and Other Substance Misuse

"I drink a lot and I have used drugs to help me with the anxiety I feel about the bullying in my past."

Numerous studies detail an association between bullying as victim, bully, or bully/victim and substance use in childhood (Higgins, Khey, Dawson-Edwards, & Marcum, 2012; Luk, Wang, & Simons-Morton, 2010). In my study, some adult participants reported using alcohol, other drugs, and food management to quell the feelings of anxiety or depression they experience related to bullying episodes from their childhood. Other research substantiates these findings. At this point, research on the consequences to adult mental health demonstrates long-term correlations between childhood bullying and outcomes such as anxiety, substance abuse, depression, and adult conduct disorders (Biebl, DiLalla, Davis, Lynch, & Shinn, 2011; Farrington & Ttofi, 2011; Kim, Catalano, Haggerty, & Abbott, 2011; Smokowski & Kopasz, 2005; Sourander et al., 2007). One inquiry investigated bullying during 5th grade and its relationship to later heavy drinking and marijuana use. The sample was from the Raising Healthy Children project and included over 900 children. The study determined that "childhood bullying was significantly associated with violence, heavy drinking, and marijuana use" in adulthood even after controlling for other risk factors (Kim et al., 2011, p. 136).

Emotional Problems and the Development of Psychiatric Disorders

"I am a cold person because of it (bullying)."

"It has virtually destroyed my spirit."

"I have panic attacks and an anxiety disorder because of bullying."

Research indicates there is a greatly elevated risk of developing adult psychiatric disorders for those who were involved in bullying as children (Copeland, Wolke, Angold, & Costello, 2013). A Finnish study examined the impact of bullying and victimization on boys over a 15-year period into young adulthood. The long-term results found that those who were classified as frequent bullies when they were 8 years old had developed a personality disorder. Those who were frequent victims had an anxiety disorder, and those who were considered bully/victims were more aggressive than any other group (Sourander et al., 2007). In my study, Chris explained that she experienced bullying and harassment throughout her school days. It affected her overall physical and mental well-being. She said, "Bullying had an extreme impact on my psychological health, anxiety, and the obsessive compulsive disorder I had. Bullying exacerbated it all. I developed depression; people thought I might be bi-polar. I developed an eating disorder as an adult. I was bullied for being overweight. Then I developed bulimia. Now I have panic attacks. But even with this, I see that I am a survivor; I see positive things in my life as a result." The impact on Chris is severe as a result of being bullied as a child. While she does not meet the criteria for PTSD, she might be a candidate for adult post-bullying syndrome.

Feelings of Anger, Rage, and Revenge

"When I was bullied, I held back my aggression and turned it in on myself."

Children who are bullied and sexually harassed often feel shame that can lead to anger and rage. Those feelings often do not dissipate. Those with adult post-bullying syndrome can experience feelings of anger and rage when they ruminate on past bullying. Feelings of rage can also occur when similar situations present themselves. One adult said he "can't stand to be around anyone who looks like a frat boy." Another is triggered by athletes because of the bullying he endured at their hands. Often adults with APBS check out their school time bullies on FaceBook but not out of friendship or mere curiosity, rather with thoughts toward revenge. They are hoping to find that their tormentors are doing poorly and thus feel that the bullies got what they deserved. The person with APBS feels vindicated when this is the case. Of course some adults have been able to move past what occurred to them and have even befriended former bullies online.

Body Issues

"I've tried starving myself so I would never be bullied again."

There is considerable research on the issue of weight bias, bullying, and the immediate impacts on children's well-being. Adults with APBS continue to have body image issues carried over from their days of being bullied as children. Bullied, sexually harassed, and "teased" about how they were built or how they looked, these adults are left with lasting impressions. They conclude something was and still is wrong with them to have received this kind of treatment. In other chapters we see that people who have been bullied still do not consider themselves to be acceptable. People who have been bullied based on being overweight seem to be particularly subject to a lifetime of concern about body image. One woman in my study said rationally she knew that she was thin enough now as a 5'10" 125-pound adult, but could not feel adequate or comfortable with herself because she feared a new friend or friends might begin to exclude her based on her looks.

Positive or Unexpected Aspects

"I feel proud of having overcome being bullied."

"Being bullied for me was a positive thing because I learned how to cope with criticism and to stay humble. I see that I need that, it's useful, in all kinds of relationships: with friends, at work, or with my partner."

There are positive aspects, or unexpected outcomes, seen in adult post-bullying syndrome. Numerous people reported finding inner strength they believe they would not have discovered otherwise. They figured out how to take control of their own lives so that they were no longer helpless. They noted that they had developed empathy for the vulnerable where they thought they might not have. Importantly, most were committed to doing something important with their lives. Sometimes this was to prove their bullies were wrong about them. But whatever the reason, it was a crucial outcome for many of the participants with APBS. As you will read throughout the book, there are copious examples of people enduring the negative aspects of APBS and using the positive aspects to better their lives. It was very interesting to find this positive feature along with the negative aspects of APBS.

Matt, age 27, is a good example of the impact of childhood bullying that can result in APBS. He said:

Since I am the youngest in my family, I caught the most grief about being little and young which created insecurities about my physical build. I also would be insecure about my strength because my brother used to beat up on me physically which led to lots of anxiety, anguish, and the feeling of helplessness. When I was in middle school, I was bullied by one kid in particular. I never knew when it would happen. This kid would threaten to beat me up and sometimes he would trip or push me. I felt helpless to prevent it and to make it stop. My friends and I were what I would call just regular guys, so I never figured out why it happened. Much of my rage towards others growing up was due to these feelings, feelings of being dominated by everyone in my life, family and friends alike. I was also poked fun of in early high school days because I was weak, scrawny, little, perceived as inadequate, etc. Ultimately, I began working out in sophomore year and saw results. Needless to say, I was hooked. I was hooked on the feeling I got from being stronger than others and looking bigger than others. I still, to this day, enjoy that satisfaction. I go to the gym every day and lift weights. I have less of the inferiority complex I once did. Now working out is more for self-gratification that I am doing something healthy and beneficial for myself. It has become a great outlet for stress, anxiety, insecurity, and emotional distress. It's also a decent ego boost. However, I think I use it now less as a need for ego than for my own self-image: what I think of myself and not what others think of me. Eventually, I became someone in high school who people were envious of and afraid of messing with. It was powerful. It felt good. However, it wasn't addressing the underlying problem: the emotional pain of being bullied. This led me to abuse substances to feel more accepted by my peers in my college days. I had insurmountable insecurities due to bullying, so substance abuse allowed me to, in my mind, "be myself." I made irrational and unreasonable decisions while under the influence. The emotional pain seemed to get deeper because I didn't address any of the issues behind it.

I believe this is why I fit in so well as a pledge to my fraternity. Hazing was just another day in the life of Matt. It was normal. It fit, it was comfortable, I was used to being abused, but this time when I was being yelled at and messed with it was actually for a purpose: to become a fraternity brother. But because of the screaming, yelling, physical torture and emotional pain, I decided I had to make friends with it. That way I gained control over it. I gained power and the drive and will to survive it. I never truly got used to being teased and mocked outside of the fraternity. I pretended to not care and the emotions of shame, anger, rage, annoyance seemed to go away. I think that was due to an emotional deadness I felt towards being bullied. I was dead to it until I got older and realized all of this and realized that I don't care about the thoughts of others, only about my own perceptions of myself and how those in my life who mean the most to me perceive me.

Matt also experienced emotional bullying at the hands of his now ex-girlfriend. Believing at the time that he could trust her, he allowed himself to be open with his thoughts and feelings. He allowed himself to be "100% vulnerable with her" and she turned that against him. He says she treated him terribly. Now he can hardly recall any memories of his time with her because he believes he has suppressed those memories out of necessity. Matt continued, saying, "I have problems in relationships. Trust is a big deal for me." One of the ways that Matt deals with the aftermath of bullying is through drinking. He says he knows that alcohol is a problem for him.

At this point, the positives Matt sees are that he is aware of his sensitive nature and is determined to treat others with respect. Further, he insisted that, despite it all, "I am going to do something with my life." After talking with Matt, I told him that much of what he described fit a pattern I was seeing in many others with bullying experiences from their childhood: adult post-bullying syndrome. His immediate response was one of relief. He said: "It makes me happy to know that it's not just me with all of these issues and thoughts and that they are not synonymous with my true identity and personality." This is a very profound statement. It means that previous to our interview Matt had considered that all of the troubles and issues he carried were central to his basic self. As a result, for many years he held a negative sense of himself. Now, he realizes that the feelings he has are outgrowths of bullying events and he can begin to read-just his thinking about himself in an affirmative and constructive fashion. Matt described many of the attributes of APBS. He is one among many, many people who experience these same symptoms and consequences due directly to childhood bullying.

Adult post-bullying syndrome and PTSD do share some common features. Rage that burns quietly or can flare up at any point may be present for both. Trouble sleeping, substance misuse, feeling negatively about oneself, avoidance as a coping mechanism, and difficulty in relationships are possible in both APBS and PTSD. However, there are aspects of APBS that are unique, as described above. Some people with APBS turn their misfortunes with bullying into something positive. A person with APBS could experience PTSD symptoms and could be diagnosed with this condition. The reverse is not necessarily true, as PTSD can be acquired in a variety of ways including living in dangerous communities, surviving an environmental threat, and being in a war zone. Potentially no bullying would have taken place.

Just as we did not know the numbers or the full extent of the impact of PTSD when it was first identified, the same is true with APBS. This concept is new and is just being introduced here. I am not proposing it as a diagnosis. At this writing, I have identified some variables that seem to be associated with APBS, but the numbers or percentages of people suffering with it are yet to be determined. In subsequent chapters, you will encounter people for whom the idea of APBS might apply. It is important that the syndrome be recognized and that it become part of the conversation about the aftermath of childhood bullying. It does and will apply to many people. At this point in time, we are not aware of the numbers of people affected or the risk factors involved. As such, this syndrome requires much further research. Healthcare professionals always need to know what, exactly, they are dealing with in order to provide any effective help. It is critical that health practitioners and the general public begin to recognize adult post-bullying syndrome. In doing so, people's suffering can be interrupted. What adults might see as a positive aspect of APBS can be emphasized and enhanced. Importantly, they will not have to suffer alone without acknowledgment of their pain.

The next chapter discusses one of the major reasons that bullying occurs. Being different in any way provokes aggressive responses, some slight, some great, in children and even in some adults. In this chapter, we see some of the adverse effects in adult life for those who were singled out as different when they were children or teens.

CHAPTER 3

Being Different

The Traces That Difference Leaves Behind

"A strange animal among other animals (is) feared and hated for his strangeness."

Pearl S. Buck, *Peony*

Anything that is different can be perceived as a threat to our safety and comfort. From an ethological perspective, difference and weakness threaten the health and well-being of the herd. Those that are sick or lame are left behind or actively cast out to keep predators away from the majority. It is an evolutionary strategy that ensures the safety of the group. Bullying is a mechanism to put anyone who is different outside of the herd, to correct for difference, or to manipulate them into changing to the norm. However, unlike other mammals, when our group members live through exclusion by the majority, there are consequences both to the bullied and to the bulk of human society.

Expressing even the smallest difference can be dangerous for children. One woman, age 40, recalled that when she was in middle school "a group of girls came after me to beat me up for dressing too nice. We were all from a poor neighborhood, so I guess they thought I was trying to act above my station."

A 30-year-old woman who works as a teacher's aide confided, "I dressed differently from the other kids in elementary school. So I didn't fit in. The kids ignored me and wouldn't play with me." Again in middle school, "I never fit in with either the popular or the less popular kids. No one physically or verbally was mean but they wouldn't include me or would purposefully leave me out or ignore me. Some kids would pass notes around and make sure I wasn't involved" in whatever activity they had planned. She was never able to figure out what was wrong with her that the others did not want to be around her. She said that by high school she stopped trying to fit in with anyone because "I got the feeling I never would," so she began to hang around with much older people and people from other high schools. The sense of isolation she experienced back then is still palpable today. The idea that there was and is something wrong with her continues. She commented that she has a hard time fitting in to any social group and has difficulty making friends. How has this kind of treatment affected her intimate relationships as a grown woman? She disclosed, "I seem to always choose partners who are mean to me. I guess I feel I should take what I get from them." She has deep-seated problems with trusting anyone and believes this stems back to the numerous instances of exclusion throughout her school days.

More drastic differences can elicit condemnation as well. This was the case for Christina Hendricks. An actress in the television series *Mad Men*, she experienced unremitting bullying when she was in high school. She explained, "I was a goth kid. I dyed my hair about 42 different colors, shaved it at the back and wore black make-up. Kids can be pretty judgmental about people who are different. But instead of breaking down and conforming, I stood firm. That is also probably why I was unhappy" (*Huffington Post*, 2012).

SHAME

Shame and difference of any sort tend to be inextricable. Often, victims of crime, such as assault or sexual abuse, carry a sense of shame associated with what has happened to them (Yoon, Funk, & Kropf, 2010). They do this despite the fact that the shame for the violent act belongs to the perpetrator. The question lingers: "Why me?" Victims answer this by deciding that they did something wrong or something is fundamentally wrong with them (Perren, Gutzwiller-Helfenfinger, Malti, & Hymel, 2012). They decide there is something different about them from other people, something that caused the victimization in the first place. Victims of bullying, exclusion, and harassment also feel high levels of shame that last well into adulthood (Carlisle & Rofes, 2007). They might experience shame connected with some aspect of themselves that is considered different in comparison to culturally acceptable standards such as their body image, their physical abilities, or something as essential as their basic personhood.

Sam, age 58, disclosed that he was regularly hit by a boy in middle school. The boy considered Sam to be different because they came from separate ethnic groups. Sam was "picked on" and hit by the other boy for over two years with no one putting a stop to it. Sam was also hit on a regular basis by his mother. He came from what he describes as "a very physical family." Eventually, Sam began to punch his younger brother as a means to take out his own frustrations about his treatment by his mother and by the boy at school. In Sam's case, there was no one to defend him and his reaction was equivalent to the "kick the dog" syndrome—passing along to the next weaker in line what has been meted out to you. I asked Sam if he ever told either of his parents about the boy at school. He shook his head and he responded with one word: "Shame." His shame was compounded, he feels, by the fact that by high school he began to hide from this boy and others who might do the same thing to him. What is the impact on personal development of this sense of shame? Does it become an ingrained part of the self? How does it affect other decisions that a person makes during school years and after? Sam believes shame is a part of his most basic self, his essential self now as an adult affecting all aspects of his life.

I had the opportunity to interview Rebecca. Rebecca, 57, also still lives with shame from her school days and her family history. The youngest of three children, she was bullied and sexually harassed at school. She was bullied at home by her older two siblings, who were 7 and 10 years older than she was. Their bullying stemmed from general family dysfunction. The father was employed irregularly. The family could not count on a steady income. Consequently, they lived with a constant state of anxiety. Rebecca became the brunt of the tensions. She was a cute and lively little girl, different from her siblings. But this difference only made her more of a target. This kind of personality might have provided some comic relief, but in her family there was too much upheaval. For some children, school is an antidote to the toxicity of home life. There, if they are lucky, they can blossom in the presence of kind teachers and positive role models. However, for Rebecca, this was not the case. She had a difficult time academically and so she was not one of the teachers' favorites. She had a hard time sitting still and earned a reputation of being a "wanderer," out of her seat and migrating around the classroom talking to other students. By the end of elementary school, she had sprouted up to her almost full adult height and was physically well developed. All of these factors brought negative attention in the form of bullying and sexual harassment from her peers as well as from some of the teachers. Rebecca describes this treatment as continuing throughout much of high school until her peers caught up with her in their own bodies. However, even before graduating, there was a toll to pay. Rebecca began smoking by middle school and drinking by first year of high school. She drank on a regular basis. This wasn't hard to accomplish, as her parents had alcohol at home when there was a paycheck. By the time she graduated, Rebecca had a "drinking problem." As an adult, she is an alcoholic and has been in rehab five different times. She is also addicted to painkillers. She can go for years without drinking or using and then relapses, like many others with this disease. The difference for Rebecca is that she attributes the first drinks not to adolescent exploration but to the need to numb out. The need to quiet her mind from the taunts of teachers and kids propelled her toward her initial experiences with alcohol. And it worked. She feels a great deal of shame about the things that were said to her when she was bullied and tormented as a child and also about being an alcoholic. It is difficult for her to separate one from the other. In listening to her describe this, it seems as if shame, nothing else, is at the core of her being.

In recounting his experiences, one man said, "I wasn't able to protect myself from bullying in late elementary school. It made me fearful and brought a sense of shame. I had a difficult time in preadolescence; I felt weak and ashamed. I still carry it with me."

What can seem trivial, such as making fun of some aspect of a person, can be a cause for shame in a child. This shame can last for a very long time. A woman, 33, reported, "I was bullied intensely in elementary school because my hair was not straight and it wasn't like the other girls. It was bushy and thick. Now even as an adult, I continue to feel ashamed when I am with people who don't have hair like mine." She went on to say that because the bullying was done by the popular kids, she wanted to be popular, too. So she became a bully. Interestingly, she did not express shame over bullying others, only over the aspect of herself that led to being victimized.

Shame and Aggression

Shame is both an outcome and a precursor of bullying, harassment, and violence. It leads to low self-esteem and acting against oneself in the form of self-sabotage, depression, and anxiety. It can lead to acting out in the form of seeking justice, retribution, and revenge. Often, anger and rage reside at the core for someone who has been repeatedly shamed. Some people will act out with retaliation. When we see children or adults who do retaliate, they may feel shamed to a greater degree by peers or school personnel. Shame is linked with aggressive behavior toward others

(Aslund, Leppert, Starrin, & Nilsson, 2009; Butterfield, 1995; Gilligan, 1996; Stuewig, Tangney, Heigel, Harty, & McCloskey, 2010) and toward self in the form of suicide (Coggan, Bennett, Hooper, & Dickinson, 2003; Kanetsuna et al., 2006). Children who are victims of bullying and harassment are made to feel ashamed of who they are. They feel ashamed, hurt, and confused when they are shunned by their peers. They feel ashamed that they are singled out for taunting, and they feel ashamed and angry that they cannot figure out how to make it stop. Shame plays an important role in the enactment of bullying as retaliatory aggression. Ahmed and Braithwaite (2005) found that children who bully are displacing the anger they feel as a result of being shamed by others. On the other hand, children who manage their shame in more socially acceptable ways are less likely to become bullies or act out in any kind of violent manner.

Being rejected, humiliated, ridiculed, and held out as "other" or different leads to deep feelings of shame. Aslund and colleagues (2009) found that adolescents who were insulted and shamed by others were inclined toward aggression and that there were significant social status differences. Their study included a sample of almost 5,400 teenagers ages 15 to 18. The inquiry controlled for variables such as social status of their families and with their peers. It also looked at verbal as well as physical aggression based on shaming experiences. In general, the more shaming experiences the adolescents encountered the more likely they were to be aggressive. Further, those students who had both high family and high peer group status or were considered low status in both categories were at higher risk for aggressive behavior when shamed than the students in the middle. Somehow being in the middle status for family and peer group hierarchy seemed to serve as a protective factor against shaming that could lead to aggression. There were also gender differences. Boys who were considered in the low status group for both family and school were most likely to engage in physical violence, while girls from the high status groups were most likely. For verbal aggression, both boys and girls from the high status groups were much more inclined to deal with shaming experiences via verbal retaliation than any other group. As these researchers point out, "Shaming constitutes a social threat" (p. 9), and as such people must figure out a means to deal with it, some solutions being more mature than others. For a fascinating account of the foundation of a culture of shame and violence in our country, see Fox Butterfield (1995), *All God's Children: The Bosket Family and the American Tradition of Violence*. Winner of the Pulitzer Prize, it is an immensely interesting and very readable account of the connection between honor and vengeance from the southern tradition and how it has influenced American life. In the Old South, men challenged one another to a duel to the death. This was to preserve their honor in the face of real or perceived disrespect. From this example, we see a cultural basis for aggressive acting out based on shame. Another interesting book on how shame is connected with violence is Jonathan Fast's *Beyond Bullying: How to Break the Cycle of Shame, Bullying, and Violence* (in press). Fast also cites historical and cultural issues that unite these factors.

Shame and Guilt

There are those who think that shame is the other side of the coin of arrogance (see Morrison, 2014; Tangney & Dearing, 2002). When you see someone who is arrogant, the theory is you are seeing someone who has been shamed and who might be considered shame-based. How do shame and guilt interact? When someone has a healthy sense of self (is not shame-based), and he does something wrong, he experiences guilt. If you have been shamed much of your life, your capacity for guilt is diminished (Tangney & Dearing, 2003). Those who are most shame-based are most able to commit acts of violence because they have less intrinsic capacity for guilt. The theory continues, if you have the capacity for guilt, your likelihood of committing acts of extreme violence is lessened (Stuewig et al., 2014). The absence of guilt is a precondition for shame-related violence. In attempts to replace the shame-base that many criminals experience before they are ever convicted, some prisons provide educational opportunities. Studies have found that those prisoners who complete a college degree, or in some other way are able to gain self-respect while in prison, have a much lower recidivism rate than the general population of inmates (Chappell, 2004; Vacca, 2004).

When people have been shamed from the beginning of their lives, it becomes almost impossible to feel guilt. What they feel is shame. When people are humiliated, they become shamed. Some people try to overcome shame through arrogance; some may overcome shame by dying in acts of glory or misplaced "glory," such as are witnessed in acts of extreme school violence.

Shame and Trauma

Shame has many adverse effects, and one is that it can result in trauma. Matos and Pinto-Gouveia (2010) conducted a study to explore the premise that "shame episodes can have the properties of traumatic memories, involving intrusions, flashbacks, strong emotional avoidance, hyper arousal, fragmented states of mind and dissociation" (p. 299). With 811 participants, their research results showed that early shame experiences can result in traumatic memories. Further, these kinds of memories produce feelings of shame that carry over into adult life.

BODY IMAGE

"A friend of mine was always bullied by a group of boys in 3rd grade because she was tall, thin, and gawky."

Children can be ostracized about their body when it deviates from the norm or what is seen as "typical." In a study by Jansen et al. (2014), obese elementary school children were more likely than overweight and normal weight children to be both victims and aggressors of bullying. In their research about bullying and weight, Fox and Farrow (2009) found that overweight or obese preadolescents, ages 11 to 14, were more likely to be verbally and physically bullied than other children. They also had greater body dissatisfaction, lower self-esteem, and less overall sense of self-worth. As children grow, body shape and size become of particular importance. Adolescence is a time of great change to one's body. Puberty means development of secondary sexual characteristics that are, for the most part, noticeable to others. Teens who develop sooner than others, later than the norm, or who are more developed or remain undeveloped, are likely targets for bullying and sexual harassment by peers and sometimes by school personnel (Cunningham et al., 2010; Shakeshaft, 2004).

Sandy, age 29, confided, "I have extreme issues with my body image and self-esteem as a result of the ridicule I experienced as a child in elementary and middle school. I avoid getting involved with skinny or slender men for fear that someday they will just end up rejecting me because of my body shape or size. So I am beginning to notice that I tend to sabotage relationships to protect myself from future rejection. I want to be the one who gets out first."

Numerous research studies demonstrate a statistically significant correlation between being overweight and being the target of bullying (Brixval, Rayce, Rasmussen, Holstein, & Due, 2011; Lumeng et al., 2010; Puhl & Latner, 2007). Weight concerns, childhood obesity, and bullying are linked together and constitute a prevalent public health problem. Children with chronic conditions such as obesity are at a particularly increased risk of peer victimization (Lumeng et al., 2010; Sentenac et al., 2012). This is not a surprise in a culture that makes a fetish of thinness. A "Barbie Doll" figure is the epitome of female body shapes. Being criticized about weight is a unique form of bullying that often leads to ongoing problems (Sentenac et al., 2012). Nelson and colleagues (2011) conducted a study of preadolescent children that looked at the criticism they received about their weight and the subsequent dissatisfaction they felt about their bodies. They found that, compared with preadolescents who were not bullied about their weight, criticism about weight was a significant predictor of body dissatisfaction, problems with body size perception, and low self-esteem. A similar relationship was noted in a study of almost 5,000 7th through 12th grade students. Boys and girls "teased" about their weight demonstrated "low body satisfaction, low self-esteem, high depressive symptoms, and thinking about and attempting suicide, even after controlling for actual body weight" (Eisenberg, Neumark-Sztainer, & Story, 2003, p. 733). This was true for all racial, ethnic, and weight groups in the study.

I had the chance to interview Delia, a 26-year-old African American woman who told me her story of being bullied in elementary school. She was overweight, so the children engaged in physical and verbal bullying toward her. She said, "They would hit me and run away thinking I was too fat to chase them. They thought I was a pushover. They would pick fights with me and verbally harass me." Luckily, she is an intellectually gifted person. As a result, eventually she attended a public high school specifically for gifted students where there was a great deal of cultural diversity. Here she was allowed to be herself. There was a high level of acceptance and respect for differences in others. It was in high school that she began the process of accepting herself "with all my imperfections," because she was accepted and excelled there. Still, she is very clear. If she is in a relationship with someone, she does not like to be picked on, and it is likely to bring up insecurities when, and if, it happens.

Emily is 28 and attended suburban schools for her whole K through 12 career. She was tormented about her weight in both elementary and middle school. The kids had a favorite nickname for her: "thunder thighs." Finally by high school she stood up for herself by calling out another girl who was talking about her behind her back. The other girl ended up crying, so this is an incident in which Emily considers herself to have been a bully. She never told her parents about any events of bullying because she felt too embarrassed. Now as an adult, she can see the damage. Emily said, "I am very self-conscious about my weight whenever I think about getting into a relationship with anyone. I automatically feel inferior and expect that, at some point, they will make fun of my body." Another way in which bullying has affected Emily is in her decision-making. She has felt too timid to venture much out into the world. She sticks pretty close to her city of origin. She feels it is familiar to her and she does not need to face the dread of getting to know new people who might ridicule her.

Liz, a graduate student, is 27, and she still has a great deal of anger from the times she was bullied because of her weight. She has not been able to forget or forgive those involved. They made her life miserable. Liz grew up in a former Soviet-bloc country, where she was bullied by kids over her weight and ostracized by teachers who said she was "dirty." Her family moved to the United States when she was a teenager, and she was bullied here as well. She said, "I realize that due to my history of being bullied, I've turned to using aggression as a coping mechanism. This has led me to bully others." Liz also related that her anger has made her more controlling in all of her relationships and it is for this reason that many of them do not succeed. For Liz, being the target of bullying and weight gain became a vicious cycle. She turned to chocolate and other sweets for consolation from the terrible taunts and physical bullying by other children. To this day, she still turns to food when she is having a hard time controlling her emotions. She is adamant that her use of food as a coping method started with harassment by peers and teachers. To compound the issue, her grandmother had dubbed her the "strong child." So she didn't want to express her unhappiness at home; she desperately wanted to keep this good title and consequently developed what she called "emotional reserve." Even though she acquired negative eating habits, she did not share her feelings of shame and sadness at home. Only now is she beginning to accept that it is okay to have and deal with emotions. And only now is she beginning to trust that others want to be her friend. She has "hundreds" of friends on FaceBook but she said that even with hundreds of new friends she never feels accepted enough or supported enough.

Many people in my research were bullied due to being overweight but a minority reminded me that those at the other end of the spectrum are bullied too. In our country, we tend to think of "weight problems" as revolving around being overweight or obese, unless someone is clearly anorexic. Sophie, age 42, is a high school teacher. During her formative years she was bullied in a variety of ways based on her very thin body type. She has a small frame ("like my maternal grandfather") and she is just naturally thin. This was perfectly acceptable at home, and she would never have seen this as a problem except for her treatment by peers at school. Sophie stated, "I internalized the bullying and this prevented me from trying new activities. It resulted in lower self-esteem and self-worth." What did Sophie miss out on as a consequence of not trying new activities? We can only wonder how her self-worth would have been impacted in a positive manner if she had not experienced this type of bullying when she was so young and impressionable. Similarly, an African American woman related this about her experience: "I was never physically bullied but the verbal bullying affected my low self-esteem a great deal. It also made me so self-conscious about my appearance, especially my weight. I was very skinny, I had little hair, and bad skin. Now as a 35-year-old woman, I have just learned how to feel comfortable about my size and body image. Skinny is not in for African Americans."

Height and Weight

Caitlin, age 22, discussed the impact of repeated bullying by girls at her school. Caitlin told me she was always very tall for her age and a little chubby. Even in elementary school she was bullied over it. She remembers distinctly a group of girls, led by a rather short one, who made fun of her "to no end" about her height and they ganged up on her repeatedly to do this. By junior high, they continued but added another component. The same ringleader told everyone that Caitlin liked a particular boy and that she was "embarrassing herself for thinking he could ever like her." Caitlin continued, "I felt like I had no friends." This is an especially egregious situation for someone in junior high school, where acceptance and having a group of friends is paramount in a teen's thinking. She said, "I still remember how bad I felt. Logically, today, I know that I am thin. But being called fat for so many years has left a lasting impression on my body image. I am very self-conscious about my height and weight. I pray that when I have children they won't have to go through the same things I did." She went on to say that she has great trouble trusting others and assumes that her friends do not actually like her. Further, due to her negative body image, she has turned away potential intimate partners fearing what their remarks might be about her. Some days she feels so negatively about herself that she decides not to do something or go somewhere based on fear that no one will want to talk with her. This may seem like an extreme or atypical reaction. Unfortunately, it is a story I heard over and over again in my discussions with people about their bullying experiences and how it is still with them today.

ACADEMIC PROWESS

An African American man, age 32, who worked as an accountant, related,

"I got in a lot of fights in elementary school. Older boys picked on me and I had to fight back. By the time I was in middle school, I was known for doing well in mathematics and the other boys tried to intimidate me to fall back in the pack. It is never okay to be at the top academically. It seems to threaten most of the other kids. So they tried to intimidate me, to get me to change, and I could tell they didn't like me because of it. I kind of felt sorry for myself, and that has lasted with me. I always wonder why they did it; they could have tried and done well in school themselves. Other than sometimes feeling sorry for myself, I'm not sure of the impact on me. I did eventually forgive them, but it did take me some time to do that."

RACE

Race and bullying are intimately linked due to the persistence of racism in our culture and others. But what is the difference between racism and bullying based on race? Hatred is a defining characteristic of racism. Someone is hated solely as a result of belonging to a particular racial group. Racial bullying is based on racial characteristics or perceived differences in behavior. In either case there are sad outcomes. Goldweber and colleagues (2012) examined the connections among bullying, race, and urbanicity for over 10,000 middle school students. They found that African American middle school students were more likely to be both victims of bullying and bully/victims based on race than Caucasian or Hispanic children. Race and school connectivity are risk factors for bullying involvement. A Canadian study indicated that while African Canadian students were both bullies and victims of bullying, the amount of bullying based on race appeared to decrease when they felt connected to their school and when there was a high level of teacher diversity in the schools (Larochette, Murphy, & Craig, 2010). These studies describe overt racial bullying. However, there are more subtle forms of bullying connected to race also. One young woman in my study, age 29, grew up in an urban area and attended a racially divided school district. She reported that in middle school her best friend was African American and she would be teased constantly because the girl was her friend and she, herself, was white. After all of the "teasing," the way she viewed others who were different changed. Before that, she never thought anything of racial difference until her peers began to point it out. Consequently, after a while, she and her best friend began to drift apart due to the stress. She says that since that time, she has never been close to someone from a different race. This is, indeed, a loss on many levels for this young woman.

Ana, age 24, was bullied in elementary and middle school. The bullying always consisted of racial slurs and epithets meant to hurt her. In middle school, she was also beat up on the school bus due to being Hispanic. Today she is apprehensive at the beginning of establishing friendships. Most certainly, she does not trust females who have the same physical characteristics as those who bullied her. In this way, she is excluding whole groups of people for consideration as friends in order to protect herself from the harm they *might* bring her.

A Native American woman, age 23, shared, "I was bullied throughout school for being Native American. I went to small, rural schools in the Northeast. People would call me inappropriate names and they would mock me with what they thought were Indian gestures, calls, and dance moves. It did have an impact on me but not what they would have wanted. It made me even more proud to be Native."

DISABILITIES

Disabilities can cover a broad range from those that are obvious to those that are unseen. Children with emotional, intellectual, learning, or physical disabilities run a greater risk of bullying involvement than their peers (Glumbić & Žunić-Plavović, 2010; Sweeting & West, 2001). Farmer and colleagues (2012) compared students with disabilities and those without. Their findings indicate that children in special education were more likely to be both victims and bully/victims than other children. Further, children on the autistic spectrum have a high rate of victimization (Sreckovic, Brunsting, & Able, 2014). Their difference seems to be particularly aggravating to adolescents who conclude they bring bullying on themselves by their out-of-the-norm behavior (deLara, 2002). Having a chronic condition or disability increases the intensity and prevalence of bullying victimization. Pittet, Berchtold, Akré, Michaud, and Suris (2010) compared children with chronic conditions with those in a control group. What they found was that the kids with chronic issues were at greater risk of being bullied and of experiencing multiple forms of bullying. Further, research has found that children with disabilities who are bullied do, indeed, carry consequences into adult life. Hugh-Jones and Smith (1999) found that over half of the participants in their study who stammered experienced the effects of their prior bullying. The effects were specific to their personal adult relationships. However, even what adults might consider minor issues of difference can be challenging for children. A 25-year-old woman conveyed this example:

"I came from a blended family. My parents were divorced and when my mom re-married, my stepfather brought his son into our family. He was a great kid;

I really liked him and I was proud of him. He had a learning disability and a slight speech problem, though, so kids made fun of him. Whenever I saw it, I would stick up for my new step-brother. One time I did this to a friend who was dissing him and after that, she began to actively ignore me and to stop including me in anything fun. She managed to get her friends, and all of my former friends, to go along with her for all of 6th grade. It still hurts when I think of it. It is so painful for a kid that young to be left out. I so much wanted to go to the parties and the sleepovers. I know I did the right thing; my parents were proud of me. But I wish the cost wasn't so high. Today, I am very sensitive to rejection or exclusion—and I probably see it where it doesn't exist."

I did not ask specifically about disabilities in my study, and no one self-identified, but interested readers could profit by obtaining Dr. Faye Mishna's book *Bullying: A Guide to Research, Intervention, and Prevention* (2012).

A BULLY AND GUILT

Charlene, is African American, 44, and a school counselor. She described her history with bullying and the guilt she is left with:

"I have memories from my own childhood about how I bullied and made fun of kids who had disabilities and who appeared 'different.' That experience has shaped who I am today. The reason that I used to pick on these kids was because I did not understand their disability and why they were different from me, and many kids felt the same way. The kids who were autistic were such easy targets for us. As I got older I felt bad and guilty about what I did. I never thought of myself as a mean person. Now as an adult, I work with adults with disabilities. You might think this is sort of ironic. It's how I can make up for what I did. It's how I give back."

ECONOMIC STATUS

Research indicates a relationship between poverty and bullying; children who are poor may engage in bullying or delinquent behavior (Shetgiri, Lin, Avila, & Flores, 2010; Stevens, Morash, & Park, 2011). At the same time, kids who are poor come in for an inordinate amount of bullying (Eamon, 2001). They don't have the "right" shoes or clothes. They can't keep up with current trends for any material object that is prized by adolescent society or the greater society for that matter. It is harder to understand when kids who are wealthy are subjects of bullying, harassment, and social exclusion. But this can be the case. Lisa grew up in a small rural community where most people just scraped by. Her family, though, was wealthy by community standards. Lisa states that her family did have a decent amount but that they were "quiet about money." They lived in a very large house; one that none of her classmates had seen before. Their homes could not compare. One day on a 6th grade field trip, the bus drove by Lisa's house and her teacher pointed it out to all the students. After that she was placed in the "you guys are rich" category. On first consideration, it does not seem like such a bad thing, especially when compared to the torment faced by poor children when attention is drawn to their homes by peers and bus drivers. As I have pointed out in previous research, school bus drivers can function as either friend or foe to vulnerable students (deLara, 2008). For Lisa, this was a day that changed her life. Once kids decided she was rich, they also decided she was "different" and that led to jealousies. Two girls, in particular, were envious and pretended to befriend her. They ended up spreading what she described as "terrible sexual rumors" about Lisa. She was called awful names that completely demoralized her. The end result of the rumors was rejection and exclusion. She still had two friends who stuck by her, but her circle of friends was reduced dramatically. Now as a 29-year-old adult, Lisa cried on and off in retelling her story. Lisa shared, "I had thoughts of wanting to hurt myself. You want it to go away. I kept thinking—'How can I make it go away?'" She went on,

"I had to learn how to use my gut instincts—who can I trust? I still get triggered by it. It takes me back to my middle-school self. It's still there. I have a huge emotional response when I think about it. I still worry that people will make fun of me. I always feel that way, especially in an environment with a lot of women. I think 'Is that person making fun of me?' I do understand that I had something that other people didn't have—it created jealousy. But there still is this feeling of powerlessness. I should be able to say something to someone who's bothering me. I can't. I wish I could do that."

SMALL DIFFERENCES

Tiffany is now 30 years old, but she remembers distinctly the bullying incidents that happened for her when she was in elementary school and middle school. She attended what she described as "medium sized" suburban, public schools. It was her inclination and behavior to try to stick up for other children who were harassed, but then the bullying would be directed toward her. Because she had visible facial imperfections and dark facial hair, she was picked on mercilessly by the other kids. She was constantly teased for not wearing the right clothes, the clothes of the popular group. The impact from this kind of ridicule is that Tiffany is very self-conscious about her appearance, perhaps more than most people. She finds it extremely difficult to get ready for work or anything else. She believes that this is due to the persistent "teasing" about her appearance. Consequently, she states, "I spend a ridiculous amount of time getting ready and making sure I look okay to leave the house. I am constantly picking at imperfections on my face. Since I take forever to get ready, this hinders some plans and makes my friends and my boyfriend upset. I refuse to go out into public if I don't feel my physical appearance is up to a specific standard. So I have missed some very important events as a result." This is a sad commentary. Tiffany is left with sometimes crippling effects of the bullying that she endured. When we hear this account, we can only wonder how many other people are living with the same feelings and reacting in the same ways to try to preserve a sense of safety and dignity. Without knowing anything about this person's background or childhood experiences, we might be tempted to label her vain or narcissistic, but that would be missing the mark. She has learned these behaviors to take care of herself. Her attempts are meant to avoid further bullying in her life.

BEING DIFFERENT IN SEXUAL ORIENTATION

With more states sanctioning the marriage of same-sex couples, it seems the stigma for difference in sexual orientation is lessening. As further evidence of the decreasing stigma, popular television programs feature gay couples. At the same time that this is true, children and adolescents are still subject to taunts and comments meant to degrade them about their sexual orientation or perceived sexual orientation (Berlan, Corliss, Field, Goodman, & Bryn Austin, 2010; Meyer, 2015). Though there was a question in my study asking, "Were you bullied due to your sexual orientation?" only a very few answered "yes" to this. Some people answered that they were called "gay" or "lesbian" but not that they were bullied or harassed for their orientation per se. This could be due to the age of the people in my study or perhaps due to the fact that they did not "come out" during high school. Or perhaps they simply did not want to answer the question. We do know that lesbian, gay, bisexual, transgender, and questioning (LGBTQ) students are more likely to have unexcused absences from school (Robinson & Espelage, 2012). They are more likely to be threatened with a weapon than are heterosexual kids, they are four times more likely to attempt suicide, and they are five times more likely to miss school due to fear for their safety. They spend much of their time just trying to figure out how to be safe in school, severely impacting their ability to concentrate on academics, and nearly one-third of LGBTQ teens drop out of school due to harassment and fear for their personal safety (GLSEN, 2005; Ryan & Futterman, 2001). Further, Berlan et al. (2010) examined the relationship between sexual orientation and bullying for adolescents. Among the over 7,500 teenagers ages 14–22 who participated, data indicated that there were statistically significant differences concerning bullying and victimization between heterosexual and sexual minority teens.

Christopher, Sexual Orientation, and Bullying

Long-lasting impacts and trauma can be associated with bullying due to sexual orientation (Rivers, 2004; Roberts, Austin, Corliss, Vandermorris, & Koenen, 2010).

Christopher, 30, is a very dedicated social worker. He shared this articulate story with me:

> When I started to think about what I wanted to share about my experiences with bullying and the lasting effect they have had on my adult life, I first thought about being different. Being different means so many things when I think about my life. I first knew I was different in preschool. At the age of four I only wanted to play with the little girls in my class and for whatever reasons I failed completely to bond with the little boys. I could not understand why the boys did not want to play with My Little Ponies, which at that time was my pastime of choice. While I knew I was different then I had not yet been exposed to enough societal pressure to force me to make an attempt to conform to the gender imposed socially acceptable norms that would plague me throughout my entire child and adolescent development.
>
> I remember when the bullying began. I grew up in a very small town. With only a handful of kids in my peer group I was bused nearly thirty minutes to a school with a graduating class of less than ninety students. In this environment gossip and hearsay spread quickly. In the sixth grade students in my school moved from the elementary school to the high school building. Elementary school provided a kind of protection. I remember kids being mean to each other from time to time

but overall I loved school until transitioning to the high school building in sixth grade. The turning point for me occurred in sixth grade in the days leading up to Valentine's Day. One of the upper level classes raised money for a class trip by selling carnations for a dollar to be delivered on Valentines to whomever the sender wished. In an effort to participate, I decided I would send a flower to my friend at the time. So I bought my flower to be sent to a male friend. Too naïve to realize how this act would be interrupted by my peers I sent my friend a flower not knowing that this simple action would lay a path of bullying that would impact the remainder of my school experience and have lasting effects to this day.

By sending the flower, within minutes, it seemed everyone in the school had labeled me queer. Except queer was not the term they used (or at least not in the context I use it to explain my sexuality today). Faggot seemed to be their word of choice; I remember being called this the most throughout school, but there was an assortment of others. Then there was a period of time when a group of male peers took to calling me Christine. Throughout this time, I withdrew a great deal. Most people in my life including my parents didn't seem to worry about me much. This was likely due to the fact that I hid my depression well. I maintained excellent grades ranking amongst the best in my class. I took piano lessons from a woman in town at which I excelled and won awards, and I volunteered at my grandmother's nursing home. The common theme however was that in those areas I was either working independently or interacting with people outside of my peer group. When it came to peer interaction my development was substantially impaired. I was painfully shy at school. I did manage to make a few friends to sit with at lunch, but I never once spent time with a friend outside of school. I never once was invited to a party. There was also a clear theme with my friends. My friends were women, many of whom I imagine could write their own chapter on the impact of bullying into adult life. We bonded together more out of need for survival than common interests.

The hardest part of the day was always gym class. Boys and girls physical education was separate so what few supports I had were gone, and I was forced to take on alone the taunting of adolescent boys in an environment where locker room behavior is all too literal. It was in the largely unsupervised locker room where I remember the majority and the more extreme bullying I experienced. Name calling was pretty standard but in the locker room things were escalated. Specifically I remember two different occasions when my street clothes were taken. Once they were thrown down the hall, the other time they were thrown into the shower causing me to spend the rest of the day in my gym shorts and t-shirt. Boys would describe and accuse me of obscene sexual acts and laugh as

I held back tears. Once I even recall a boy exposing himself to me and saying to everyone that he bet I wanted to give him oral sex.

I would stay after school almost every day to practice piano in the music room. In the small sound proof room I would plunk away on the piano and process the day. I will say there are days I would cry. Mostly I was just thankful that the day was over and I would soon be headed home.

My parents knew that I struggled with bullying but I never made clear to them the extent to which I was struggling. And they were content to believe that my grades and involvement in piano were indicators that I was doing well enough.

The irony of all of this was that despite living in an environment where everyone knew I was queer, I was more confused about my sexuality that anything else. The bullying made me fight what I knew was true. I can't say I wanted to belong to my peer group, but I wanted so badly for the bullying to stop. I felt if I could change myself, if I could stop these thoughts, these attractions, I could curb the bullying. I could at the very least fade into the background and just get by. As a result my sexual development was also delayed. I did not even make an attempt to date or reach a single sexual milestone until my later years of college, and even then it was in an effort to pass for heterosexual and further repress my sexuality.

Needless to say, I graduated from high school. The bullying was largely over, however the consequences both direct and indirect were just beginning. Despite being accepted to a number of schools my mother, both out of concern and out of her own inability to accept the impending adulthood that was before me, insisted that I go to community college and live at home for my freshman year of college. Her reasoning was that I was too shy and that I lacked the maturity to be successful living in a dorm. Community college in my hometown was referred to as "grade 13." This was because in a small economically depressed town like the one I grew up in most people who went to college went to our local community college. Any hope I had of starting over with a new peer group was gone. My classes were filled with the same peers that I had known since kindergarten. I will say that they seemed to lose interest in picking on me, but they weren't friendly either.

It was during this time that my depression began to turn to anger. First the anger was largely projected on to my parents. I blamed them for not letting me go away to school for what I perceived would have given me a fresh start, in some way erasing the history of high school allowing me to grow and flourish. My relationship with my parents became strained to the point where they made the decision that I could go to a local state college about forty minutes from their house. They also encouraged me to get an apartment and live there on my own. I leapt at the chance to escape, but without my parents around to take the brunt of my anger I turned on myself.

Throughout high school, I coped with the stress I experienced in part by eating. On graduation from high school I weighed over three hundred pounds. During my sophomore and junior year of undergrad I would lose nearly a hundred and thirty pounds. While this was initially viewed as a healthy thing, as people learned how I lost the weight it became clearer that I was far sicker than they realized. Undergrad for me was not about parties and making friendships that lasted a lifetime but it was about going to school continuing to work hard for high marks and about sleeping. For two years that was almost all I did. My sleep was broken up by class and studying but rarely anything else, not even meals. If I ate one meal a day that was a big eating day. As I lost weight I started to get positive feedback from people and I fed off of it. Each person's comments about my appearance gave me the attention that I guess I did not know I had been craving from years of being taunted and teased. I continued to take more extreme measures to lose weight until in the summer between my junior and senior year I fainted at my summer job after barely eating for three days. It was at this point I entered mental health treatment for the first time.

I finished undergrad becoming healthier and made the decision to pursue graduate school. I moved away from my home town area for the first time and I really began to flourish. Free from that environment and the memories associated, I was able to accept my queer sexuality and come out over the course of my two years of graduate school.

If I have one regret in life it would be that it took until I was twenty-three to come out, the depression that had been built over all of those years was so debilitating that I missed out on having the college experience that people talk about so fondly. When I did come out however I came out in an environment that was able to fully support and accept me. I know that would not have been possible had I come out earlier.

Now looking back as an adult I can draw connections to facets of behavior that I can directly link to bullying. I remain a rather shy and introverted person. I know that I am able to open up when I feel confident in the information that is being discussed. In my professional life I am able to feel comfortable in nearly any situation because I know that I am very capable in this arena and that I have earned the respect of my colleagues. Contrast that however with a cocktail party in which I know very few people, I am likely to be found clinging to the people I do know, or sitting awkwardly scanning the room, observing people who seem to have been born with an ability to make small talk that I can only hope to acquire someday.

There is another important result of my bullying, one that is more internal. While I believe my experience with bullying is what made me such an empathetic person, it is also what has made me so self-critical. I am the first one to point out my flaws and I often struggle to take compliments and accept positive feedback. I constantly question if I am doing enough to please people, and I know that sometimes I try too hard and it can be off putting. I know that when I make mistakes people do not necessarily feel badly toward me, but still there is this sense of wanting people to be happy with me at all times for fear that rejection is only one screw-up away.

I still continue to have struggles with depression, thankfully it has never reached the point it did when I was in undergrad. I know now what my warning signs are and have developed a tremendous support system and self-care routine. In a way I have embraced my bullying. While my current job does not always allow for it, I jump at any chance I have to work with queer youth. Being able to provide them with the support I needed at their age allows me to reclaim some of the power that I didn't have in school. It allows me push back in hopes that something positive will have come from my struggles."

Christopher's story is heartbreaking. He suffered years of torment from his peers based on difference—difference that he could not change or subjugate, much as he may have wished. It is painful to think of a young boy dealing with this level of sadness and doing so essentially by himself. We can see the lifelong impacts of depression, influence on self-concept, and still feeling ill at ease in social situations. At the same time, Christopher is left with a strong willingness and ability to help others in similar circumstances to those he withstood. He is a person of courage and dignity despite years of humiliation.

Perceptions

Perceptions, too, of a person's sexual orientation or gender identity can cause lasting damage. Taylor, age 28, suffered through much psychological bullying in middle school. Her classmates circulated a rumor that she was lesbian. It became a topic for discussion every day for about 3 years. She remembers feeling so alone and on guard all the time. Her peers would make comments to her and make up stories that involved seeing her with other girls. The harassment would occur most often during unstructured, unsupervised times of the school day. She told her parents about it and they suggested seeing the school counselor, which she did. They also started driving her to school so she did not have to endure the bullying and harassment on the school bus. Taylor still thinks about what happened "weekly, if not more." She is left wondering how her behavior is perceived by others. She has never been comfortable in close relationships with other women because of the fear she felt in school. She worries that someone will start rumors again. Today Taylor has very few female friends, having never learned how to have healthy relationships with women.

DIFFERENCE AND THE BEHAVIORAL IMMUNE SYSTEM

Being different, in almost any way, can trigger what Schaller and Park (2011) called the behavioral immune system. In this hypothesis, staying away from differentness (a person with a wine-stain birthmark on the face for example), is meant to preserve the physical health of an individual or a group. How might this apply to preserving other aspects of well-being of an individual or a group? Such as emotional well-being or a sense of safety?

If applied to the phenomenon of bullying, the behavioral immune system hypothesis implies that people are most prone to bully others as a way of minimizing contact with them. Jane Goodall (1988), world-renowned primatologist, observed situations in which an ill chimp was either excluded or actively ostracized from the rest of the troop. This is quite like children who ostracize their peers for any forms of difference such as being on the autistic spectrum, having a disability, or having a mental illness. Children will ostracize others for lesser forms of difference like dressing differently than the norm.

Shying away or staying away from those who exhibit differences, isolating those who are different physically, emotionally, or behaviorally, seems to serve a function in adolescent society as it does in society in general. In my research with adolescents I have found that they place high value on being able to predict the behavior of their peers. They are clear that with the advent of deadly school shootings, this is necessary. So, as a means of staying alert, they consciously observe their classmates, are aware of those who tend to act out violently, and calculate the numbers of times per week that unpredictable behaviors occur. This peer predictability, this mindfulness of others serves, they believe, a protective function (deLara, 2002). Societies and cultures work hard to prescribe and enforce norms of acceptable behavior. What are the reasons for having these norms in the first place? They provide predictability, which is useful in a civilized society. In the United States we can expect that everyone will drive on the right side of the road while we are traveling at high speeds to reach our destinations. If there were no norm or law pertaining to it, driving would be chaotic, unsafe, and life-threatening. We expect that the police will intervene if someone threatens us or our property. In order to preserve civil behavior and life, norms and rules abound. Safety first is a highly valued commodity in a well-run society. This is all on a more or less conscious level of thought and action. Predictability is a cornerstone of a safe society.

On a less conscious level, do we, as Schaller and Park imply in the behavioral immune system hypothesis, discriminate against people who are different in behavior or in appearance, to protect ourselves from a felt or perceived disease? Do we experience literal "dis-ease," which we attribute to something emanating from the "other" person? Many people are uncomfortable around someone with a disability. The discomfort can stem from numerous factors and questions: "Should I help him with the door?" "People are looking at her; does she mind?" "What if this happened to me?" The last question reflecting self-concern is paramount to the discussion of avoiding or isolating those who are different from ourselves. Despite our best intentions and most rational thinking, do we at a subconscious level attempt to protect ourselves by staying away?

According to some research, our ancestors developed strong responses to signs of sickness in others, including birthmarks (Schaller & Duncan, 2011). Further, as discussed above, animals also demonstrate strong avoidance of those who may be ill based on their behavior. Being "other" or being perceived as different comes with grave consequences for individuals, communities, and societies. Difference is the basis of racism, heterosexism, and many other "isms." Adherence to "isms" leads to rejection and exclusionary practices in interpersonal relationships. It also leads to acts of bullying and greater violence. Unfortunately, just as adults have been unable to overcome their fear of difference or their reluctance to be inclusive, children do not fare any better at school—a microcosm of the greater culture. Victims are left with numerous, detrimental lifelong outcomes.

In this chapter we have seen example after example of how being considered different from others can precipitate shame, bullying, and harassment. Next, we explore how bullying in childhood affects adult development and adult behavior.

CHAPTER 4

People-Pleasing Versus Revenge

Consequences on Development of Being Bullied

"Do not scorn the weak cub. He may become the brutal tiger."
Mongolian proverb

"Felt betrayed, shame, embarrassment, figured out how to survive, became a people-pleaser." These are just some of the responses I heard when I asked people the broad question "If you were bullied, what impact did it have on you?" I was surprised at the range of reactions people had to being involved in bullying. From my own clinical practice, I was well aware of the kinds of psychological impact kids experience at the time and then carry with them as adults. I was not prepared for the extent, depth, and breadth of reactions that I encountered from the hundreds of people involved in my study.

During interviews, I started with the question "Were you bullied in elementary school?" I was struck by the number of people who responded "Yes" to this question and how vividly they remembered bullying incidents in kindergarten and 1st grade. Some described what might seem innocuous events like being called names on the school bus. But if this is your first exposure to school and your first exposure to verbal abuse, it is memorable. Some described physical bullying that would be considered assault if it happened to an adult. Often this would take place on the playground, where supervision was minimal or where there were adults who did not intervene. It makes you wonder what adults are thinking when they see a little boy on the ground being kicked and punched by others. Do they think it is just "rough-housing?" I wonder if they think it is not painful for the victim because he is little. Do they believe that little children don't feel helpless and terrified in situations like this?

Children who are mistreated at school by peers, and by teachers or other adults, are at special risk of unhealthy development that continues into adulthood (Bentall, Wickham, Shevlin, & Varese, 2012; Copeland et al., 2014; Kim, Catalano, Haggerty, & Abbott, 2011; Shonkoff, Garner, Siegel, Dobbins, Earls, Garner, . . . Wood, 2012). Their sense of security and identity are shaken. Abused children attempt to understand the reasons behind their treatment and most often conclude that there is something fundamentally wrong with them. This sad and inaccurate conclusion leads to an adult with a fragmented self: one self that is tarnished or shame-based and one part of the self that is overly inflated or elevated (Herman, 1992). Neither one is an accurate representation of the true person. These adults struggle throughout life to try to integrate the two aspects of themselves wondering "Am I no good?" or "Am I really talented and remarkable?" Neal, age 51, gives a good example of this. He said: "I was sexually harassed in middle school. I was one of the so-called sensitive kids who played an instrument in the school orchestra and I didn't play sports. So I was called all kinds of names and they were mostly sexually derogatory. Now as an adult I struggle sometimes thinking that I'm not worth much and other times I think that I am better than other people. Then I feel arrogant and go back to thinking I'm not much good."

There are all kinds of developmental impacts on adults resulting from childhood bullying. In a conversation one 58-year-old man said, "I think that bullying can be either physical or psychological abuse. I was beat up pretty much every day after school. Back then, we rode our bikes back and forth. I had a nice one and I now realize that the kid who was beating on me was envious. I was little for my age in elementary school and I did have a big brother, but he couldn't be there every minute. The impact for me? I learned to size up a situation quickly and avoid a bad one if I could. I am slow to make friends now and I don't trust easily."

Another developmental impact can be seen with teenagers who seem to be too eager to graduate from high school. We might think: "What's the rush? Attending college or otherwise moving into adult life isn't that easy. Stay in high school as long as you can and enjoy yourself." That view is uninformed. It does not take into account the fact that older teens and young adults may be trying to extricate themselves from dysfunctional environments. I had the chance to interview many college students who graduated from high school early. These students said they purposefully graduated as soon as they could from their high schools to escape their tormentors. For the most part, they were finding a better fit for themselves at college. Students who cannot graduate early to escape may become those who drop out of school, leaving a resounding impact on their future development.

PEOPLE-PLEASING

Becoming a "people-pleaser" is often the result of being bullied, harassed, and shamed as a kid. Feeling rejected by others, people try desperately to be accepted. We all know at least one "people-pleaser"—their efforts are usually quite obvious. Women frequently report, "I became very promiscuous (as a teenager) and this has had its own problems now that I'm an adult. I thought I could be accepted by the boys, at least."

I had the privilege of interviewing many delightful people who demonstrated considerable insight. Chris, age 26, was studying for her PhD. She related that she was bullied and harassed by other students throughout elementary school and then on into high school. She gave these examples:

> "I attended a small elementary school. On one occasion, my classmates were throwing pencils and erasers at me during a quiz. When I began crying, the teacher pulled me by the ear to the front of the classroom and reprimanded me for the disruption, telling me that if I were 'normal' then I wouldn't have these problems. She asked: 'What's wrong with you?' I ran out of the class, out of the school, and hid in the woods until the principal found me. I was returned to my classroom. The most disturbing aspect of all was the adult involvement. My teacher in 3rd grade was an awful person. I got detention for crying in class or whispering 'shut up' to the kids who were making fun of me. Then the principal would yell at me for the same thing."

Chris thought she had told her parents all of the incidents. But it turned out she had not told about running out of school. She got to the point where she stopped telling her parents because she said she realized "there was nothing they could do. They had exhausted all options. They talked to everyone." The only thing left was going to another school. Chris felt she knew it would start all over again with a new bunch of kids. So she stayed in the same school district. She said, "When I went to middle school and high school, the bullying continued. I thought it might stop because these schools were pretty good size. But the kids called me 'weird' and a 'freak' and said that I used drugs. They whispered and laughed when I went by and this continued until I was in my junior year of high school. At that point, I think they just literally forgot how it all got started."

When I asked her about the impact of so many years of this kind of treatment, she said,

> "I have devastatingly low self-esteem. I think it is directly from the bullying in 3rd grade. I have the best parents and family you could want. But from the bullying, I am an extreme people-pleaser. I am always willing to say yes. It leaves you open to being walked on. It affects my ability to trust anyone. It impacted my self-esteem in this way: *I will never fully be able to be okay with me.* Even when I think I am, if something happens, I think it has to do with some inherent flaw in myself and I get into immediate self-loathing. I think I always have to defend myself even for the smallest thing that doesn't require a defense. My boyfriend points it out. He tries to tell me: 'You don't need to defend yourself.'"

Many of the respondents in the study ended up with low self-esteem and became "people-pleasers" as a result of being bullied and harassed. Low self-esteem, shame, and being "a people-pleaser" are inextricably intertwined. People who have low self-esteem do not think that others will want to relate to them based on their own merits. They believe that their only chance of being accepted by others is to make them happy. People-pleasers do this often at their own expense in terms of their well-being. They may be sacrificing their own chance at personal integrity and authenticity. One person put it this way: "When I was in high school, I adopted the values of the 'popular group' in order to be accepted and included by them. I have no true sense of myself or my own values."

INTERPERSONAL BALANCE AND INSECURITY

Finding a sense of self, a sense of authenticity, and an authentic voice are fundamental jobs for adults in all stages of development and, once achieved, imply a developmental milestone. This true sense of self can lead to feeling centered and garners a sense of well-being. It is impaired for many adults who were bullied and harassed as children. They shared:

> "I can't seem to find a balance. Sometimes I feel really walked on and other times I am mean and abusive."
> "Some days, I am stronger for it (the bullying), but also I think I am harsher toward others."
> "I grew up to be insecure, always feeling like an outcast, rejected, left out, and different somehow from other people."

So many of the participants in this study described their reaction to the bullying and harassment they had in school as deciding to "be nice." But is this "being nice" genuine or a protective device? A perfect example of this comes from Bethany, age 32:

> "I still worry that people will see through me to the 'real me' or the part of me that made me get made fun of. To protect myself, I decided it was in my best interest to be overly nice and to make sure everyone was comfortable. I realize, as an adult, that this has come at a price to myself. Sometimes I wonder who I am really. Would I have been this accommodating if I hadn't been so abused in school? It is still my best defense."

Judith Herman (1992) in her book on trauma describes childhood victims of abuse as performers. They are forever on the alert for what may be required of them and seek to please others in order to avoid further abuse. As a result, as adults they typically perceive themselves to be inauthentic.

SOCIAL ANXIETY

We have all noticed infants and little children who are hesitant or reluctant around others. We tend to classify these children as "shy." Indeed, there is a great deal of research on people who are shy by temperament; they were, in essence, born that way. Can it happen that an otherwise outgoing child becomes shy and withdrawn as a result of interpersonal experiences at school? (see Prior, Smart, Sanson, & Oberklaid, 2000; Sanson, Hemphill, & Smart, 2004).

Social anxiety is the most common anxiety disorder (Stein & Stein, 2008). People experiencing it are worried about and fearful of criticism and judgment by others. For some it can be disabling; for others it can lead to developmentally inappropriate conduct. One woman offered the following comment:

> "After the bullying began in junior high school, I began to develop social anxiety and became much more quiet and shy. Before the bullying, I had been outgoing and expressive. I started over-thinking every word I said. I became extraordinarily passive so it was less likely that I would be cast out for my opinions. Then, I got involved with peers who were not the best influence on me just to be accepted by somebody. Even today, I avoid conflict at all cost."

From this comment, those like it, and from another large study of adults (Boulton, 2013), we see growing evidence that childhood bullying may produce social anxiety that extends into adult life. Though I didn't ask, several people volunteered that they "ended up in therapy," either when they were children or as adults, to deal with the impact of bullying at school and to deal with the social anxiety they still experience.

SELF-MEDICATING

People self-medicate for all kinds of reasons. Some they are aware of and some they are not. Self-medicating was a recurrent theme in answer to the question about the impact of bullying. As adults, people who were bullied experience feelings of anxiety and sadness so self-medicating with a variety of substances from food to alcohol and other drugs is a common escape. The following are typical responses:

> "I am a very anxious person now. I think it is a direct result of being bullied and harassed for so many years in school. I see that I do a lot of self-medicating. I know it's not a good idea, but it helps me get through the day."
>
> "I still food binge as an adult to cope with the feelings of sadness and loneliness that began when I started being bullied and sexually harassed."

Self-harming can be a way of attempting to self-medicate for emotional pain. Studies reveal that more than half of those who engage in self-harming practices were victims of bullying (Fisher, Moffitt, Houts, Belsky, Arseneault, & Caspi, 2012). There are no drugs currently available that treat self-harming behavior specifically. When physicians become aware of self-harming, they typically prescribe antidepressants or antianxiety medicines. However, studies indicate that only 3% of physicians are ever aware that their patients self-harm (Whitlock, Eckenrode, & Silverman, 2006). When physicians are not aware, people may continue to self-harm and to try to deal with their emotions through other means of self-medicating. Self-medicating has an impact on development. While individuals are medicating with food, other substances, or through self-harm, they are not dealing directly with the pain in their lives and therefore they are forestalling healthy development.

REVENGE

"When I was in elementary school, I was bullied about how I looked. When I grew and was considered pretty, I was a huge bitch! I ignored and excluded those who had bullied me and made them look stupid whenever possible. Revenge was sweet!"

Female, 19, Hispanic

Humans have an innate sense of reciprocity and fairness. All societies have set up systems of justice to deal with grave interpersonal violations. However, when these systems fail, thoughts of revenge against self or others are activated (Bloom, 2001). Many authors have written about the importance of the concept of revenge (see Seton, 2001). Revenge can function to help maintain a person's sense of self when he is being beaten down by others. Fantasies of spiteful actions serve as a protective factor from lapsing into a deep and intractable depression. Thoughts of revenge or actually taking revenge are linked to deliberations on fairness and justice. It is important to remember that for children fairness is a paramount principle. Adults and peers should beware a child who feels he or she has been treated unfairly. With their undeveloped sense of morality, children and adolescents, who experience unfair treatment at the hands of others, are liable to take matters of justice into their own hands. Righting a wrong is acutely important. When no adults administer justice for perceived offenses, certain children will act of their own accord and feel entitled to do so (Black, Weinles, & Washington, 2010). This is often what is happening when a child brings a gun to school (Apel & Burrow, 2011). We have seen numerous examples of gun violence in our nation's schools based on a young person's need for righting a wrong through revenge.

Lawrence Kohlberg, American psychologist, described the moral development of children and adults in terms of stages. In the first stage, a person's morality is really only concerned with avoiding punishment, and in the second stage morality is concerned with anything that is in the person's self-interest. The third stage is focused on interpersonal relationships, so moral development is based on group standards, group norms, or the Golden Rule. The next two stages have to do with maintaining social order, the social contract, and individual rights (Kohlberg, 1991, 2008). According to Kohlberg, when children or adults act to take revenge, they are still located at a lesser level of moral development. While this may be true, in terms of the immature thinking of adolescents, we can speculate that teens may believe they are acting in accord with their own sense of what is right and wrong in interpersonal relationships. It is not a stretch to imagine that their own code of morality feels violated when they are excluded, hazed, bullied, and tormented. Acting out with revenge is a way of sending a message to the group: "You weren't supposed to do this to me. You all did me wrong."

As adults, some victims feel a great deal of satisfaction when they find out that their former bullies are not doing very well. They feel a sense of vindication. Some consider this a form of revenge. This raises the question: "How does the search for vengeance fit into adult morality?" The Hammurabic Code of the ancient Babylonians, dating back to 1772 B.C., provided a strict interpretation of revenge. If someone caused the loss of an eye in another person, then their eye would be put out too. The same held true for a death (Cloke, 1993). The Pharisees of the Old Testament adopted this dictate, and consequently they held to a public policy of reciprocal behavior: "an eye for an eye." While most societies considering themselves to be civilized seem to have abandoned this idea in principle, individual actions along with certain national political policies act in accord with this concept.

From the kinds of comments that you have been reading about in the book, you can understand how teenagers, with their limited repertoire of responses and feelings of powerless, gravitate toward feelings of revenge. Adults who are continually disrespected, too, entertain these fantasies. However, we expect adults to be in control of their thoughts, feelings, and actions. Sociologist Scott Melzer (2013) describes the idea that some people need to exorcise the demons of being emasculated via fighting as adults. Men who were bullied in their youth may not exact revenge on their perpetrators, but find relief from the pain they experienced by joining Fight Clubs. Men in urban, suburban, and rural areas risk great physical harm to bond with other males, something they did not have as kids, while at the same time instating a sense of accomplished masculinity. Young men may feel emasculated due to the bullying they encountered and try to gain a sense of masculinity by literally fighting back. Others may exorcise their sense of emasculation by using their unique talents and skills to become successful adults. One such person is author and software developer Oliver Emberton, who wrote a piece entitled "What Are Bullied Children Like as Adults?" (2013). In his story, he describes numerous instances of being bullied and harassed. Everything from being held underwater until he went limp while others laughed, to being vastly outnumbered in fights, to verbal torments that were perpetrated against him as a child. He believes that this was because he was half-American and a scrawny red head. He was convinced that the "outside world" wanted him dead. He says: "I'm sure bullying affects everyone differently. But for me, it grew to feel like a thousand furious suns burning in my chest. A source of immense anguish, and immense motivation. In a word: *fury*." Emberton used the fury to good effect. He employed his brain power to build a software company and make a success story of his life. He contends that the fury he felt has not faded, but it has lost "nearly all of its bitterness." He ends the piece by saying: "I'm Facebook friends today with people who bloodied my nose at school. But who they are and what they did doesn't bother me in the slightest. They're not the same person anymore. And neither am I." It may be true that he is not the same person as he was and that his bullies are not either. But to say the bullying no longer "bother(s) me in the slightest" may be lacking in a bit of self-examination, as Emberton says he is still feeling the fury.

Revenge. Thinking about it and getting it are featured prominently in the responses of people who participated in my research. It made sense to me that when I interviewed teens in the wake of Columbine, they expressed these kinds of sentiments. Kids would say, "I think about getting revenge all of the time." They would say they understood how "a Columbine" could happen, how someone could be sent over the edge by being the brunt of chronic bullying. A study was conducted with a nationally representative sample of over 2,000 secondary school students by Harris Interactive and Alfred University. When asked why school shootings occur, a majority of the students answered: for revenge. One male student commented, "I would never do it, but every day I think about getting that kind of revenge on the ones who bully me" (Gaughan, Cerio, & Myers, 2001). One college senior I interviewed said, "When the massacre happened at Virginia Tech, my friends thought the shooter must have been crazy, but I empathized with him and the guys at Columbine. There's only so much you can take. There were definitely times when I was bullied that I wanted to take a baseball bat to people." Is this kind of sentiment a natural response to chronic bullying or an aberration? We don't really know the answer because we don't really know the numbers of teens (or adults) who harbor thoughts of revenge when they are mistreated by anyone.

But when I began to hear the idea of revenge from adults, I wondered how they would execute this. George Herbert, 17th-century clergyman and poet said, "Living well is the best revenge." Many of the people I interviewed took this to heart. They determined as children and teens to "be somebody," to "show them" by achieving success and happiness in their lives. This is not the revenge of children who think in terms of negative retaliation. But people see it as a form of revenge. People's faces move from sad and hurt when describing the incidents of bullying they endured to radiant when they describe what they have accomplished. They are so pleased with the revenge they can exert over their victimizers. They may have lived in fear and pain then, but they live well now.

FOLLOWING FACEBOOK "FRIENDS"

FaceBook has made its own contribution in the domain of bullying. It is here that young people and even adults can torture one another with their postings around the clock. Of course FaceBook is not the only social medium about which such a claim can be made, but it is prominent enough that pediatricians now recognize a syndrome called "FaceBook depression." This is exactly as you can image: a child or teen suffering from a true depression based on treatment received via FaceBook messages and postings (O'Keeffe & Clarke-Pearson, 2011).

However, there are other uses for FaceBook in the realm of bullying. As adults, some victims have actually accepted invitations from their former school bullies to be Facebook friends. This seemed to be more true for men and women in their 20s and early 30s than for older people in my research. This may be because this group is disproportionately represented on social media. It may also have to do with a changing idea or definition of what, exactly, constitutes a friend. This will have to be something for later research. However, I was intrigued by how many in the study regularly peruse the FaceBook pages of their school tormentors. What they shared with me is that they are hoping their bullies are not doing well in life. They describe this as "sweet revenge" and, indeed, they are not really all that surprised to see the bullies have messed up their lives. They are happy, some are elated, that those who made their lives miserable are finally miserable themselves. They have finally gotten what was coming to them for their terrible behavior. A person can go from great sadness in relating their stories of being bullied to bright smiles, in a short minute, when describing the "good news" they find on FaceBook.

Chris, who calls herself a "people-pleaser," commented, "I check up on my bullies on FaceBook to see what they're doing and I say to myself, 'hah you're only doing this meager thing with your life and look at me!'" She also shared that her former bullies, now as adults, have friended her on FaceBook. She said: "I think this is very interesting. I was shocked that they did this. My initial reaction was I don't want to friend them, but then I thought I can see what they are doing. Every once in a while, I compare myself to them. I think it is Facebook stalking." She wants to know how does this one look? How is that one doing? When she sees that one of the bullies is not so successful, she confesses that some part of her is very glad.

She still wishes them ill and does not want them to be happy. This kind of sentiment was not at all unusual. To "forgive and forget" was not a typical reaction. Perhaps it takes the passage of time to move into forgiving. Most of the participants in the study who had been bullied did not forget—they recalled the bullying they experienced instantaneously. They did not need to search their memories.

Once in a while, bullies figure it out as adults and take responsibility for their actions by offering an apology. Victims, in that case, often come to a different resolution. It is easier to forgive someone who is asking for forgiveness and who seems to understand the pain that was caused. Chris said this happened to her. One of her bullies became friends with her sister and reached out to Chris. Her feelings about this young man completely changed after his sincere apology. She no longer wishes him ill. Victims may also find out, as Chris did, that their bullies were victimized too at home or at school.

IMPACT ON EMPLOYMENT

Bullying in childhood creates problems in employment as an adult. One very large study of over 53,000 adults in Finland found that among people with long-term unemployment, 29% reported being bullied at least once a week during their adolescence. This considerable statistic indicates a relationship between school bullying and unemployment in adulthood that is significant (Varhama & Bjorkqvist, 2005). In our own country, we know that thousands of students do not attend school every day due to fears for their safety, and the dropout rate in our schools is impacted significantly by bullying (Centers for Disease Control and Prevention [CDC], 2009). This is an especially profound problem when we consider that the task of elementary and secondary schools is to get our children prepared to enter the workforce as healthy adults. Other research has demonstrated a direct link between bullying and ultimate educational attainment (Due et al., 2011). Then as a result, bullying indirectly affects the wages a person is able to garner during adulthood (Brown & Taylor, 2008). Further, people with a history of being bullied are more likely to be fired and to go from job to job than people who were not targets of bullying (Sansone, Leung, & Wiederman, 2012). Consequently, in this way, victims of bullying in childhood become victims in the workplace as adults.

In my research, I began to wonder what impact, if any, being bullied as a child, might have on a person's choice of career or employment. Many people leaned toward a job in the helping professions. I believe this was partly to gain an understanding of what had happened to them as children and partly to prevent and correct the harm that they uniquely understood.

Jamal is a good example of the interplay of bullying and the impact on employment. Jamal is a 33-year-old, African American minister. He lives in the suburbs of a large metropolitan city with his wife and child. He remembers being bullied as a 13-year-old as clearly as if it just happened. He told his story of bullying and intimidation with great seriousness, for the most part. But one part of the story involved a misunderstanding about someone else's girlfriend. In that event, his friends and cousins, some of whom were gang members, came to his aid and intervened at school. About this particular incident, Jamal laughed and said: "Even athletes (those who were threatening him) don't mess with gangsters." While the bulk of the bullying felt like it happened yesterday, he says that he feels at peace with it. There are some important reasons for this. One is due to his spiritual practice, but an equally important reason is because he became friends with the boy who tormented him. Jamal was bullied by Leon, someone who used to be his friend. The friendship went awry for many months. It began with sarcastic and derogatory comments. For example, whenever they would be at the playground playing basketball or in the neighborhood field playing football, Leon would say: "Jamal is a punk, I'm going to whoop his ass . . . I dare him to say something. My brother and I will kick him and his brother's ass!" There were other times when he would be walking around the neighborhood alone or getting off the bus, and Leon (and a cousin or friend of his) would see Jamal and chase him home. For a very long time, Jamal lived with the anxiety and fear that he would be jumped and beaten by a multitude of people. Since Leon would pick on Jamal typically when Leon showed up at the playground, Jamal's strategy was just to leave and head for home even if he was enjoying himself. Leon had people in his family who were members of a gang, so that really intimidated the young Jamal.

In Jamal's family, it was customary to take action if someone was "messing with you" or disrespecting you in any way, but especially if someone "put their hands on you." If that occurred, the family advice and expectation was that you would fight back. If you did not, and the abuse continued from the other person, the shame would be on you. Jamal remembered, "My mother would often say to my brothers and me, 'Never run from a fight, because if I find out you ran from someone you are going to have two fights: first with me, then with the person you ran from!' So, with that in mind I never really saw telling my stepfather or mother about Leon's harassment or more importantly my feelings of fear." As a result, when Jamal was bullied, he was in a bind. He was not inclined toward violence and at the same time, the family expected him to meet violence with violence. With all of these factors happening, he felt very lonely, sad, and afraid. One day, fear turned into anger. Leon and a cousin chased Jamal down the street and into his house. Jamal had had enough. He grabbed a knife from the kitchen and went out to find and confront Leon. Sure enough, soon Leon and his cousin came back to start their heckling again. Jamal was waiting for them. Just then, Jamal's best friend came around the corner into sight. When he saw what was about to happen, he intervened immediately by tackling Jamal to the ground. As a result, no violence ensued. After that incident, oddly enough, Leon wanted to be Jamal's friend. That moment resolved any future conflict. To this day, Jamal is not sure why. He speculates that it may be because Jamal showed his willingness to do whatever was needed against being bullied any longer. Or maybe Leon worried Jamal was too crazy to have as an enemy.

As Jamal described it, depending on gang involvement for assistance was a dangerous thing. When Leon called his cousin for help, he was also calling his cousin's whole gang. Jamal says about this, "My older brother was in that same gang, but I didn't identify with it. That was my brother's thing. Though my brother was in a gang, I never took that as an opportunity to bully anyone." When I asked Jamal about the general impact now in his life of the bullying he endured, he shared,

"I'm at peace about it. It's a moment in my life I can reflect on. It's a teachable moment for me as a parent and for other young people. I grew up in a relatively poor neighborhood but always had my needs met. I'm in a good place now. I wish I could have told that 13-year-old me that things would turn out well. Life really does get better if you make some conscious decisions to make it that way . . . to be strong. Grabbing a knife was out of character for me, it was a drastic measure."

Grabbing a knife was a child's response for self-protection in a terrible situation. It is also a good example of how children can turn to violence to take care of themselves and of how this momentary decision can change a life course forever.

I also asked Jamal if he saw an impact on his friendships, and he immediately responded,

"The concept of friendship is very sacred to me. I can count my friends on one hand today. Friendship is a major investment; sometimes the return isn't there on a friendship. People who are transparent I feel **safe** with. There are a few people in life that can handle who you really are. There are very few people who get that Jamal. I don't let them in. I can give ya'all the public Jamal but not the private me. Do you deserve to be let in that close? I have a few friends that I call."

The need to keep the true or private self separate from the public one is a concept that I came across time and again as people talked about the long-lasting impact of childhood bullying on adult development and relationships. For Jamal, a public self and a private self are clear and distinct entities. Bullying has affected him in terms of closeness with others and in terms of the numerous examples of bad decisions he can offer to the children who come to him for guidance. Jamal sees a clear link between the bullying he endured and his choice of employment positions.

So many factors influence the psychological and physical development of each person moving into adulthood. Some of the impacts on development of sustaining bullying and harassment during childhood were discussed in this chapter. There is a substantial impact on self-esteem and then on the presentation of self in everyday life. From people-pleasing to thinking about revenge, adults deal with the consequences in their own unique ways. This leads us to the question "What are the consequences in adult relationships?" The next chapter focuses on adult friendships and intimate relationships.

CHAPTER 5
Consequences in Relationships

"Et tu, Brute?"

Julius Caesar, Shakespeare

hildren start life as very trusting people. They have to; they're totally dependent on those around them to meet their needs and to treat them well. When children are loved and their needs are met, they learn to trust others. When they are maltreated at home, they learn not to trust. A trusting child can also learn not to trust as a result of mistreatment at school. For a child whose sense of trust was intact before going to school, encountering bullying and harassment can lead to issues of trust and problems with self-esteem. These themes surfaced over and over again in my interviews.

How does trust impact relationships? Ideally, we tend to think of a friend as someone we can share important aspects of our lives, someone who will have our back and generally be kind in a world that might otherwise not be. Most of us consider a friend to be like a safe haven. In short, a friend is someone you can trust.

What happens when this is not the case? While it was not unknown in the pretech age that a school friend might betray you, it did not seem to be an everyday event. Loyalty, and especially loyalty to friends and the group, was considered a priority. At this point, if a friend is upset with you, everyone in your circle and beyond can know about it. Cell phones and other media make circulating a rumor instantaneous. Friends may be called on to take sides. Or worse, one person is just excluded. Your friend or former friend may post very hurtful comments on social media and if there is an embarrassing picture or video, it can go viral.

This raises the questions: What happens when friendship is disrupted and betrayed through bullying, exclusion, rejection, and harassment? How do people contend with the humiliation and the rejection? The answer is complicated. Some children have such resiliency that they seem to be little affected. Some utilize cognitive mechanisms that allow them to reframe what has happened (deLara, 2008b). Some children have the support of understanding parents and go to them as a resource (Bowes, Maughan, Caspi, Moffitt, & Arseneault, 2010; deLara, 2012). However, there are numerous children who do not have these kinds of strengths and supports. They are the ones who are at risk for poor developmental and mental health outcomes (for more information see the Search Institute).

Being unable to trust others emerged as a major theme in the interviews I conducted. One woman, age 25, said, "I don't make friends easily and I'm not willing to trust people until I really know them." This short sentence was uttered by hundreds of people interviewed in my study. Another woman said, "I rarely trust women my own age and I rarely get along with them. This is a direct result of being bullied constantly in school." One man, age 37, said, "I seek out few friendships with guys. I think this is rooted in the bullying I got by other boys when I was a kid."

Others said:

"I feel helpless when it comes to making real friends. I just want to keep up appearances and look like I have friends but I never connect with them due to fear of rejection. Being bullied made me hate people."

"I find it hard to let people in and always keep people at a distance."

"I never trust anyone and feel that they are going to hurt me or not like me. I always feel like I'm being judged."

Research on childhood experiences of violence and the ability to trust later on indicates that trust is severely impaired for those who experience aggression in any form. Over 11,000 adults were interviewed in a study conducted in England investigating any links between childhood happiness or unhappiness mediated by violence and adult outcomes. One of the outcomes that was measured was the ability to trust others in relationships. The researchers found that, even controlling for social demographics such as income, adults who experienced violence in their childhood were significantly less able to trust others than their counterparts who had a violence-free childhood (Bellis et al., 2013).

DATING AND BULLYING

Gender identity and sexual orientation are typically solidified during adolescence. From early adolescence to the start of early adulthood, most people are exploring romantic and intimate relationships. Dating is an integral part of healthy development during these time periods. Adolescents and young adults whether lesbian, gay, straight, bisexual, transgender, or questioning try on various relationships to come to a determination about who they are as a sexual person and to figure out their compatibilities. In our culture, dating by adolescents and young adults is a part of normal development (Newman & Newman, 2014). When dating is hindered or interrupted, we consider normal development to be impaired (Collins, Welsh, & Furman, 2009). Dating in the United States either in couples or in groups typically begins to occur sometime between ages twelve and seventeen or eighteen (Newman & Newman, 2014). However, being the object of bullying by peers can be a deterrent. A 22-year-old male college student said, "One consequence I can see of being bullied when I was younger is I have not begun dating yet because I feel my self-esteem is too low to have a healthy relationship with anyone." He was a senior at his university and about to graduate. He had missed many opportunities that the college environment provided.

Adolescent dating is meant to be the prelude to the development of healthy adult relationships. Unfortunately, there appears to be a direct link between bullying and dating violence (Ellis & Wolfe, 2014; Foshee et al., 2014; Josephson & Pepler, 2012). When teens decide to "hang out" or move into an exclusive relationship, they take a risk in terms of how they might be treated by their dating partner. Adolescents engage in behaviors that can have unintended consequences. For example, we know that teens send sexually suggestive pictures or messages to their current partners (Onugha & Finlay, 2012). This can come back to haunt them in the form of "revenge porn" when the relationship breaks up (Stroud, 2014). Posting revenge porn on Internet sites is a relatively new form of bullying. Adolescents are also subject to other forms of aggression during dating. For example, teen dating violence can begin with so-called teasing and name-calling, both of which people tend to see as "normal" in adolescent relationships. According to a 2008 CNN survey, 69% of those sexually active at age 14 experienced abuse from their dating partner. Sixty-two percent were verbally abused by being called stupid, worthless, or ugly by their dates. Unfortunately, most parents seem to be unaware of these undercurrents in teenage relationships (CNN, 2008). In a nationwide survey, 9.9% of high school students report being hit, slapped, or physically hurt on purpose by their boyfriend or girlfriend in the 12 months prior to the survey (Centers for Disease Control and Prevention [CDC], 2010). Unhealthy, abusive, or violent relationships can cause short-term and long-term negative consequences to personal development. Victims of teen dating violence are more likely to do poorly in school, show earlier sexual debut, and engage in binge drinking, suicide attempts, and physical fighting. Victims may also carry the patterns of violence into future relationships (CDC, 2010; Silverman, Raj, Mucci, & Hathaway, 2001).

DO YOU SEE ANY CONSEQUENCES FOR YOU IN RELATIONSHIPS?

A European study was conducted in 2004 with adults who were victims of bullying as children. The research team found that victims, as adults, expressed considerably more emotional loneliness, and reported more difficulties in maintaining friendships, than nonvictims (Schäfer, Korn, Smith, Hunter, Mora-Merchán, Singer, & Meulen, 2004). For more information on the aftermath that can result from bullying, I asked each person this important question: "If you were bullied, do you see any consequences for you in relationships?" A few in the study reported some positive effects (which are addressed in the chapter "Unexpected Outcomes"), but the great bulk of people in the study who were involved with bullying reported lowered self-esteem that resulted in a significant and noticeable impact for them in their relationships. These statements were typical:

"I have very low self-esteem so I don't feel like I deserve a good relationship."

"My self-image is messed up. I never really believe that someone likes me. That makes it difficult for me to be in a relationship."

"I was bullied emotionally all through grade school as I was developing a sense of who I am. I think in reaction to this I developed an outgoing, interesting personality so I have lots of friends. But I feel it's all a show and that someday people will see through it."

Because the question was asked in an open-ended manner, people talked about consequences they could see in their friendships and intimate relationships. Some people had great difficulty establishing either kind of relationship. It is interesting to see that people were aware that the low self-esteem they suffered left them feeling less than deserving of a good relationship and, also, cognizant that a relationship, friend or intimate, might not work out well for them. One woman responded, "I cannot maintain relationships because my self-perception is terrible. People no longer want to be around me."

FRIENDSHIPS

Men, Friendships, and Childhood Bullying

It is rare for men to have close friendships as adults. In our country, men in heterosexual relationships count on their female partners for most if not all of their closeness and intimacy needs. This phenomenon is seen in other countries as well (Ryan & Mulholland, 2014). Why is this? As children, boys seem equally capable as girls of having friends. They, too, have playmates. What happens to them? It appears at least one variable on their ability to connect and manage friendships as adults may be a result of the bullying they experience as children. One man expressed the sentiments of many others I interviewed when he said, "I was bullied by my friends. Now I have trouble having guy friends because I'm afraid it will happen all over again." This makes clear that he is concerned about a reoccurrence of something very troubling in his childhood. It appears also that he is avoiding the possibility and that perhaps he still has not figured out how to stand up for himself against those who try to put him down.

Todd has a similar issue. Todd, age 26, attended schools that he described as multiracial. In elementary school, he was bullied by two boys in particular. He is white and they were Native American. By the time he went to middle school, the bullying continued, but the two boys began to gain respect for him based on his athletic abilities on the lacrosse field. Once he proved how much of a contribution he made to the team, all of the bullying and harassment stopped. However, in high school he experienced several incidents in which his best friends turned on him and got others to go along by pranking him over a period of time. They would also engage in physically assaulting him on the playing field whenever they got the chance. Today, he says that what happened in high school with his "friends" has really impacted him in how much he lets himself attach in friendships with other men. He disclosed, "I either feel rejection or anticipate rejection, so I keep limits on my friendships with men. I see that I am cut off in many ways. I just can't attach in ways that I used to before what happened with my friends in high school."

Michael, age 41, also has problems with adult male relationships. He was bullied for being "different" in elementary school due to having an ethnic last name and not being good at sports. In middle school, he was made the brunt of jokes for not wearing the "right" clothes. By the time he got to high school, he was not directly bullied as he had been in earlier grades, he was just generally avoided. He was a social outcast. The bullying and harassment were carried out by other boys. There were a few girls who intermittently talked to him or befriended him for a short while. Consequently, as an adult, it is with other men that he feels great unease. He says that it is extremely difficult for him to trust men, so he tends to avoid anything more than exchanging a few pleasantries at work.

ACCEPTANCE AND REJECTION

Children and adolescents want to be accepted by their peers. Developmental psychologists recognize that feeling accepted is a basic human need (Baumeister & Leary, 1995; Rohner, 2004) and may be fundamental for adequate psychosocial development (Baumeister & Leary, 1995; Kurzban & Leary, 2001). Psychologist Stanley Coopersmith's work with children and teens details the activities and adversities young people will take on themselves to be accepted and included. In virtually every culture studied, kids who are rejected turn out badly. Ronald Rohner, an anthropologist who studied over one hundred cultures around the world, found that rejection can be described as a "psychological malignancy" (see Garbarino & deLara, 2002). Children and adolescents demonstrate basic psychological needs for safety, belonging, autonomy, and competence (DeWall, Twenge, Gitter, & Baumeister, 2009), and schools that provide these basic needs reap the benefits in terms of respectful relationships among students and between students and adults (Schaps, Battistich, & Solomon, 2004).

Interpersonal rejection experienced through bullying and exclusion can lead to feelings of intense rage and aggressive actions either toward self or others. Being victimized by peers is seen as both a cause and a consequence of later aggressive behaviors as well as being a cause of depressive symptoms (Perren, Ettekal, & Ladd, 2012). Of those children victimized by being bullied, 30%–45% are classified as socially rejected over the next 4 years of their lives (Leary, Twenge, & Quinlivan, 2006). Further, victims who experience a sense of loss of control over their lives can feel they have nothing to lose by being aggressive toward others.

The research literature on this paints a clear picture. If you are bullied as a child and you see it as your fault, you are likely to internalize feelings of blame and shame. If you believe it is the fault of the bully, you may have aggressive feelings. If you see it as both "It is my fault" and "It is their fault," you may have both sets of feelings to contend with as you move through life (Boulton, 2013; Perren et al., 2012). Consequently, using properties of social cognitive theory (Bandura, 1991) and attributional theory (Perren, Gurtwiller-Helfen, Malti, & Hymel, 2012) with children who have a high degree of social-emotional intelligence can be helpful for those children to mitigate the negative effects of rejection they experience. However, because most children do not report bullying to any adult (deLara, 2012; Mishna & Alaggia, 2005), they are left without professional intervention to try to figure out for themselves how to deal with the consequences of shame, anxiety, self-blame, and anger.

While it may seem to achieve the opposite outcome from what they are trying to accomplish, children who are shamed, bullied, harassed, and excluded may react with aggression to contend with their rage. In studies by the US Secret Service, 75% of school shooters are found to be victims of bullying at school (Vossekuil, Reddy, & Fein, 2000). This was certainly the case at Columbine High School, where, in 1999, two boys who were bullied, tormented, and ostracized for four years by the school athletes decided to take revenge by shooting 13 people at their school (Garbarino & deLara, 2002; Hong, Cho, Allen-Meares, & Espelage, 2011).

Ostracism, a type of rejection, is part of the lexicon of bullying (Williams, Forgas, & Von Hippel, 2005; Williams & Nida, 2011). When someone is being ignored, shunned, or ostracized by an individual or by a group it can be difficult to substantiate, and therefore it is quite easy to deny that anything like this is happening. So the shunning and ostracism can continue without any fear of recrimination by those in charge. It becomes institutionalized as part of the way that the system functions. Ostracism can take many forms, including cyberostracism, but it typically has three specific purposes: one, as a rehabilitation method to correct undesirable behavior on the part of the person targeted for ostracism; two, as a means to eject the person or group from the greater group or organization; and three, simply as retribution for a perceived threat or injury (Dixon, 2007; Feinberg, Willer, & Schultz, 2014; Williams et al., 2005). Gibbs and Roche (1999) wrote about this in *Newsweek* magazine immediately following the incident at Columbine, when they reported the following quote from one of the athletes there:

> "Columbine is a clean, good place except for those rejects [Klebold and Harris]. Most kids didn't want them here. Sure we teased them. If you want to get rid of someone, usually you tease 'em. So the whole school would call them homos, and when they did something sick, we'd tell them, 'You're sick and that's wrong.'"
>
> see Garbarino & deLara, *2002, p. 79*

This quote is a clear representation of ostracism and rejection. It also meets the purposes of ostracism that Williams and others have listed.

In her book *Ostracism: The Power of Silence*, Williams tells the poignant story of an Aboriginal inmate at a prison in Australia. The prisoner had ostensibly tried to escape captivity, but was found between two sets of barbed wire fences. He was picking up litter when guards came for him and he did nothing to resist them. His "escape" was merely an attempt to determine for himself whether he truly existed. In prison, no one looked at him, talked to him, or bothered with him in any way, leaving him to wonder about the reality of his existence (Williams, 2002).

Helplessness, despair, and a sense of invisibility typically result when someone experiences ostracism over a long period of time. Some people will begin to question whether they even exist. Such is the power of this form of rejection on the human spirit. The anger that develops from rejection and bullying can last for many, many years. I have found that it has a corrosive effect on the relationships a former victim tries to establish as an adult. Friends and intimates are held at arm's-length, and their actions are scrutinized for any signs of rejection, exclusion, or maltreatment.

One of the effects of rejection appears to come in the form of defensiveness. Think of the scenario in which a person has been physically hit—more than once. If he sees a hand coming his way, the instantaneous reaction may be to duck or to block the blow in some way. Similarly, people figure out a way to protect themselves from verbal blows or even when they perceive that there may be an "attack" imminent. The majority of the people I interviewed in my research said that they consider themselves more defensive when they relate to others as a result of the bullying they endured. Certainly, when they hear an insult or something that borders on insulting, they become defensive. This is an interesting concept. As adults in our culture, we are allowed to defend ourselves against a physical attack and this is seen as justified. But when an attack is verbal and we defend against it in kind, we are labeled with the pejorative term "defensive." Defensiveness is considered a negative trait. Indeed, when attacked verbally, most people would like to be able to respond in a calm and collected manner instead of getting worked up emotionally. However, if the seeds of needing to defend yourself have been planted early, it is difficult to overcome that defensive reaction. Another form of self-defense can look like this: "I'm not very open to truly being myself because I still feel like I have to put on a front of being perfect so people don't think less of me or make fun of me." Putting on a front or trying to be perfect are additional ways to defend yourself against rejection by others.

I have found that those who were excluded or rejected by peers as children and adolescents can experience particular difficulties in establishing and maintaining healthy adult friendships and intimate partnerships. They are fearful that they will be rejected all over again and, as a result, they tend to be clingy or maintain too much distance. They can become inveterate people-pleasers in an attempt to hold on to friends and intimates at all costs. Conversely, bullied children as adults can keep a good amount of emotional distance from others, not allowing friends or intimates close to their inner thoughts and feelings. This is an example of attachment theory gone wrong. When John Bowlby and Mary Ainsworth originally conceived of this theory, it was as an explanation of the importance of a child's attachment to a secure caregiver early in life. In order for a child to develop in a healthy manner, be able to navigate relationships well, and balance that with independence, attachment theorists believe that children must be able to count on at least one adult who will provide for their needs in a caring and consistent way thus producing a secure attachment—the basis for all future healthy development (Ainsworth & Bowlby, 1991; Bowlby, 1969). Later, this theory and its implications were extended to adults and their relationships (Hazan & Shaver, 1987, 1994).

Essentially attachments are either secure or insecure. Bowlby (1973) and others (Bartholomew & Horowitz, 1991) described the idea that children have a working mental image, a representation, of attachment that consists of two parts: one, how the child sees other people, and two, how the child sees himself or herself. Based on these internal representations and on the interactions the child has with others, he or she comes to some critical conclusions such as, "I am lovable because someone important responds lovingly and consistently to me (or I am not because they do not)" and "People can be trusted (or not)." These very important life messages, developed in infancy, carry over into later childhood and into adult life.

What I have found in my research is that even those who feel very securely attached to their parent(s), and believe that they have a good, healthy, positive relationship with their parents, can still end up with insecure attachments in primary relationships as adults due to the bullying and torment they experienced as children and adolescents. They were unable to hang on to the internal representation of themselves as "lovable" and of others as trustworthy after experiencing many instances that demonstrated the opposite. Then, these adults may move into insecurely attached relationships.

STATISTICS

In my study, 37.6% of the more than 800 participants said there were consequences for them in their relationships as a result of bullying. Their ability to trust was compromised. Thirteen percent of respondents found a noticeable impact on their ability to trust others in both friendships and intimate relationships. The data revealed other significant problems specific to this category:

11% said they were very self-conscious in relationships. As a result they were aware that they wanted people to like them and were "people-pleasers" or their self-consciousness took the form of keeping people at a considerable distance.

10% suffered from low self-esteem in relating to close friends and intimate others as a result of bullying. For some this translated to "I don't deserve a good relationship."

8% were very sensitive to rejection and criticism by others and some responded with anger and defensiveness.

7% of respondents experienced considerable social anxiety that interfered with their relationships.

4% found themselves in abusive relationships as either the victim or the perpetrator.

3% mentioned attachment problems specifically, saying they never wanted to be in any relationships at all or, conversely, that they never left a relationship even if it was not good for them.

A very small percent (2%) admit to being controlling in their relationships in an attempt to ensure that they are never victimized again. These responses all came from the question "Do you see any consequences for you in relationships?" I believe that the percentages would be higher if I asked specifically about self-esteem, sensitivity to rejection, social anxiety, attachment issues, and attempts to control others.

TRUST IN ADULTHOOD

There are long-lasting outcomes that show up in adulthood as a result of bullying and betrayal experienced in youthful friendships or peer relationships. The primary toxic outcome is on a person's ability to trust others. The following responses were typical:

"I no longer trust people. When I walk into a room and people are laughing, I freeze because I think it could be about me."

"Being bullied made me not trust certain females that fit the same characteristics as my high school bully."

"Because my friends in school hurt me so badly, I think my friends now are being fake or conspiring about me."

"Although it was more than 15 years ago that all the bullying and harassment happened, I still remember the mean things that the kids did to me and it affects my ability to fully trust my friends today. I keep them all at arm's-length."

Sean had some similar experiences with "friends" and others. He is a 22-year-old college student at a highly competitive Ivy League university. Sean experiences bouts of consuming rage, flashbacks, and terrible nightmares. His girlfriend has urged him repeatedly to get some kind of counseling help. Sean contacted me after hearing me speak about my research on high school bullying. He asked to meet to discuss his experiences and hoped it might be helpful for my work in bringing about change in the schools. We met and talked about the bullying he endured from 6th grade on, and Sean described long-lasting effects on him. Though he is only 22 years old, he revealed ways in which he feels he is changed forever.

The first thing you need to know about Sean is that his appearance is so "normal." I mean by this that he does not have any outstanding characteristics that anyone could point to and say, "Oh, no wonder he was bullied at school." He isn't short or tall. He isn't heavy or very thin. He has no noticeable irregularity that might have caused him to become a target for bullying or harassment. He is bright and personable with big blue eyes, an open face, and an engaging smile. Sean is handsome and shy, and very polite. Sean described having flashbacks about a terrifying episode of bullying in the boys' locker room of his high school. During the course of a regular school day when Sean was 15, he was the victim of a surprise attack by several of his "friends" along with other members of his sports team. About eight young men, ages 15 to 18, wrestled him to the floor, some held him down, and stripped off all of his clothing. One boy threw his clothes out into the hallway. Because he was in excellent physical condition and "felt that something worse was about to happen," Sean fought with all his might to throw off the perpetrators and run out of the locker room—naked. He gathered up his clothes and dashed into a nearby empty office. Fighting back, Sean believes, saved at least a shred of dignity. During all of this, the coach was nowhere to be seen. Since that time, he has had flashbacks and all the symptoms of post-traumatic stress disorder (PTSD). Further, he fantasizes about killing the ringleader of the bullying.

Athletes are "privileged" according to Sean. They are given special status in high school and even at college. They have the best locker rooms and the best equipment. "It's really sort of sad," Sean said, because once they leave school, "they're nothing special, just dumb jocks." When Sean spoke about this time, his face was sad and perplexed and he looked much older than his 22 years. His eyes were cast down as he recalled the event in vivid detail. He can see it and remembers it, all of it, clearly. His sadness, he said came from many thoughts and feelings. One of the boys was "my best friend at the time. I could never understand why he did that to me. I could never understand why any of them did that." I asked if, afterward, any of the boys ever apologized. Sean said one of the boys had. I asked, "Did you believe him?" He said, "No. It wasn't sincere. A couple of years later that guy got expelled from school, got some girl pregnant, now he's a bum." I wondered, at that point, if that was the one and only incident of that sort of bullying for Sean. He said, almost astonished at my question, "Oh no! I still had to get through all the rest of high school!"

Sean was raised Catholic, to be "nice," and as he said, "The 'Do unto others' thing is important in my family." That he was brought up with this belief system actually cut both ways for Sean as he tried to navigate the system at his school. In the end, it probably saved him from doing any serious harm to those who were tormenting him. He freely admits that he often "fantasized about killing some of those kids." And he says, "I wondered if it really would be wrong. I mean if someone constantly torments you." So he struggled with the moral aspects of his possible retaliatory actions. He did not appear to struggle with or have any moral compunction about his homicidal fantasies. He said it just seemed normal to him to think about it because people were harming him every day. And because he was so very angry, helpless, and "crying all of the time on the inside."

Sean described his school district as a mix between the "have's" and those whose income was more moderate. Some kids came from "million dollar homes," but he never thought that the bad treatment he received was as a result of income issues. He certainly was not poor. He was from a middle-income family. He said that his family did not flaunt the money they did have, that was not their value system.

"They would just think less of me."

When I asked Sean if he ever told anybody at school what was happening to him, he replied,

> "No. They would just think less of me. One time I told the gym teacher that two boys pushed me into a gym locker. I had to stay there pounding to get out till the kid who owned the locker came along. The gym teacher blamed me, saying, 'You shouldn't have tried to see if you would fit in there.' That's what these guys told the teacher—that I wanted them to put me in there! They were older athletes and he was a coach. Guess who he believed? So I was blamed. After that I stopped even considering telling anyone."

Sean felt he would not be believed, he would risk being blamed, and he would look weak and stupid in the eyes of both adults and other students if he said anything. It was soon after this locker incident that Sean "got heavily into the martial arts." He studied several different forms by the time he graduated from high school and settled on Krav Maga, a form of self-defense used by the Israeli army. Sean is convinced this style of self-defense is the most effective for the kinds of bullying that take place in schools. For being held down or for headlocks, he said a student with a good knowledge of Krav Maga can get away and protect himself. His suggestion is that this martial art form should be taught to all American school children so that they can protect themselves from bullies during the school day.

He told of other incidents. He spoke of regularly being dragged into the boys' bathroom right before math class. There would be a group of between three and six guys hanging out near the restroom. Sean drew a map of the hallway for me, showing the closeness in proximity of his math classroom and the boys' bathroom. He told the poignant story of approaching the classroom, seeing his teacher standing in front of the door, being so close, and not being able to get there before encountering the bullies waiting for him. They regularly held him upside down in one of the toilets. How he wished the teacher could have seen what was happening and intervened. He wished that she could have known what was going on before class so many days. We have to wonder: how did Sean concentrate in math class after these events of terror in the boys' bathroom?

Yet again, he never said a word to this teacher or any other teacher. This raises an important developmental issue. Many adolescents believe either consciously or not so consciously, that the important adults in their lives, their parents, their teachers, should just know what is happening to them. When their adults do not know, adolescents feel angry and betrayed by these same, often very well meaning adults (deLara, 2012). This childlike characteristic or belief that parents or parent-figures are all-knowing omniscient, and should be omnipresent, is a significant component to consider in the effort to build effective safe school programs (deLara, 2012). Of course if asked, adolescents will admit that it is necessary to tell an adult before someone can actually know what is happening and intervene. However, that is a very rational perspective, and adolescents just like adults are not always rational. In events that involve harm and the need for protection, they are just learning how to take care of themselves and are looking to adults for intervention and modeling.

"The Bus Incident"

One day in 11th grade when Sean was riding the bus back from school, a boy about "twice my size started choking me." The attack was unprovoked. Sean decided that he had to fight back to save his life. Sean had never told his parents that he was having any kind of trouble at school. Eventually they found out about the bullying through this incident, when he finally decided he couldn't take it anymore and fought back. Sean rationalized it was permissible to fight back to save your life. When I asked Sean why he never told his parents any of the incidents, he said, "What could they do? If they went to the other parents, it would only make it worse for me. I couldn't see what they could do to stop it." Sean's dad would come home from his day at work and "be all happy and smiling. He'd just ask me how my day was and I'd go off on him! My dad didn't know why, but I couldn't stand it for anybody to ask about my day. It was terrible and I didn't want to talk about it." Sean said he was angry and depressed. When he got home from school, he would go into his room for hours. He confided that even though his mother was trained to "see the signs," she did not see them in him.

The incident on the bus when Sean was being choked and fought back to save his life was a turning point for him. He felt that this is when he finally began to stand up for himself. He knew that because of the school's zero tolerance policy (anyone involved in a fight would be put on suspension) he risked a black mark on his "permanent record." For Sean this meant he also risked not being able to get into a top-tier university, his life's dream. But in this situation, he knew he had to take that chance. He knew there would be no college for him at all if he did not survive the bus ride. So after thinking all of this through, while being choked, and with no intervention forthcoming from other students or the bus driver, he fought back. Sean felt that he was in the right for taking defensive action despite the school policy. As a result, he said, "I wasn't so worried." When his mother and father were notified, Sean's mother went to school to advocate for him. Because his mother was familiar with district policy, she appealed to the principal to forego the usual disciplinary action of suspension. As Sean reported it, his mother said to the principal, "What would you want your own son to do in the same circumstances?" The principal responded, according to Sean, "Punch the kid in the nose and make him stop." Sean was given the sentence of a 7-day exclusion from the "privilege" of riding the bus to and from school. After that, Sean said he was no longer afraid at school. He was a junior. He had proved to himself that he could take care of himself, even in the worst of circumstances. Subsequently, when kids came down the hall and pushed into him, he would trip them in such a way that it looked accidental. Soon everyone knew to stop trying to intimidate him; everyone knew that he would fight back. On top of that, Sean is convinced that "the administration finally realized about particular kids and what they were doing." Then the administrators in the school began to intervene with the troublemakers instead of blaming Sean for all of the terrible things that had happened to him. His face was a mass of smiles as he recounted this triumph. How liberating it must have been for him. After years of torment on a daily basis, he had finally been set free. Some of his liberation came at his own hands, of his own making, some from help and intervention by his mother, some from the realizations of administrators. Here is a good example of how parents who are aware and are willing to be good advocates for their high school children can make an enormous difference in their lives. This is often a necessity, as some areas and times of the school day are basically unsupervised and incidents of unprovoked bullying and violence are commonplace (deLara, 2008a; Garbarino & deLara, 2002; Vaillancourt et al., 2010).

"Long-Lasting Impact?"

I asked Sean if he felt there was any long-lasting impact on him or on his decisions as a result of the bullying and harassment that he endured for so long at school. Quickly he answered, "Yes. I don't trust people. I don't talk to people I don't know easily." Sean said, "I never go after someone to be my friend. If they want to be friends, they have to come after me."

He explained further, "I notice that almost all of my friends are girls." Luckily, that seems to be okay with his girlfriend. When I asked him if he had a theory about why that was true, he said, "Sure, no girls have ever treated me the way guys did in high school. I can hardly stand to be around fraternity type guys. They were the same ones in high school (who bullied him). They make me feel actually sick to my stomach when I see them."

WITNESSES

A great deal of research focuses on why witnesses stand by and watch bullying instead of intervening. Some antibullying programs are aimed at engaging bystanders to eliminate bullying. While this may seem laudatory, research studies to date do not find a positive correlation between peer or bystander intervention and the cessation of bullying victimization (Frisen et al., 2012). Whether or not this is an effective strategy remains to be seen. In the meantime, there are reasons that kids give for their actions or inaction. Those who don't do anything when they see bullying or harassment are concerned that they will be victimized next if they defend the victim (Garbarino & deLara, 2002; Gianetti & Sagaresse, 2001) or think the situation does not really involve them and that the bullying is not severe (Cappadocia, Pepler, Cummings, & Craig, 2012). Those who do intervene do so out of empathy for the victim (Barchia & Bussey, 2011) and a sense of social justice (Cappadocia et al., 2012). Whatever the reasons, bystanders or witnesses end up with long-lasting psychological consequences that impact their abilities in friendships. Mary tells of her experience as a young teen and how it has affected her today at age 57:

"Over the years I have felt really guilty for being a bystander and not standing up for others. I guess in that way I was a participant too, but I didn't think of it like that back then. I carried awful messages back and forth between groups of girls. I didn't realize it but I think that I did it to be safe and avoid becoming the next target of the groups. I've hated the life of silence that I led and the feelings of weakness that have accompanied it. Although it was so many years ago, I still remember the mean things they did and it affects my ability to fully trust the friends I have today. I keep them all at arm's-length. I am so cautious about who I let enter my world. I am always anxious about what others will think of me and I find myself trying to please everyone. It is exhausting."

Vincenza, age 27, experienced bullying while she was attending the 8th grade at a Catholic middle school. The year before, she and two friends ruled the school and were considered the popular group. They received good grades, played school sports, and had their pick of spots in the cafeteria. The girls never spent a Friday or Saturday night without plans. The group was always together, and they were selective about with whom to spend time. All of the teachers knew them and had high hopes for their futures. The group seemed to be treated in a more positive manner than other students. For all of these reasons, Vincenza loved 7th grade. Her euphoria came to an end the summer before 8th grade. A nasty rumor was circulated about her, from an unknown source, that she had tried marijuana with some children in the neighborhood. This was not true, however the rumor spread like wildfire. All of the people she had known her whole life stopped talking to her instantly. When she got to 8th grade, students wrote on her locker, threw garbage and already-chewed gum at her in the hallway, defaced her notebook, and verbally attacked her at any chance. They also enlisted the help of older students, teachers, and coaches to add to the bullying. Vincenza walked through the hallways terrified, at an elevated state of arousal, the entire school day. Because the girls who were bullying her were the high-achieving athletes with well-known families, everyone believed their description of the facts. Teachers would no longer help after school, and her coach recommended that she stop playing sports now that she was a "pothead." Not a single person helped; instead they joined in on the bullying.

The bullying happened solely at school until the Internet infiltrated everyone's home that year. In 7th grade they had dial-up Internet, which limited the amount of time that could be spent on the computer. Over the summer, her family put in cable Internet, which enabled "away messages" for AOL instant messenger and constant communication in the new cyber world. Over the summer, Vincenza had been using the Internet to speak to her friends. However, with high-speed Internet, bullying could infiltrate her home. She was attacked on instant messenger from unknown screen names multiple times per day. By the time she would ask the attacker to "please stop and leave me alone," the screen name would be deleted with a new one taking its place. She could not escape the incessant bullying now that it was occurring inside her safe haven, her home.

The bullying also took place while being transported to and from school. Because the families lived in the same neighborhood, everyone carpooled. The girls who bullied her told their parents about the "bad seed" she turned out to be, and the adults believed them. All day these girls would bully her until everyone piled into whichever mom's minivan. During the ride home the girls would be nice and ask about her day, hiding their true behavior, their public ridicule. Vincenza knew that no one would believe the terrible things that the "perfect" girls would do during school and at their computers. She did not tell a single person about the bullying. These girls had been her only friends since she was little. She knew no one else at school. Also, she reasoned, if the girls' parents, the teachers, and coaches were either avoiding her or adding to the bullying, who else could she tell? Vincenza was always close to her family, but the summer before 8th grade was the same time her father left the family. She felt that everyone had more important things to worry about than her concerns. It was the worst year of her entire life. She believed all of the terrible things all of the kids, teachers, and coaches were saying about her at school. She thought, "If all of the adults in my life are avoiding me and ignoring the ridicule, it must be true." She began to believe, "If even my father left me, what kind of person am I?"

Finally, Vincenza talked with her mother and they decided it would be better to transfer to the public school in her district. Immediately on hearing this, the girls befriended her again. They apologized for not being friends but never owned up to any of the bullying antics. Vincenza forgave them and transferred to public school for 9th grade. There she was accepted, applauded for her academic abilities, and joined various sports teams. She began seeing a clinical social worker to deal with the trauma of the bullying and the losses associated with her father. She remembers feeling happy again. Vincenza got her confidence back and she said this allowed her to meet the man she would marry. They have been married for three years and have "an amazing and trusting relationship." Though she went through a great deal of anxiety and depression, she sees herself as a stronger person at this point. At the same time, now as an adult she reports having a much more difficult time trusting people outside of her immediate family. She has become a person who only allows one or two friends and family members in her life. She remains untrusting of other people. Some of this is culturally derived from her Sicilian family, which generally keeps to a very close circle of "insiders" and is wary of "outsiders." While this is a cultural belief that she subscribes to, she also believes the trauma of 8th grade still has an impact on the intensity in which she holds this conviction. There are very few people in her life she trusts implicitly. She says, "I have a shorter fuse for individuals with any lack of loyalty." Vincenza believes her experiences have changed how she will eventually deal with her own children. She relates, "I understand completely what it is to feel like you are in a room screaming for help and have no one glance in your direction. I will have empathy for adolescents. I want to be that one person who listens to the hardships and relentless fear that bullying causes."

INTIMATE PARTNER RELATIONSHIPS

In the best of all circumstances, an intimate partner relationship, a couple of long-standing, or a marriage is based on friendship. What happens to a close couple when one or both members have been involved with bullying as children and teens? How does it affect the relationship? Research is beginning to investigate the associate between bullying and later intimate partner problems (Corvo & deLara, 2010; Falb et al., 2011). Some of the people in my study were willing to share their experiences.

We met Chris, age 26, in a previous chapter. She was bullied pretty consistently from 3rd grade on. Subsequently, she always puts other people first before herself. She sees herself as a "people-pleaser." The bullying and harassment she sustained had a big impact on how she sees herself in her most intimate relationships. She believes she is with her boyfriend because of some of the events that she went through as a kid. She considers him her "rock." But at the beginning, she put up with a lot. He has a temper due to his own issues from childhood. He was never abusive, but it was difficult to be around his pent-up anger. Being a people-pleaser with low self-esteem does lead to accepting poor behavior from others sometimes. Chris says that if she did not want to make everyone and everything better, she would probably have walked away from her boyfriend. Today, she's very grateful she didn't do that. He has made significant changes in his behavior, and the two of them are extremely supportive of one another.

Here are other typical responses to the question, "If you were bullied, do you see any consequences for you in relationships?"

ONE MAN, AGE 43, SAID, "When I was bullied as a kid, I was meek and didn't stand up for myself. I was always seeking approval from other people. Now I am dominant and strong-willed in my relationships. I rarely allow another person to have any control or decision-making power. I feel the need to be in constant control over my environment so no one can harm me. When I let my guard down, I notice that I become anxious and afraid."

A WOMAN IN HER EARLY 30'S SAID, "Being bullied caused my anxiety and the approval-seeking that I have to this day. I am unsure of myself and that has led to unsuccessful relationships. It significantly impaired my ability to form and maintain relationships now as an adult."

A MAN IN HIS 50'S CONFIDED, "I was bullied throughout elementary school. I think it did toughen me up but it also made me violent as an adult. I was aggressive in my intimate relationships from the time I was twenty until I was about thirty-five."

Ann is 51 and works as a teacher's aide. She is married and has two middle-school-aged children. Ann attended schools that were racially diverse. She reports that she was bullied in middle school and high school by a group of girls who continually picked on her. She was also bullied by one of her teachers in middle school when she gave incorrect answers. Ann had forgotten about all of the mistreatment until her older child started middle school, then the memories came back to her. She remembers that she handled the bullying by "getting small," trying to make herself as inconspicuous as possible. She retreated inside and she never stood up for herself. Ann has carried this over into adult relationships. She was emotionally and physically abused by her first husband. She is emotionally abused by her current husband, and there have been questionable incidents of physical abuse in this marriage as well. She is still not good at standing up for herself. She never learned how. Ann did tell her parents, but they never did anything about the incidents in school. At this point, the major issue in her life is about trust. She focuses on and asks herself, "Who can I trust?" She thinks about this in her friendships and tries to figure out what she can rightfully expect in relating to others. She thinks about how her childhood bullying has affected her behavior in her marriage. What is clear is that she cannot, as yet, trust herself or count on herself for protection.

We tend to think that it is only women who find themselves in abusive relationships and situations but Jim, age 36, shared the following:

"I have found myself in abusive relationships. I didn't leave because I was too fearful to be alone and I didn't trust my own judgment. My fears of being alone and my desire to always have an intimate partner are driven by my need for security and reassurance. I never felt secure in who I was growing up. The bullying did that to me. It has affected my ability to feel comfortable in any intimate relationship I've had as an adult."

For Jim, and many others, it feels better to stay in a familiar relationship, even though it is abusive, than to risk another one where you don't know what kind of torment you will face. Jim's reactions and fears of being alone are markers of attachment issues in his life. He would be considered to be "fearfully attached" in relationships. This particular kind of reaction is seen in others who have been bullied and has been described in international studies as well (Schafer et al., 2004).

Daniel, age 35, a corporate manager, was bullied throughout elementary and middle school. Being bullied was his first memory of any kind. The bullying began as early as 1st grade, when he was pushed around and beat up by a boy on the playground. The boy attacked him, producing long scratches and bleeding on his face. As a little child, Daniel had no idea of what had provoked the boy, but he remembers feeling terrified. It changed something very profoundly for him. He stated, "It introduced unpredictability and fear into social relationships I hadn't had before." He said that although his parents knew he was unhappy during elementary and middle school, they never really asked what it was about and he does not believe they could have done anything helpful in any event.

He was victimized by individuals and groups of kids while at school and on the school bus. He describes himself as a pacifist and conflict-averse. Thinking about it as an adult, he has determined that this is part of what made him a target. He was "systematically" bullied and intimidated on a daily basis by a group of five or six boys who were his same age. Daniel describes them as "violent athletes." They were all in his class and he was far ahead of them academically. Daniel surmised, "This was the other part of being singled out for bullying. At the time, I wasn't exactly sure why I was being picked on to this extent. I didn't apply much thought to the situation; I just tried to get by day-by-day. I certainly never figured out how to stop it. It never occurred that I might have the power to put an end to it." Daniel said that if any adults were aware of what was going on, they never stepped in to intervene on his behalf. In fact, the gym teacher saw him being "nailed" each time the class played dodgeball, but he never did anything about it. Daniel described this teacher as "unsympathetic" to his plight.

One incident occurred for Daniel when he was in middle school. A boy who was part of his social circle started picking on him. Nothing really much, as Daniel recalled, and nothing like what he had been subjected to in elementary school. But it pressed some buttons for him. For one thing, he had thought he was in a safe environment. He related this:

"Anyhow, I suddenly snapped, and all the rage I have inside from all this [bullying and harassment] came to the fore, and I just started whaling away at this kid, hitting him over and over. After a bit of that, during which he was so surprised he just sat there and did nothing, I walked away and sat by myself in the hallway. Steam was practically venting out my ears. He and I never talked about that incident afterward, even though we continued to be in the same social circle for several more years, and the incident never repeated itself. I think he was basically a good kid, and has turned out well as an adult. I think he was just indulging in a bit of 'social dominance play' or whatever one might call it. Interestingly, I don't remember him unkindly. To his credit, I suspect that he understood very well what had happened and learned from it. This was one time I was really moved to violence as a result of being mistreated."

The bullying at Daniel's schools took many different forms and could not be considered good-natured teasing. Daniel said the bullying was mean-spirited and revealed the bullies to be "bad to the bone." While he was the victim of a degree of interracial bullying, the primary harassment came from other white children. Daniel got a bloody nose on several occasions in middle school. This was produced primarily by kids he described as "white, affluent, hockey players. They were all rich, privileged, violent, jerk athletes." Their bullying was centered around issues of homophobia. Daniel said he began to notice his sexuality in 8th grade when he developed a crush on a girl. Despite this obvious crush, the boys who targeted him would ask repeatedly, "Are you gay?" According to Daniel, the boys did not have much of an idea themselves what they meant. Daniel's reaction was "passive incomprehension." He did not answer and just tried to ignore and put up with what they were doing. At the same time, he conveyed to me, "I hated those kids with a passion. Even today, if I saw them, I would have trouble controlling my emotional response. I don't feel forgiveness. I would still be very tempted to hurt them or sabotage them in some way. I feel deep-seated anger and hatred. I still hate rich kid hockey frat-type boys and men. I experience an immediate stereotype and think, 'This is someone I hate.'"

Along the way, Daniel started taking karate lessons and became a black belt. He also felt that the lessons had some important moral codes and values and gave him the ability to protect himself from the threats of others. Finally, before high school began, his parents moved and he started at a new school district. There, he found friends with similar interests, and the bullying and harassment he had experienced as a result of his academic prowess ended. He said he is grateful for attending this school, otherwise he could see himself becoming "a hermit" as an adult.

Daniel saw the special treatment of athletes continue when he went to college where he, and others, experienced a vague threat from the athletes who lived on their dormitory hall. Daniel said he has always resented how academia elevates athletes over all other students.

There have been tremendous consequences in his personal life as a result of the chronic bullying. Daniel listed consequences for him that are absolutely enormous. The impact of bullying in his life can be seen in his social relationships, in academic environments, in employment decisions, in his politics, and in his couple relationships. Daniel said, "All of this has had a profound impact on my personal relationships. I keep a degree of dissociation from those I am involved with. I am emotionally distant in order to preserve my safety." This "dissociation," as he calls it, has led to problems in his closest intimate relationships. He is never quite able to trust his partners and expects that, at some point, they will hurt or betray him.

In his own words, Daniel said:

"I definitely don't deal with conflict at all well in social situations. I observe that other people can get into an argument then the next day they have forgotten about it. For me, those angry words echo in my brain and it is difficult to resolve—I want people to apologize—but the echo still reverberates for me. I seek out relationships with people who are pacifists. If I do get into a conflict with a friend, I walk away from the friendship forever. I have abandoned many relationships over the years. I feel pretty comfortable with it. Ok, I'm not friends with this person anymore—no second chances, no remorse. Maybe it indicates an emotional disconnection. But I feel there is an endless supply of friends in the world. This propensity hasn't prevented me from having lasting friendships and they are completely non-confrontational. We have never gotten into a fight."

"Intimacy is very difficult"

"It extends to my friendships with women as well. Intimacy is very difficult for me. One of the reasons I decided to marry my wife is because she is so non-confrontational; she avoids most issues. At the same time, I can talk to her about things; we discuss, but we never shout or anything like that. So our marriage works. I had a relationship before I got married but the first time we had a fight that sabotaged the whole thing. I tried to get past it and we stumbled on for a while. When there is a fight, I feel unsafe. I perceive the other person to be untrustworthy and unpredictable. It's sort of sad and impressive that one little argument could change a whole relationship. It's the way I've dealt with employment situations too. The first time something comes to a head, I walk. Then I feel like I have some control."

At least in the examples above we see men who are in relationships or attempting them. Some research describes the impact of rejection and bullying as so devastating that relationships are not even considered. Gilmartin (1987) described research in which shy males were compared with non-shy males using the Eysenck Personality Questionnaire. The study found that those who were "social isolates or outcasts" in childhood and who recalled "stressful and non-supportive relationships" with peers were much less likely to participate in "courtship, marriage, and family formation roles" than those who had not been bullied (p. 467).

Infidelity

Is there a connection between childhood bullying and infidelity in adult life? When individuals feel comfortably close and emotionally secure in their relationships, their risk of infidelity is greatly decreased (Mikulincer & Shaver, 2003). Consequently, we might speculate that individuals who no longer feel close, whose comfort level, security, and trust have been shaken in their friendships, run the risk of later infidelity in intimate relationships. This makes sense. When you are committed to a friend and you are betrayed by being bullied or rejected, you are learning that fidelity is not the most important component of a relationship. It makes sense also as you strive to find someone, or more than one someone, to accept you and be available to you that issues of fidelity may become problematic. Trust is a vital component in friendships, and if you have been bullied, rejected, or intimidated in some way by a friend, this trust has been violated. Social learning theory indicates that we learn from each interpersonal interaction and we learn how to treat one another (Bandura, 1969). The result, for some people who have been bullied and have lost trust is to keep a certain emotional distance in all of their relationships.

Infidelity can take many forms, but it may be conceptualized as an emotional affair or sexually intimate affair with someone other than the primary partner in a relationship (Fish, Pavkov, Wetchler, & Bercik, 2012). Studies about infidelity often look at this phenomenon through the lens of attachment theory. Attachment theory contends that the connections made in infancy with primary caregivers have considerable impact on the relationships we form in adult life (Powell & Ladd, 2010). Attachments, though varying in description, are either secure or insecure, as discussed earlier. Whatever type of attachment we are able to form as infants and toddlers is the basis for our sense of acceptance as a person. When infants develop insecure attachments, they end up with a belief that they are unlovable. Research indicates that victims of childhood bullying often have insecure maternal attachment (Seibert & Kearns, 2015; Walden & Beran, 2010). Also, children with attachment problems are more likely to demonstrate poor impulse control and lack empathy for others' feelings (Bowlby, 1969; Corvo & deLara, 2010). Poor impulse control and the poor ability to understand how a partner might feel about being betrayed through infidelity may factor in later when opportunities for cheating present themselves. Further, bullying victims demonstrate difficulties with attachment in romantic relationships. They are likely to be overly anxious, worrying they will lose their partner and face abandonment, or overly independent, creating too much distance in the relationship. Consequently they have trouble finding a balance that works well (Fish et al., 2012; Powell & Ladd, 2010). Either way, attachment issues combined with bullying victimization can produce problems in adult relationships. An example of this can be seen with Evan. Evan was the victim of years of bullying in elementary through high school. He is 45 and has been married for a number of years. However, he said he has had the following attitude about infidelity since the beginning of the relationship. He explained:

> "I am certainly willing and interested in having sexual relationships outside of marriage. What does this say about me and bullying? I think I have a less than full commitment to my marriage. I feel like I need to keep some distance from my wife. Having relationships outside allows me that distance and I don't feel dependent on her to be my best friend or my only friend for that matter. I saw what happened when I was bullied as a kid and thought I could count on my friends to be there for me. They weren't. Now I am old enough to take control of my life."

Evan's statement shows considerable insight into the connection for him between his bullying experiences and his leanings toward infidelity in his marriage. Of course, this attitude and behavior can result in devastating outcomes for Evan, his wife, and his family. Here is another way in which childhood bullying can scar an individual and come into play in adult relationships.

There are thousands of other Daniels and Evans out there. People so traumatized by the maltreatment and betrayal of close friends and intimates that they keep themselves emotionally separate at some level. There is a wall, even if it is invisible. The wall goes way up when they are hurt or perceive that they are about to be abandoned. Then they make a hasty retreat behind the wall for protection. Their friends and intimate partners may end up wondering why. What has happened? What did they do that could have resulted in this kind of fracture in the relationship? This points out again how important trust is in a relationship, how it gets irreparably damaged in bullying and harassment situations, and how crucial predictability is as the courier of trust in most interpersonal relationships.

The next chapter addresses some of the physical health and mental health issues that are the result of bullying in both children and adults. We see the long-lasting impact of bullying on the body and the mind.

CHAPTER 6
"Angry Words Echo in My Brain"

Health and Mental Health Impacts

"Evil dwells in the heart of man, words cut deep, what you don't know won't hurt you, but it may be killing your children . . . These truths are carved in flesh."

Babbi J., 2003

When most people think of bullying they envision a single incident; the child deals with it, and everyone moves on. However, experiences of bullying and harassment can lead to physical, mental, and emotional harm, whether the child is a direct victim, a bully, or a witness (Fisher et al., 2012). No one can dispute that the bullying that occurs in schools precipitates anxiety among many children and teens (Leone, Ray, & Evans, 2012). Numerous research studies document the psychological consequences for a child's mental health as a result of bullying (Biebl, DiLalla, Davis, Lynch, & Shinn, 2011; Heikkila, Vaananen, et al., 2012; Schneider, O'Donnell, Stueve, & Coulter, 2012). Some research looks at the stability of mental health problems that may continue into adolescence stemming from childhood bullying experiences as bully, victim, or both (Biebl et al., 2011; Burk et al., 2011).

While research with children has established numerous psychological consequences that result from being bullied, interestingly, all parties (victims, bullies, and witnesses) may experience adverse effects. This is not surprising when we consider that some children inhabit all of these roles. Depression and anxiety are common, but children also suffer with the following:

- Lower self-esteem
- Greater unhappiness

- Greater social isolation
- Greater susceptibility to peer pressure
- Impaired academic performance
- Skipping school
- Greater likelihood of dropping out of school
- High probability of suffering from injuries—accidental and those per-petrated by others
- Use of medication for nervousness and sleep problems
- Increased likelihood of using substances
- Self-harming behaviors
- Suicidal ideation
- Homicidal ideation
- Suicide attempts
- Homicide attempts

(Anthony, Wessler, & Sebian, 2010; Arseneault Cannon, Fisher, Polanczk, Moffitt, & Caspi, 2011; Bowes, Joinson, Wolke, & Lewis, 2015; Fitzpatrick & Bussey, 2010; Jokinen, 2015; Kendrick, Jutengren, & Stattin, 2012).

This raises the question: Is a person's well-being affected for life as a result of these childhood experiences that impact their sense of safety and self-worth? Can bullying affect mental health and even physical health into adult life? My own research and that of others indicates the answer is a resounding Yes. Research is just beginning to have a clear view into the effects of bullying and harassment that may begin in childhood and become evident in adult life. In fact, the long-term impacts on mental health from childhood bullying can surpass even those that result from maltreatment by adults. In a study of over 4,000 people in England and over 1,000 in North Carolina, researchers found that those who had been bullied as children by their peers were much more likely to suffer from anxiety, depression, and self-harming behaviors when they were adults than those who had been physically, emotionally, or sexually abused by adults. The findings held true after controlling for several factors such as family social-economic status, family instability, and gender (Lereya, Copeland, Costello, & Wolke, 2015).

ADVERSE CHILDHOOD EXPERIENCES

Children who have been mistreated and subject to certain kinds of del-eterious situations are said to have undergone adverse childhood expe-riences (ACEs). In 1995–1997 the Centers for Disease Control and the

Kaiser Permanente Health Organization began a comprehensive study of the childhood experiences of 17,337 adults. Bullying was included as an ACE. The study also looked at their current adult health status. Almost two-thirds reported at least one ACE with more than one in five people reporting three or more ACEs. What the researchers discovered was there were multiple short-term and long-term health and social problems associated with adverse childhood experiences. The health problems reported by the participants occurred at a greater rate than for the general public and led to earlier death than typical for people of the same age. Among the health problems that led to a poor quality of life and early demise were:

- Smoking
- Alcoholism and alcohol abuse
- Chronic obstructive pulmonary disease (COPD)
- Depression
- Illicit drug use
- Ischemic heart disease
- Liver disease
- Risk for intimate partner violence
- Multiple sexual partners
- Sexually transmitted diseases
- Suicide attempts (Centers for Disease Control and Prevention [CDC], 2013).

These outcomes are typically considered to be public health issues. However, as Cronholm, Ismailji, and Mettner (2013) point out, "In reality, there exists a 'public health paradox': What are conventionally viewed as public health problems often are also unconscious attempted personal solutions to long concealed adverse childhood experiences (p. 273)." This is an especially important idea. We tend to think of most of the health problems listed above as free-standing. In other words, as having nothing to do with childhood issues or problems. Some are easier for us to make a connection to childhood such as intimate partner violence (where this behavior was perhaps viewed at home). But the ACE study changed our outlook so that the link between the hardships of childhood and consequent adult medical conditions is now well recognized. One of the categories that the study looked at was "recurrent humiliation." This is considered an ACE and it is certainly experienced by bullied and sexually harassed children. During research, surveys were given to participants and then scored for ACE. The scores for those who were repeatedly humiliated were positively correlated, in adulthood, with depression, alcoholism, gastrointestinal problems, drug abuse, promiscuity, violence perpetration, impaired memory of childhood, and suicidality.

There is a cumulative effect of trauma, hence the need to know and try to replace or prevent ACEs with positive experiences. Adverse childhood experiences lead to disrupted neurodevelopment. Stress is a part of life for all children, so there is a degree of stress that is normal and tolerable. However, overwhelming stress is toxic for healthy development and damaging to neurological structures in the brain, leading to dysregulation in stress response systems. Children subjected to this kind of trauma have difficulties in a range of developmental domains. Adverse childhood experiences lead to "adverse brain development and lifelong problems in learning, behavior, and physical and mental health" (Cronholm et al., 2013, p. 274). Maltreatment in childhood (bullying, sexual harassment, and other ACEs) can lead to trauma and PTSD. When this occurs, it creates neurobiological changes in the brain. The changes in the child's brain affect the child's development and set it off course. These developmental shifts show up in behavior and in overall health. Health impacts can be physical or psychological and extend into adult life. Maltreatment in childhood then has lifelong consequences. These consequences, and their sequelae, should be considered a public health crisis. Authors of the ACE study point out that it is of great importance for medical professionals and clinicians to ask their patients about any adverse childhood experience in their lives—and about how it has affected them as adults. A similar study was conducted in Sweden. This longitudinal study followed over 14,000 children born in 1953. The researchers were looking at health and health-related outcomes over the lifespan for children who were at the bottom of the social order at school. They found that adults who were mistreated through marginalization or exclusion as children reported many more instances of hospitalization than those in the study who were not isolated. Further, as adults those who were bullied through exclusion were twice as likely to be at risk for mental illness, four time more likely to develop diabetes, and nine times more likely to develop heart disease (Almquist, 2011; Almquist & Brännström, 2014). Australia has often been at the forefront of research on bullying and its consequences. One study polled almost 3,000 adults in South Australia to determine the health issues of those who had been bullied as children. Those adults had "significantly poorer mental and physical health compared to those who had not been bullied" (Allison, Roeger, & Reinfeld-Kirkman, 2009, p. 1163). These researchers suggest that because school bullying can lead to a lower quality of life in terms of health concerns, it should be looked at as a preventable public health issue.

SYSTEMIC RESPONSES

It may be difficult to understand how childhood bullying can actually result in a negative influence over a person's biological systems, but research has begun to investigate this closely. Copeland, Wolke, Lereya, Shanahan, Worthman, & Costello (2014) explored the ways in which experiences of bullying affect systemic inflammation. They interviewed children and young adults at various points in their development for the study. What they found was that in young adulthood, those children who were bullied showed greater levels of C-reactive protein in their blood than children who were not bullied. C-reactive protein is a definitive marker for systemic inflammation. Though this protein rose for all participants in the study as they got older, those who were bullied showed the greatest increase. Bullies showed the lowest levels of C-reactive protein into adulthood. The study carefully controlled for other childhood adversities, substance use, other health factors, and individual body mass index. Basically, the bullied continued to show higher levels of C-reactive protein into adulthood leading to continuing systemic inflammation. Systemic inflammation results in a person's immune system being on chronic high alert, and this kind of response can lead to the development of several forms of disease in the body. Further, it is important to note that other somatic symptoms may appear for those who have been bullied including poor appetite, headaches, sleep disturbances, abdominal pain, and fatigue (Sansone & Sansone, 2008). In another study, Ouellet-Morin and colleagues (2011) looked at twins who were bullied to determine any systemic differences between them and a control group of nonbullied twins. The results indicated blunted cortisol secretion in the bullied twins. This basically means that their neuroendocrine system was adversely affected by the bullying they experienced.

Cerebral Changes

We have long known that childhood sexual abuse affects changes to the brains of those who are victimized (Andersen et al., 2008). It turns out that even verbal abuse by classmates, though it may seem to be ubiquitous, appears to damage and change portions of a child's brain as well. Neuroimaging scans have explored this link and discovered damage to the corpus callosum area of the brain. This area is important because it connects both hemispheres of the brain and is responsible for multiple neuronal networks. Unfortunately, damage to the corpus callosum increases the risk for ongoing psychological problems (Teicher, Samson, Sheu, Polcari, & McGreenery, 2010).

ANXIETY AND DEPRESSION

While some research may not find as many physiological issues of concern for bullies as for victims (Copeland, Wolke, Lereya, Shanahan, Worthman, & Costello (2014)), other research demonstrates the correlation of mental disorders with being a bully in childhood. A very large national survey of almost 64,000 children in the United States found 15.2% between the ages of 6 and 17 were labeled as bullies by their parent or other guardian. These children had various mental health diagnoses. Those who were depressed, anxious, or had ADHD were three times more likely to be a considered a bully (Benedict, Vivier, & Gjelsvik, 2014). On the other hand, there are abundant studies demonstrating that children with ADHD, depression, and anxiety are bullied by others (Bogart et al., 2014; Hong, Kral, & Sterzing, 2014; Redmond, 2011). Some studies point out the circular nature of bullying. Timmermanis and Weiner (2011) studied the activities of children with ADHD and discovered that they were both bullied and bullies. As Kylie, age 30, told me, "Bullying has been such a normal part of my life that I sometimes have a hard time distinguishing between when I was a victim, bully, or bystander." This demonstrates how difficult it is, if not implausible, to try to place children in one group exclusively.

Anxiety is an aftermath of bullying for many. Children who are chronically exposed to real or perceived threats learn to react with anxiety in a wide variety of situations (Gladstone, Parker, & Malhi,2006; Nansel et al., 2001). Children who experience bullying anywhere on the spectrum, whether as bully, victim, or witness, end up with some degree of depression and anxiety (Sourander et al., 2007; Sourander et al., 2009). Those who are considered bully/victims have the highest rate of these psychiatric symptoms. At the same time, children who are victims only are at the greatest risk of suicidal ideation or action (Swearer, Collins, Radcliff, & Wang, 2011).

Social Anxiety

"I had awful anxiety about going to school. I threw up nearly every single morning of 9th grade."

Male, 36

As was mentioned briefly in the chapter "People-Pleasing Versus Revenge," social anxiety can be the result of childhood bullying and can have a powerful corrosive effect on development. When children have been victimized by bullying there can be short-term negative effects. We are now seeing evidence that many forms of so-called teasing can eventuate in adult social anxiety. Boulton (2013) found that social anxiety was predictive after testing and collecting information from people over age 23. The anxiety that remains into adulthood, based on childhood bullying, generates counterproductive coping strategies for some victims. When they face stress in social situations, they are most apt to avoid confrontation or to avoid specific social situations all together. While this may have served well in childhood, it does not provide a good basis for managing the stress in adult relationships where dealing with problems is required. Further, studies indicate that those with social anxiety suffer from problems with relaxation and they spend less time feeling happy. It also contributes to more occasions of feeling angry over the course of a day (Kashdan & Collins, 2010). Matt, age 24, is a good example of some of these effects. He said:

> "The anxiety and social anxiety I have today has everything to do with the bullying I experienced as a kid at home and at school. My self-esteem, self-worth, and self-confidence were severely impacted. Today I experience depression, sleeplessness, panic attacks, and so much stress I find it difficult to really relax. I have a great deal of trouble falling asleep, I wake up in the middle of the night, and I never feel rested in the morning. When I go on a job interview, I know what I know and what I want to say but I am so anxious that I nearly black out. I second-guess everything I say. I believe this is what has led to my use and dependence on alcohol. It helps me numb out and dull the pain."

Matt is describing all of the attributes of depression and an anxiety disorder. He is one among many, many people who experience these same symptoms and consequences due directly to childhood maltreatment by peers or parents. Among the mechanisms that people in my study used to deal with their anxiety in social settings were to become more shy, introverted, quiet, and actively avoid people, certain settings, and situations. Caitlin, 37, an office worker, carries a great deal of anxiety. Caitlin believes this anxiety stems back to when she was in high school. She had a friend who was lesbian and when her other friends discovered this, they began to call Caitlin a lesbian too. They isolated her and she felt very alone and "fell into a depression." She is always worried about what other people are thinking of her or will think of her for something she says or does. It gets in her way in social contexts and causes her to be more withdrawn and shy than she might be. Today she has issues trusting other people and experiences social anxiety.

Depression

"Bullying made me insecure and depressed as a child so I was less confident in myself. I performed worse in school and didn't want to leave my house."

Female, 20

Various studies indicate a correlation between childhood involvement with bullying and later depression in adult life. One study is particularly relevant in that it investigated 28 longitudinal studies using a secondary analysis. The findings were unequivocal. Even up to 36 years after being bullied, the researchers found that those who were bullied as children showed a statistically significant probability of being depressed when compared with adults who were not bullied. This held true after controlling for up to 20 other risk factors that can contribute to depression (Ttofi, Farrington, Lösel, & Loeber, 2011a). The other variables were accounted for, and still the results held up. This means that childhood bullying victimization is a major risk factor for depression across the lifespan and carries its own distinctive influence. Gladstone et al. (2006) did an interesting study of men and women who were in a clinic setting being treated for depression. Over one-quarter of them had experienced bullying that they considered severe and traumatic. The researchers discovered that childhood bullying was very strongly associated with several types of anxiety including state anxiety, social phobia, and agoraphobia. Further, all of them suffered from depression as well. Though this is a clinical population and not the general population, it is important to consider the correlations of comorbid anxiety and depression resulting from bullying that may exist for all adults who experienced bullying.

Tracy, 31, a florist, spoke about the bullying she received as a middle school student in France. Her parents traveled there for a sabbatical year. Though she spoke the language, she was bullied the entire school year by her fellow students. It was not that her accent was wrong. She had learned to speak from her mother, a native French speaker. It was because she was just plain "different." She was from the United States and that was enough to give her peers ammunition against her. She was never more grateful to return to school in America, where she fit in with old friends. However, for her, the damage had been done. She had lingering scars. Her grades began to slip as she relived the taunting and torment. Now, she suffers from low self-esteem, depression, anxiety, and an inability to believe that she can succeed at anything worthwhile. She attributes these mental health problems to being bullied relentlessly. At this point, she relies on alcohol and other drugs to "make me feel better" and to feel "less anxious."

SHAME AND MENTAL HEALTH

Shame is discussed in the chapter "Being Different." An internal feeling of shame over who you are is one of the long-term consequences of being bullied, labeled, harassed, and excluded. Children who merely witness bullying say they feel ashamed as a result of the experience. They feel shame in empathy for the victims and they feel shame that they do not or cannot come to the rescue (deLara, 2012; Garbarino & deLara, 2002). In a pilot study, adult survivors of bullying reported high levels of shame and anxiety based on being frequently bullied during their school years (Carlisle & Rofes, 2007). Many of the adults in my study related a deep sense of shame concurrently with anxiety, recurrent sadness, and/or depression. Bullies are a different story. Bullies do not accept responsibility for their actions but, instead, tend to externalize responsibility placing it on others. They contend that it is the action of others that causes them to act in the ways they do and they respond with anger and hostility when confronted. Further, while victims feel shame, bullies may not experience shame associated with their own aggressive behavior (Ahmed & Braithwaite, 2004; Menesini & Camodeca, 2008).

Relatively few people admit to being a bully themselves. In my research just under 20% of all participants said they bullied others when they were children or adolescents. Of that group, slightly more males than females admitted to bullying others. A certain lack of insight or of taking personal responsibility is evident in the representative quotes below:

FEMALE, AGE 24: "I used to bully my younger brother and rough house him but I don't really know why."

MALE, AGE 33: "I teased other guys in elementary school and early middle school. Looking back I never realized I was bullying because I thought it was funny. I never distinguished between popular and unpopular in bullying and I later found out that popular kids were often more upset after the fact."

FEMALE, AGE 21: "From elementary through high school, I was kind of 'the bully' I guess when I think about it. In elementary school

I chased boys on the playground and when I caught up to them, I would always kick them. In high school, I picked on people and it would sometimes upset them. But I don't think it has had any effect on me in my life—at least not that I can see."

MALE, AGE 28, HISPANIC: "I used to make fun of people but usually would tell them I was kidding. The jokes were harsh. I also bullied my younger cousins, but I think it toughened them up."

Some adults related the bullying they inflicted to the bullying they received. In this way they are talking about the cycle of violence or the bully-victim-bully cycle that we observe with many children. One young man said: "I was always left out and bullied by groups of guys. I was taunted for being smart and overweight. With all of the negative attention toward me, I began to bully and tease my younger brother and kids who were younger than I."

MENTAL HEALTH, BEING OVERWEIGHT, AND EATING PROBLEMS

"Getting bullied for so long, I had low self-esteem and through that acquired an eating disorder."

Female, 20, African American

"I continue to have a very negative body image—I also developed an eating disorder starting in late high school."

Female, 42

In the chapter "Being Different," weight and bullying were discussed. But how does this relate to mental health? In the United States, thousands of people of all genders suffer from eating problems of one form or another such as anorexia or bulimia (Peguero & Kahle, 2014; Wade, Keski-Rahkonen, & Hudson, 2011). Weight is often described as the last acceptable prejudice. In the United States, where more than one-third of adults are overweight (Ogden et al., 2014), it is still deemed "acceptable" by many to tease or otherwise discriminate against heavy children or adults. Our media and culture are deluged with images of thin people. Even very young elementary school children are weight-conscious and can be heard asking, "Am I fat?" The research literature on weight, eating problems, and bullying has shown interesting findings. Some studies say there is a substantial difference for boys who are overweight compared with girls, that gender makes a great difference in terms of impact. Other studies contest these findings and basically show no statistically significant difference in the poor effects and outcomes for boys or for girls on being "teased," taunted, or excluded over their bodies. Among the effects are an attempt at food restriction and self-imposed social isolation. Among the poor outcomes of being bullied based on being overweight are emotional problems, body dissatisfaction, low self-esteem, depression, suicidal ideation, and suicide attempts (Eisenberg, Neumark-Sztainer, & Story, 2003; Farrow & Fox, 2011; Jiang, Perry, & Hesser, 2010). Unfortunately, these same consequences can and do carry over into adulthood for some. Bullying by peers is found to be particularly pernicious for young women in the development of bulimia nervosa (Fosse & Holen, 2006; Sansone & Sansone, 2008).

AGGRESSIVE AND VIOLENT BEHAVIOR AND SUBSTANCE USE

"I have become aggressive as an adult. I'm sure it has to do with being bullied for so many years as a child. No one is going to take advantage of me now."

Male, age 43

"I drink too much. I know it. It takes care of my anxiety."

Female, age 30

When children are bullied we may be aware of immediate impacts such as sadness, reluctance to attend school, and sometimes retaliation. However, there are long-term consequences that may take the form of adult aggression and violence. Interviewing outpatients at an internal medicine practice, Sansone, Leung, and Wiederman (2013) found that over 300 adults engaged in 21 different types of aggressive behavior toward others. These included "hitting walls, intentionally breaking things, getting into fist fights, and pushing/shoving a partner" (p. 824). The longer the bullying victimization went on when they were children, the higher the number of self-reported violent behaviors. The research team compared these results with people who were not bullied as children and determined that the difference between the two groups was statistically significant. The results of this study have significance for issues of domestic violence and intimate partner violence. Other research demonstrates a troubling connection between bullying in childhood and adult criminal offenses (Renda, Vassallo, & Edwards, 2011; Staubli & Killias, 2011; Ttofi, Farrington, Lösel, & Loeber,

2011b). This seems to be particularly true for males (Renda et al., 2011). Substance use and later abuse can stem from experiences with bullying. Children who are bullies and bully/victims are at great risk for multiple types of substance abuse (Bradshaw, Waasdorp, Goldweber, & Johnson, 2013; Hoertel, Le Strat, Lavaud, & Limosin, 2012; Niemela et al., 2011). Kim, Catalano, Haggerty, and Abbott (2011) examined self-reported bullying by 5th graders and found a substantial link to later marijuana use and heavy drinking. These findings were also associated with adult violent behaviors. The research concludes that bullying in childhood is a unique indicator for adult substance use and violence (Ttofi et al., 2011b). As discussed above, anxiety is correlated with childhood bullying. A clear connection exists between an individual's attempts to quell anxiety and the use of various substances (Rivers, 2004; Corrigan, Fisher, & Nutt, 2011).

SUICIDE

"As an adult, I have contemplated suicide, dealt with low self-esteem issues and behaved rather poorly with self-destructive behaviors."

Male, age 45

Bullying and suicide are associated phenomena worldwide (Espelage & De La Rue, 2012; Smith, 2011). In the United States, the media too often contain reports of a child who has committed suicide as a result of being tormented at school. Children who are bullied articulate suicidal ideation (Heikkila, et al., 2012) and this is true for bullies as well (Holt et al., 2015). Furthermore, when a child experiences psychological or physical maltreatment through bullying, hazing, and harassment, he or she incurs a lifetime risk of attempting suicide two to five times greater than that of someone who has not been similarly mistreated (CDC, 2013). Data from the Minnesota Student Survey of 136,549 students, investigating the outcomes of adverse childhood experiences, including bullying, found correlations with suicidal ideation and suicide attempts (Duke, Pettingell, McMorris, & Borowsky, 2010). Lesbian, gay, bisexual, transgender, and questioning (LGBTQ) students report feeling unsafe in their schools at some time during the school day. This often precipitates dropping out of school (Harris Interactive et al., 2005). Being bullied and sexually harassed by their peers can eventuate in patterns of risky behavior and suicidal behavior in LGBTQ children and teens (Hatzenbuehler, 2011; Jiang et al., 2012). In the UK over half of children who self-harm in any way are victims of bullying at school (Fisher et al., 2012). In Ireland, boys who have been bullied have a four-fold increase in their likelihood for self-harm over their lifespan (McMahon, Reulbach, Keeley, Perry, & Arensman, 2012). Participants in my study expressed this association revealing thoughts of suicide that they had over the years. Longitudinal investigations find strong links between bullying victimization in childhood and adult suicidal thoughts or attempts (Copeland, Wolke, Angold, & Costello, 2013; Roeger, Allison, Korossy-Horwood, Eckert, & Goldney, 2010; Staubli & Killias, 2011). Copeland and colleagues (2013) conducted a study and found several adult psychiatric outcomes for those involved in bullying during their childhood as a bully, a bully/victim, or a victim. The researchers controlled for family issues and for diagnosed childhood psychiatric disorders. The findings point to an increased risk of depression, agoraphobia, and panic disorder in female bully/victims. Adult male victims are at increased risk for suicidality including recurrent thoughts of death. Bullies appeared to be inclined toward antisocial personality disorder. Those classified as a victim have a significant probability of developing generalized anxiety or panic disorder as adults. The rates of psychiatric disorder among victims including depression, anxiety, agoraphobia, substance abuse, and suicidality were higher than for those in the study who were not engaged in bullying. In South Australia, a study of nearly 3,000 adults who were randomly sampled discovered that adults with a history of victimization through bullying were three times more likely to acknowledge suicidal ideation compared with adults who were not victims. Additionally, the findings were stable for all age groups represented in the sample. These results were valid even after controlling for multiple sociodemographic factors (Roeger et al., 2010). Consequently, this is important information in attempting to prevent suicide and in addressing this public health issue for adults.

PSYCHOSIS

While bullying victimization can be associated with psychosis, it is important to remember that some symptoms such as hearing voices and dissociation can be signs of trauma. They are not always signs of psychosis (Longden, Madill, & Waterman, 2012). At the same time, there is an increased risk of psychotic symptoms in children and teens who have been bullied by their peers (Arseneault et al., 2011; Brent, 2011; Sourander et al., 2009). Further, children who are victimized are found to experience severe symptoms of mental illness leading to self-harming and violent acting out along with psychosis (Arseneault, Bowes, & Shakoor, 2010). The Arseneault study is especially intriguing because it investigated the experiences of twin pairs. The twin who was the subject of bullying was much more likely to exhibit psychotic symptomatology than the other twin. Other studies have found that both being a bully and being a victim place people at risk for suffering from psychiatric disorders in adulthood (Sourander et al., 2007). Bentall, Wickham, Shevlin, and Varese (2012) point out that research studies delineate a clear association between childhood bullying and abuse with psychosis in adulthood. This includes various forms of hallucinations and paranoid ideation. Collectively, these findings are evidence that childhood bullying should be considered a marker for later psychiatric problems.

CONSEQUENCES OF CYBERBULLYING

Cyberbullying is a relatively new form of torment for both children and adults. There are numerous platforms over which it can be conducted. As quickly as adults learn of one medium another pops up where children are easily able to escape adult supervision for a period of time until adults catch up. Once they are online, cyberbullying is a definite menace children face, "more often from someone they know than from a stranger" (Cassidy, Faucher, & Jackson, 2013, p. 577). According to Wang, Nansel, and Iannotti (2011), children feel helpless and dehumanized when they are cyberbullied. The CDC (2010) states there is a sense of permanence associated with cyber-attacks that feels different from traditional bullying. Victims of cyberbullying, like those of traditional bullying, report higher rates of depression and suicidality than children who are not victimized (Cappadocia, Craig, & Pepler, 2013; Hinduja & Patchin, 2010; Landstedt & Persson, 2014). However, some studies indicate that children suffer greater depression from cyberbullying than from any other form of bullying (Wang et al., 2011). "Being bullied over the internet is worse," said one 14-year-old from New Jersey who posted on a website for the Cyberbullying Research Center, a nonprofit organization dedicated to researching the effects of cyberbullying. "It's torment and hurts. They say 'sticks and stones may break my bones, but words will never hurt me.' That quote is a lie and I don't believe in it." Another cyberbullying victim, a 14-year-old from New York, said "It makes me feel bad and rather depressed. Like I don't want to be a part of this world anymore" (Cyberbullying Research Center, n.d.).

Effects of Being Bullied Through Cybergaming

Georgia, 27, a paralegal, described her experiences from elementary through college years. Sometimes she was bullied through exclusion, sometimes she participated in bullying others, and in college the worst sort of bullying and sexual harassment took place. She remembers,

I was never physically abused or pushed around at school, or home or elsewhere, although I remember often feeling hurt inside by being left alone or ignored, too shy to join in or speak up when classmates or teachers had more important or fun activities to do than spend time with me. In elementary school, you could say I was a bully. My actions at school to feel included led to participation in group bullying or gossip. The key to get in to a group was to have a good "break the ice" kind of laugh *about* someone else (like agreeing with another girl's comment about the horrible outfit someone was wearing, or joining in a game that mocked someone so that you felt better inside). As an adult, I was bullied, sexually harassed, and stalked through an online interactive game. I ended up feeling entirely ashamed, helpless, sad, and mortified. A guy was stalking me in the game and my friends told me not to reply to his "trolling" behavior. I didn't but we had a guy friend who did. He became incredibly depressed because of the abuse from this other guy, the troll. I am glad I walked away. At the time, the online world was my social world. It was terribly difficult to leave it behind but I'm glad I had the courage to do it. Now I wouldn't enter into another forum like that.

These were real people (thankfully behind computers), and this explicit and unwanted attention both confused and angered me, and quite scared me at a real, deep level. I have little doubt that if he (the stalker) could have found me in real life I would be in physical danger. I found myself making little tally sheets every few days for weeks, marking down "What does he know about me?", "Does he have enough information to find me?", and "What might he try next to get information about me from my friends?" It stressed and drained all my time, my energy, and all of my will to keep up a calm exterior for the two months that this went on. I worried about my social reputation, even a little more sometimes than my safety which looking back on it seems the silliest thing in the world. But this is probably why I did not leave the situation sooner. In that online world, my character's presence was like a life to me and I cared what people thought of me. I could be funny, well-liked, even beautiful and confident more so than I felt while going to school each day. I had to sort through every message I got from friends looking for yet another lie that the stalker had started. I would have to calm someone down after reading a terrible message of profanity generated by the stalker. All of this began to make me panic that I would lose all of my friends, that they would begin to believe the horrible things he was saying about me and wish me gone so that they could play in peace again. I typed him as a resentful stalker the year afterward when I was brave enough to look into behavioral patterns. And I spent those intervening months (and still do occasionally before I post anything online that might involve any personal information) worrying over the smallest of details that I let the world know about me. FaceBook I will never join. How much could I trust people with my personal information? How much could I trust security of online systems? I even unplugged my computer entirely every night because I irrationally thought he could hack into it if it was connected to a power source. I kept reliving the abusive chat logs that I held as evidence for a long time, wondering where I went wrong, and how I could have solved the problem better. The loss of control during the bullying frightened me, the raw violation and exposure of my inner self to some creepy stranger, not knowing how many details he knew or what he was capable of. I felt horrible inside for a long time. That this could even happen in my own room, my safe room at home—open to the world online—was frightening. I also greatly missed my online friendships after leaving, but I no longer had much faith in them by the end either— one had turned on me as another bully, a tool of stronger persuasion for the stalker, and the others had not really been able to step in and help me. This stalking event, although it has been several years, still affects me as an adult. However, I have more self-confidence now, not placing as much of my worth in what other people think or say about me, and I am able to let go of trying to control the insane actions of others. I did learn a bit, through the hurt, in the good way to stick up for myself and not be treated that harshly again without informing the police. With relationships, I feel a little more comfortable going to those in authority with problems I encounter, but relying on friends or trusting in the decency of strangers is a challenge for me. I still wonder sometimes if my wariness is a good thing or bad thing or if I just need to open up and relax and surrender a part of myself in order to get to know people. Part of me very much fears to be hurt and vulnerable again. Thankfully I have met some wonderful people now in the real world who can help me socialize and really have fun. I still have to practice though."

Although Georgia seems to be recovering from the effects of online bullying and cyberstalking and is trying to replace helpless feelings with other, more positive ones, it is evident that she is left with emotional wounds. She is trying to put aside fears, to be able to trust others. She wants to be able to relax and not experience so much anxiety in letting people get close to her while she attempts to build new relationships. Her capacity for this has been taxed based on the bullying and harassment she described. The desire to be included and not isolated, as she experienced in elementary school, quite possibly fueled Georgia staying too long in the online world. However, at this point, fear and anxiety of a future "creepy" stranger in the real world are imprints from her online encounters. Georgia's story is compelling and gives us a window into the very legitimate concerns of cyberbullying victimization and its aftermath.

HOW DOES THIS CONTRIBUTE TO ADULT ISSUES OF ATTACHMENT, HEALTH, AND MENTAL HEALTH?

"You always hear those voices [of those who bullied you]."
Female, age 55

Attachment Issues and Trust

Children who are exposed to any form of violence are more likely to suffer from attachment problems, regressive behavior, anxiety, and depression, and to have aggression and conduct problems. Disruption in attachment as a result of violence can be seen in parent–child relationships and in peer-to-peer relationships (Burton, Florell, & Wygant, 2013). Unfortunately, attachment issues play out through adult life and carry over into all important adult relationships (Alexander, 2009; Coan, 2010; Simpson & Rholes, 2010). John Bowlby's seminal research was on the importance of love and attachment. His basic premise was as humans we have an innate need to love and to be loved. This is instinctive and it allows for our survival. He theorized that children who do not receive the reliable, nurturing response they need from their mothers or primary caregiver become angry and aggressive in an attempt to make the mother respond. Of course this may elicit an angry response, in turn, from the mother, but Bowlby hypothesized that children were willing to accept any attention rather than bear the loneliness that the lack of attachment produced. The drive toward connection stays with us for life. Those who are not securely attached during infancy and childhood will continue to search for this in their relationships as they grow. The lack of secure attachment often means difficulty trusting in relationships. Further, once a relationship is established, any threat to it can result in a deep sense of abandonment or in "separation protest" that can be accompanied by rage (Bowlby, 1969, 1973, 1980). When abused children grow up, they are "left with fundamental problems in basic trust, autonomy, and initiative" (Herman, 1992, p. 110). At the same time that they struggle with issues of trust, they are desperate for acceptance and protection in intimate relationships, and are extremely fearful of abandonment by their partners. In terms of physical and mental health, much current research is devoted to the neurobiological aspects of childhood and adult attachment issues. It is clear that specific functioning of the hippocampus, a component of the brain, is associated with attachment anxiety in relationships (Quirin, Gillath, Pruessner, & Eggert, 2009). Further, other areas such as the hypothalamic-pituitary-adrenocortical axis of the human brain are activated in response to various attachment styles and patterns (Diamond & Fagundes, 2010; Pietromonaco, DeBuse, & Powers, 2013). When neural networks are triggered by concerns around attachment, emotion regulation difficulties occur. Examples of emotional health issues and attachment are demonstrated in responses like these I encountered:

> "I'm emotionally distant to preserve my safety."
>
> Male, *age 32*

> "I expect close friends or my intimate partners to betray me."
>
> Female, *age 39*

WHAT IS LEFT BEHIND?

The majority of adults in my study reported experiencing one or more negative consequences in their adult lives as a result of childhood bullying. These include poor self-image, lack of trust in others, difficulty making or maintaining friendships or intimate relationships, remaining in unhealthy relationships, generalized feelings of helplessness, anxiety, panic attacks, and depression.

> "They [her parents] helped me talk to a school counselor and started driving me to school so I didn't have to take the bus, so I could avoid getting bullied. I have been in therapy on and off for 20 years. I have post-traumatic stress disorder. I have problems with social interactions, lack of confidence. I still won't pass a group of people I suspect as a threat. I don't trust strangers. I am hyper vigilant."
>
> Female, *age 32*

"I am extremely emotionally damaged."

Male, *age 37*

In my clinical practice also, I have seen the contributions of past bullying and sexual harassment to current adult problems of social anxiety, hopelessness, poor relationships, and depression. Steven is an exemplar: Steven, age 30, came into therapy for feelings of inadequacy, pervasive feelings of sadness he attributed to experiences from his childhood, and the inability to sustain a relationship with a woman. In treatment it became clear that Steven had suffered bullying, harassment, and emotional violence throughout all of his public school years. Other boys tormented him for his lack of physical ability in gym class and lack of participation in sports—highly valued in his hometown. The girls provided their own brand of humiliation in the form of verbally shaming him and shunning him over his appearance and manner of dress. When he did manage to get a girlfriend, according to Steven, she would complain that he didn't know how to kiss and that he was not sexually adept like the other boys. Sometimes, she would make this known to others at school, providing more fodder for victimization by his peers. As a young adult currently in an intimate relationship, Steven struggles with issues of depression, of masculine identity, of confidence in his sexual relationship, and of worthiness to be in a happy, ongoing relationship at all. Consequently, he has found a partner who has similar issues. She questions her ability to sustain any long-term relationship. She believes that a happy, lifelong relationship is probably not a likelihood for her. She, too, was bullied during her high school years.

A great many people have come to see me in my clinical practice to deal with the consequences of the bullying they experienced in their childhood years. They were neither psychologically nor physically prepared to stop it when they were young. Though they have moved on in their lives and many are successful people in their professions, they are left with the damage. These scars impact their ability to thrive in relationships with intimate partners because their sense of self-esteem is still greatly affected. Some clients have chronic social anxiety that stems from their childhood experiences with bullying. The anxiety impairs their willingness to go out, to meet new people, and ultimately it gets in the way of their friendships and intimate relationships. This becomes problematic in unexpected ways. It is difficult for one spouse when the other is too anxious or too frightened of interpersonal interactions to want to go out. Even an everyday event, such as making a phone call or going out to dinner, becomes a trial for those with social anxiety. A trip to the grocery store is equally fraught with potential problems.

There are numerous consequences of bullying and maltreatment in childhood that show up as residual impacts on adult well-being, health, and mental health. Childhood bullying has disastrous effects oftentimes leading to lifelong physical health problems, anxiety, and depression. Plainly, more research is necessary to protect against permanent health impairments. The imprint of bullying leaves a deep impression. Adults shoulder this burden and transport it into every relationship and every aspect of their lives.

Sexual harassment is a form of bullying leaving many consequences for both children and adults. In the next chapter we look at the numerous instances of sexual harassment that children are met with and how adults attempt to deal with the resulting consequences.

CHAPTER 7

"I Am So Self-Conscious"

The Impact of Sexual Harassment

"I was called really horrible, profane names . . . I was so embarrassed all the time.

I was so ashamed of who I was."

Lady Gaga, March 1, 2012

Lady Gaga is a talented artist, singer, and entertainer. She said she was up all night crying when she heard the tragic news about Jamey Rodemeyer, a 14-year-old gay boy who had taken his life. He had been trying to hang on, trying to look forward in spite of bullying and harassment due to his sexual orientation. He had recently posted to the "It Gets Better" project website. This website is meant to convey that things get better as you get older and to give hope to lesbian, gay, bisexual, transgender, queer, and questioning young people. As a result of this tragedy and others, Lady Gaga established the Born This Way Foundation to encourage and empower kids to be happy and accept themselves. The lyrics in her music also encourage this. Lady Gaga has achieved worldwide fame and recognition despite a tragic backstory. When she was in high school, she was bullied and sexually harassed so badly that she felt traumatized. She made herself into a superstar despite early and chronic suffering inflicted by her peers. However, she had to endure "really horrible and profane names . . . in front of huge crowds of people." The crude comments hurled at her led to an inability to focus at school. She had been a straight-A student. She stated, "I was so embarrassed all the time. I was so ashamed of who I was." To this day, she says, "When certain things are said to you over and over again as you're growing up, it stays with you and you wonder if they're true" (Kristof, 2012). The scars and trauma are still there for this woman who is so successful and known all over the world. Even she is left questioning what is true about herself based on the cruel sexual harassment she endured in her high school days.

Sexual harassment is bullying or coercion of a sexual nature. It is one of the many forms that bullying takes. When children are at school or on the school bus, they are subjected to sexual harassment, and it does not go unnoticed. It takes a great toll on them (deLara, 2008a, 2008b; Gruber & Fineran, 2008). Sexual harassment is different from merely looking at or observing someone. Observing the sexual attributes of another person is a normal developmental phenomenon. This is how kids begin to figure out to whom they are attracted. But sexual harassment is meant to intimidate and demean. The target may end up shocked and shamed or cowering in fear. The sexual bully is hoping for this. Sexual harassment is defined as unwelcome sexual advances, requests for sexual favors, and other verbal or physical conduct of a sexual nature (Fineran & Bennett, 1998; York, 1989). The definition was originally intended for adults in the workplace but, out of necessity, it has been extended to include children in their workplace as well.

STATISTICS

Numerous children and adolescents are subject to bullying in the form of sexual harassment by peers or even by teachers and other adults at school. The American Association of University Women put together a thorough report on sexual harassment of students in 2001 and updated it in 2011. They found that in 2001 83% of girls admitted to being sexually harassed and 79% of boys admitted that they were sexually harassed at school. By 2011, those numbers decreased by about 40%. This may be due to the fact that students became more aware of what constituted sexual harassment or they had been provided with greater means to combat it via school programming. However, a full 38% of students said they were sexually harassed by teachers and other school personnel. That statistic did not change over the course of the 10 years (American Association of University Women [AAUW], 2011). The fact that school personnel engage in sexual harassment and sexual activity with children is, of course, an even greater violation of a child than peer sexual harassment. As part of the implicit social contract, children should be able to count on the adults in their lives to be trustworthy.

Sexual harassment creates a hostile environment. Children are supposed to be protected against sexual harassment by peers or adults at school under Title IX of the US Education Amendments of 1972. Even though this law has been in effect for over 40 years, recent statistics indicate the following about our schools:

- 56% of girls admit they have been sexually harassed
- 40% of boys admit to being sexually harassed (though some studies find boys are more often the target of sexual harassment than girls)
- Only 12% of students say their school does a good job of addressing sexual harassment

(AAUW, 2011; Pepler, et al., 2006; Petersen & Hyde, 2009).

Of course sometimes in an attempt to keep to the letter of the law, instead of its spirit, adults end up doing peculiar things like suspending a 6-year old boy for kissing a girl on the hand (Wallace, 2013). It is important to note that children and adolescents are not always aware that they are being sexually harassed. Several of the adults in my research said they realized that what had happened to them was sexual harassment only when they reached adulthood and could look back. At the time, they were just aware that they were being made fun of, that someone was being "mean," and that they were extremely embarrassed. Likewise, Hlavka (2014) found that girls do not name sexual harassment for what it is, but rather think it is part of normal heterosexual activity. Of those I interviewed individually, about half said they were sexually harassed at home, at school, or in the community.

IMPACT ON CHILDREN AND TEENS

Sexual harassment is an ordinary part of the day in elementary and secondary schools (deLara, 2008b; Gruber & Fineran, 2008; Meraviglia, Becker, Rosenbluth, Sanchez, & Robertson, 2003). Adults have difficulty seeing how this can be a long-lasting problem for children once they grow up. Indeed, most adults think kids are not paying much attention to the phenomenon of sexual harassment at all except when it results in a tragic outcome. However, teenagers report feeling afraid, upset, or threatened as a result of sexual harassment when they are either a target or a witness. Some describe having sleep problems due to sexual harassment, and others report not wanting to go to school (AAUW, 2011). Though it appears to be part of their everyday environment, the effects do not just roll off their backs.

Sexual Harassment is Harmful to Healthy Development

"The sexual harassment I got made me wary of people, then and now, and I struggle to feel good about myself and how I look. I struggle to get over it. The experiences I had in junior high school are as fresh to me today as if they happened last week."

Female, age 56

Sexual harassment has a profound impact on a child's conceptions of his or her body (Gadin, 2012). It can also result in a negative impact on a child's well-being and academic performance (Lichty & Campbell, 2012). Espelage and Holt (2007) report a correlation between sexual harassment of adolescents and their experience of subsequent anxiety and depression. As Fineran and Bennett (1998) stated, "peer sexual harassment interferes with and impairs adolescents' developmental progress towards readiness to become part of the adult world" (p. 63). All of this constitutes a public health concern that should be addressed in the schools and, by the time someone is an adult, may need to be addressed in counseling.

Compared to whatever might be considered "regular" bullying, sexual harassment has been shown to have more adverse effects on physical and mental health. These adverse effects are especially seen among girls and sexual minorities (Gruber & Fineran, 2008). Developmental psychologists Newman and Newman (2014) point out social acceptance by peers and adults is affected by how closely one's body matches up with the reigning cultural values. Basically, if your body is not in compliance with social norms, you are much more likely to become a target for sexual harassment and mockery. Even those who develop "too quickly" are prey. For Deidre, age 33, slow development resulted in a great deal of ridicule, as she recounted:

"In early adolescence, I was not developing as quickly as some of the others which set me up as a target to some of the other kids. I looked younger and meeker. Many of the school bullies were girls who tended to be overly developed and looked much older than their age. I can remember having very low self-esteem at that time period as I compared myself to some of the other students. I was not measuring up and it was making a definite impression on my sense of self-worth. It affected my social life. Of course I have a social life now as an adult, but it has left me with a downgraded sense of my appearance."

Even very young children experience sexual harassment. One study found that girls as young as 1st grade through 6th grade experienced verbal, nonverbal, and sexually assaultive behaviors at school. In many ways this has become normalized as part of how the system of the school operates. Sexual harassment is "a concealed phenomenon" that children are struggling to deal with (Gadin, 2012). The vast majority of middle school students in the United States are both targets and witnesses of sexual harassment (Lichty & Campbell, 2012). Once in middle school and high school, girls are more likely than boys to be sexually harassed both in person and via social media. Being called gay or lesbian in a negative way is something experienced equally by boys and girls. Witnessing sexual harassment is not an uncommon event, and it leaves students with a sense of insecurity regarding their personal safety. Even though sexual harassment has become an everyday occurrence, only about 9% of students report it to any adult at school (AAUW, 2011). Some forms of sexual harassment are actually sexual assault. Sometimes sexual harassment and sexual assault can cause so much psychological suffering that they lead both boys and girls to engage in deliberate self-harming behaviors (Landstedt & Gadin, 201).

Athletes are not excluded. Many children participate in athletic activities as part of their school day. We tend to think of the benefits to their physical, psychological, and moral development coming from these experiences. However, sexual harassment and abuse occur in all sports and at all levels with an increased risk prevalent for those athletes who rank at the very top of their sport. The physical and psychological consequences of sexual harassment and abuse are significant for the athlete and the team in terms of health and issues of integrity (Marks, Mountjoy, & Marcus, 2012).

Once at college, things don't necessarily change. Sexual harassment continues, though perhaps young adults have some better coping mechanisms than children. Research by Jordan, Combs, and Smith (2014) shows a true impact on women's academic performance as a result of sexual victimization. Yoon, Funk, and Kropf (2010) looked at a diverse group of college women to examine their experiences with sexual harassment and to investigate whether there were any kind of adverse psychological outcomes at the time. They interviewed female students from two different colleges and found what they considered an "alarmingly high rate" of sexual harassment for both African American and white women. Their academic success was altered as a result. Further, they experienced a great deal of shame and their sense of well-being was shaken dramatically.

As a result of being harassed sexually, young people often pair up, typically with someone of the opposite sex, for protection. They are looking for protection from unwanted touching, from unwanted actions, and against rumors about their sexuality or about sexual promiscuity. By doing so, they hope to stop unwanted attention and especially to stop rumors from circulating. Problematically, we know that once in a relationship, a boy or a girl may bully or harass a partner to get what they want sexually (Garbarino & deLara, 2002), resulting in early sexual debut. Research has also found that early bullying of this sort is predictive of adolescent pregnancy (Lehti et al., 2011). Consequently, the strategy of pairing up can backfire and have lifelong consequences.

Sexual Harassment and Coercion

Teens and preteens may endure significant levels of bullying behavior, including intimidation and coercion, pressuring them to be sexual before they are ready. This may be especially true for younger teens. Certainly, many people are aware of the old line, "If you loved me, you would prove it by (fill in the blank with any sexual act)." This ancient tactic is a means of subtle bullying and coercion. This approach may or may not end up in any form of sexual engagement. However, there is a great deal of research on the connections among bullying, sexual harassment, and dating violence (Connelly, Pepler, Craig, & Taradash, 2000; Connelly et al., 2014; Josephson & Pepler, 2012). Adolescents who bully their peers report being physically and socially aggressive in dating relationships (Connelly et al., 2000). In turn, dating violence is associated with increased risk of substance use, unhealthy weight control, first intercourse before age 15, adolescent pregnancy, and attempted suicide (Silverman et al., 2001). Older teens who engage in sexually harassing behavior in their dating relationships contribute to a great deal of psychological distress in their partners, leading to mental health problems (Landstedt & Gadin, 2011). Any of these outcomes has ramifications in adult life.

Technology and Sexual Harassment

Sexual harassment via technology is a more recent twist on this phenomenon. It allows for bullying through several means and can be anonymous. Children and teens can connect with one another for sexual expression, such as "sexting" or sending suggestive pictures. Further, in a recent study, teens described sending naked pictures of themselves to romantic partners and various friends and having no idea whether the pictures were forwarded on to other people (Tompson, Benz, & Agiesta,

2013). While young people are much more savvy than their parents about technology and how it works, they are typically less knowledgeable about the implications and long-range issues that can arise from any form of sexual behavior or sexual harassment through technological means. One tragic example is that an adolescent can be classified for life as a sex abuse offender, and be included in their state registry of perpetrators, by forwarding a seminude picture of a classmate. In general, we know that victims of sexual harassment can be left with feelings of shame and that their academic success and psychological well-being may be destabilized (Yoon et al., 2010). Long-term impacts of this type of sexual harassment include anxiety, depression, suicidal ideation, and suicidal behavior (Arseneault et al., 2011; Brunstein, Sourander, & Gould, 2012).

Internet and other technological forms of sexual harassment were not a formal part of my study. The majority of those who participated were not yet affected in this way by the technological age we now have. Only a few encountered this kind of bullying while they were at home or at school. Because it involves so many teens now, the consequences of sexual bullying via technology on their adult development will be an important focus for future research.

Sexual Harassment on the School Bus

Unfortunately a good deal of sexual harassment and sexual acting out occurs on the school bus. It is an essentially unsupervised area where teens and preteens are thrown in together. Sometimes, in rural areas, even younger elementary school children are on the same bus route with the high school kids. Consequently, with no supervision and rarely an intervention, sexual harassment can run rampant (deLara, 2008a). Two women provided their experiences and the immediate and long-term impact for them:

A commonplace example is supplied by Shirley, 44, African American, an administrative assistant.

"I was different than the girls on my block so I got teased a lot. I was a bit of a tomboy and loved to ride my bike everywhere. I really worked out with it. One day on the bus, this boy (who used to get teased as well, but wanted to earn 'cool' points with the girls) asked me very loudly in front of everyone, if I could ride him as hard as I rode my bike. Now I would guess I was 14 or 15, and although I wasn't sexually active at that age, I knew instantly what he meant and I was not only embarrassed but immediately threatened. I didn't respond and the rest of the way home, I just wished the bus would move faster. I was so angry at myself for not having something quick to say back, or maybe the strength to punch him in his face . . . . So now it is thirty years later and that one instance is still as fresh in my mind as if it happened yesterday. This incident only happened once, but one time is all it took to stick."

Linda, age 44, a physician's assistant, offered another example.

"I realize that the sexual harassment that occurred when I was in middle school has had a pretty big effect on my development. For one thing, it made me feel bad about myself and I didn't like the kind of attention it called on me. Two boys on my bus were always grabbing at me and trying to touch me sexually when I walked by. I made an effort to sit in the front of the bus but it wasn't always available. I tried telling the bus driver but he didn't do much. Now, after all of these years, I still feel bad about myself. One result is that I don't speak up in a room full of people even if I have something to say. I don't want to call attention to myself. When I think I might and that I should, my heart starts to pound so hard. I just stop myself. I can see where this gets in my way; I end up frustrated and unhappy in these kinds of situations. Another result is sort of worse. I've shut myself off emotionally to my husband, to most people actually. I just don't feel like I can afford to let anybody in. I am always afraid they will turn on me when I least expect it."

These may seem like everyday events that don't warrant this kind of response many years after the fact. However, this is the response; these are the feelings of the two women. They are merely representative of many, many others who faced the same or similar unwanted sexual attention at a very formative time in their young lives. They, like many others, are left with prominent scars that affect their lives today.

Sexual Harassment Based on Sexual Orientation or Gender Identity

Sexual harassment can come in the form of ridiculing someone due to sexual orientation or gender identity. The incidence of sexual harassment is much higher toward lesbian, gay, bisexual, transgender, and questioning (LGBTQ) youth. Youth who are LGBTQ or who are perceived to be different from the majority in terms of their sexuality are frequent targets of bullying by their peers (Fineran, 2002; Mishna, Newman, Daley, & Solomon, 2009; Morgan, Mancl, Kaffar, & Ferreira, 2011). Children and teens use homophobic sexual harassment as a way to enforce social norms on those who are engaging in nontraditional gender behaviors (Poteat, Kimmel, & Wilchins, 2011). Harassed gay, lesbian, and bisexual youth are at high risk for drug and alcohol abuse, suicide, prostitution, homelessness, and poor academic performance (Fineran, 2002; Grossman & Kerner, 1998; Morgan et al., 2011; Poteat, Mereish, DiGiovanni, & Koenig, 2011). Those who experience sexual victimization in the form of verbal abuse in high school are likely to end up with traumatic stress reactions (D'Augelli, Pilkington, & Hershberger, 2002) and mental health problems (Espelage, Aragon, Birkett, & Koenig, 2008; Gruber & Fineran, 2008). Post-traumatic stress disorder can develop and may persist into adulthood for those children who experience frequent and prolonged bullying at school as a result of their actual or perceived sexual orientation (Rivers, 2004).

Of course being called lesbian, gay, bisexual, or trans, when used as a way of demeaning a teenager, can have not only detrimental but disastrous effects on development. Some teens who are inaccurately labeled as gay move into a heterosexual intimate relationship before they are really ready. They do so to try to prove to others that they are straight and to stop being tormented and sexually harassed (deLara, 2008b). Some gay teens become promiscuous in heterosexual relationships in a similar attempt. They want to cast away any aspersions on their sexuality (Harris Interactive, 2005).

Gender identity and sexual orientation are usually solidified during adolescence. Adolescents and young adults, whether lesbian, gay, straight, bisexual, transgender, or questioning, try on various relationships through dating to come to a determination about who they are as a sexual person and to figure out their compatibilities. However, being the object of sexual bullying by peers can be a deterrent to dating. One young man, age 30, confided to me that he had just recently "come out" to his family and friends that he is gay. He said that the taunts and torment he saw peers experience when they came out in high school was enough to make him hide his true self until his 30th birthday. Finally he felt secure about himself and believed he could endure any humiliation that might come his way.

Megan, age 28, was sexually harassed by classmates who started rumors that she was a lesbian. This became a topic every day for about 3 years. She was never physically assaulted but felt alone and on guard all of the time. Kids would make comments or make up stories about her being with other girls sexually. Then they would harass her during unstructured and unsupervised times of the day at school. They made her feel "less than" and unaccepted. She says she still thinks about it on a regular basis. She still worries about how her behavior is perceived by others. She has never been comfortable in close relationships with females because she was always afraid during school that people would start rumors again. This difficulty continues now. Megan has very few close girlfriends. She believes this is because she still feels uncomfortable never having learned how to have healthy relationships early on.

Sexual Harassment and Suicide

In recent years we have seen notoriously bad results of teens and young adults being persecuted over their sexuality. The tragic example of Jamey Rodemeyer is cited above. Teenagers and young adults contemplate and commit suicide due to terrible treatment by peers and by adults who should know better. Week after week we hear of another tragic event where a young person full of promise has ended his life after chronic torment. The list is so long it is disheartening. It is because of these outcomes that the "It Gets Better" project was started by author Dan Savage. Numerous people have uploaded their own stories to encourage others, but waiting for adulthood to begin is often too long a wait. Tyler Clementi was just a 1st-year student at Rutgers University when he took his own life in response to sexual harassment. We tend to think of college campuses as tolerant and liberal, and this is often true. However, this was not true for Tyler Clementi, a bright student and aspiring musician. His roommate, Dharun Ravi, and hallmate, Molly Wei, secretly filmed him having a sexual encounter with another man. Tyler was so embarrassed and so shamed that shortly thereafter he committed suicide by jumping from the George Washington Bridge. (First he posted his intentions on FaceBook.) Both hallmates were charged with invasion of privacy, but since Wei turned state's evidence against Ravi, she faced community service only. Ravi was tried on several counts of webspying and found guilty. He served 20 days in jail and was released with a sentence of community service (Parker, 2012). A study of almost 38,000 lesbian, gay, and bisexual youth shows that they are significantly more likely to attempt suicide than their heterosexual peers by a rate of 21.5% to 4.2% (Hatzenbuehler, 2012). The fear of discovery, the shame associated with discovery and rejection, and the constant torment all play a part in these suicide attempts.

Self-Perception and Sexual Harassment

How do young people process this type of intimidation when it is aimed at their developing physical and sexual self? Research by Cunningham et al. (2010) indicates that an adolescent's perception of his or her own sexual attractiveness can play a key role in experiences of sexual harassment. In their study of middle school students they found that those who considered themselves to be more attractive than their peers also more often were bullied, more often bullied others, more often observed sexual bullying, and more often had friends who participated in sexual harassment than peers who rated themselves just average in attractiveness.

School Personnel and Teacher Sexual Misconduct

The vast majority of teachers and other educators are caring professionals concerned for the well-being of children in their charge. However, children are not immune from sexual harassment by adults during their school day. Studies of 80,000 schools found that more than 4.5 million students are subject to sexual misconduct by an employee of a school sometime between kindergarten and 12th grade (Hill & Kearl, 2011; Shakeshaft, 2004). This translates to nearly 10% of students being targets of educator or other school personnel sexual misconduct sometime during their school years.

When a teacher sexually harasses or assaults a student, the question arises about whether or not the school district should be held liable for the teacher's actions. A decision by a Louisiana appellate court in the 2009 case of *T.S. v. the Rapides Parish School Board* found, definitively, yes. A 15-year-old girl was forcibly kissed twice by her teacher, a popular coach for the girls' track team. The teacher's actions left the victim feeling "shocked, embarrassed, and upset" by the events. She also "felt ashamed and guilty as though she had done something wrong" (Teachers College Record, 2010, p. 630). When adults at school engage in sexual harassment and misconduct they place a terrible psychological burden on children and adolescents. At the very least these are psychological injuries. They interfere at the most basic level with children's ability to trust others and to move through normal stages of development at their own pace. This young woman experiences recurrent nightmares of what happened to her. Her first kiss was forced on her by a married man whom she should have been able to trust. Her family sued and won a financial judgment on her behalf from the school district. In instances of sexual harassment or sexual assault often the victim bears the shame that rightfully belongs to the perpetrator. This young woman carries a legacy inflicted by her teacher. She did not have the option to experience her first kiss with a person of her own choosing. Whether or not the school district is held accountable or a student receives a monetary award does not repair the losses experienced by a child sexually mistreated by an adult. The result: Now she is distrustful of men and dating situations.

These kinds of behaviors raise questions for us. If sexual harassment is almost normative in our schools, how do children and teens deal with this? What is the impact on young people who are sexually harassed? At the time, the impact affects individuals differently. Some young people will act out sexually, becoming involved with various sexual partners in an attempt to prove their attractiveness. Some will become angry, some depressed. Some will try isolating themselves, declining invitations to socialize, and hiding their bodies in baggy or ill-fitting clothing. We know that these are some of the consequences of sexual harassment that occur at the time (deLara, 2008b).

However, what are the repercussions in adult life? What do adults tell themselves about their physical selves and other aspects of their sexuality if they were mistreated and intimidated sexually as children? A'isha, age 24, is a schoolteacher. She had several experiences of invasions of her personal space and boundaries when she was a child. She was bullied and sexually harassed. She shared a few of these experiences with me. As she told me her story, she became very agitated and her eyes welled up, obviously reliving the events:

"When I was in 2nd grade, this girl would try to touch me in inappropriate places. I was scared to tell anybody but I finally told my mom. My mom went to the school to complain that it was going on and it became a huge issue. No one did anything at the school. It was ignored, so she continued to try and I had to do the best I could to take care of myself. Then at 16, there was a guy. The same situation with the 2nd grade girl happened with him. I was walking to the store and he saw me. He pushed me to the side of a house. No one could see us; no one could help me. He was trying to put his hands on me. I kicked him hard and I got away. I saw him some time later and he ran away when he saw me. There was an impact on me then and now. Then I was really cautious in gym class. I was basically hiding when we had to change before and after the class. I was afraid somebody might try something with me. Now, I can see the influence in what I wear. I have to protect myself. I have to cover up in terms of my dress. I do wear shorts, but long ones. I don't wear low cut shirts. I don't want to give the wrong message. Since the second grade incident where the girl invaded my space, I know it can happen. It had a big effect on me; I still think about it. Some people who were mean during grade school, I have friended on FaceBook, but I wouldn't want to friend her (the 2nd grade girl). I still feel angry, scared, and vulnerable when I think about her. It takes me a while to trust others based on these incidents. I haven't been in a long-term relationship yet because of these issues. I think, 'Can I trust this person? Or is he just trying to manipulate me?' It takes me a long time to trust.

"I am very cautious who I talk to. I put on a strong tough image. I don't let everyone in. I have to give them 'an interview.' I want to find out if they are going to respect me and my boundaries or try to take advantage of me. I can't believe it but I still have flashbacks about these incidents. The setting, working in the school, brings it up for me too. It's been 17 years since the first incident . . . and it's still all there."

Trauma and Sexual Harassment

As we see in the incidents and reaction by A'isha, sexual harassment can be experienced by the victim as traumatic. This kind of trauma can influence how others view the victim and even their willingness to interact with her or him. Elizabeth is an example of this. Elizabeth is a 32-year-old attorney. Her practice is centered on child advocacy. When she was in middle school she was the subject of an especially pernicious rumor that had long-lasting impact on her social life and on her developing sense of herself. She shared this experience:

"A boy who had a crush on me in 8th grade decided to tell a few girls in our grade that he and I had a sexual relationship. He went into great detail about the night we supposedly spent together. The rumor then spread to other people like a virus, and very quickly I was labeled the 'class slut.' My reputation was greatly diminished and some of the girls in school didn't want to talk to me. They began to un-invite me to parties and events. After a number of months of dealing with the constant whispering behind my back, the harassment started to become physical. Before this it was just words and although they hurt, I tried to let it go, brush it off. Since we are taught as children, ignore it and it will eventually go away, I hoped for that. It didn't happen and ignoring made it worse, because people believed it was true."

Elizabeth finally decided to talk with the principal at school hoping for some relief from the bullying, exclusion, and sexual harassment she was experiencing. Unfortunately, the principal insinuated that Elizabeth brought this on herself and offered her no help. Now she not only felt blamed for her own victimization, but she felt more alone than ever.

I asked Elizabeth about the effects of this early experience on her development. She said,

"At a young age, I learned to deal with my own traumas and solve my own problems, because I felt abandoned by adults. It was easy for me to lose myself for a long time, and feel like I was the terrible person that everyone kept talking about. I felt unprotected and silenced for so many years that life constantly felt like a tornado ripping me apart. Eventually I was able to clean up the destruction and move past this part of my life. This kind of bullying experience helped to shape me into the person that I am today. It is important to me to help people get justice in their lives."

Elizabeth's psychosocial development was impaired, at that stage, as a result of the bullying, sexual harassment, ongoing social exclusion, and inappropriate adult response that she encountered. Not being able to count on adults had both positive and negative consequences. The negative: She felt "unprotected and silenced." She felt "abandoned." This is not what we want for our children. The positive: As an adult, though she bears the scars, she can face trauma and surmount it. She has regained much of what she lost in those formative years and has a very promising career in front of her.

Does Barbie Contribute to Sexual Harassment?

Barbie dolls may be an inadvertent contributor to the problem of sexual harassment and body image issues. In the United States and in other countries, children play with Barbie. Playing with dolls is one way that children have of thinking about themselves and thinking about themselves in relationship to other people. In terms of healthy development for girls, playing with Barbie may be unfortunate. Unfortunate because Barbie is glamorous and is depicted as the ideal young woman. This is also inappropriate given the real-life statistics that represent Barbie's body. If Barbie were a real person, some estimate she would be 6' 0", weigh 100 lbs., and wear a size 4. Her measurements would be 39"/21"/33."

I had the opportunity to interview Sarah, 51, a government employee. She told me she was teased relentlessly, day in and day out, by the boys in 7th grade. Because she had skipped two grades in school, she started

7th grade much younger than the other kids. Most of the kids' physical and emotional development was way ahead of hers. The girls had little figures while Sarah had not even started wearing a bra yet. This fact did not escape the boys and she was tormented daily about it. Finally, though she had no need of one, Sarah talked her mother into taking her shopping for a bra just to end the agony. Besides the teasing and harassment, Sarah believes there are other consequences from this treatment. First, it happened in full view of teachers. They heard every word. This alone was mortifying. The last thing a young girl wants is for anyone to be discussing her body publicly much less bringing the attention of adults to it, male teachers. Further, the teachers did not do anything about it. She clearly remembers looking to her home room teacher, a man she admired very much, to see what his reaction was to this "teasing." He noticed. She saw that he noticed. But he did nothing. Then Sarah felt doubly helpless: Helpless to get the abuse to stop by her own doing and helpless that anyone was going to come to her aid.

Sarah believes another outcome was that she accepted the first boy who came along and showed interest in her as an intimate boyfriend. Believing that she was not attractive based on the ongoing comments of peers, she thought, "This boy seems to like me despite my faults; I better stick with him because no one else is likely to want me." She was and remains terribly shy at the idea of having to be physical with someone. That feeling of mortification and fear has stayed with her. Sarah says she has suffered in terms of her body image her whole life. She commented, "While I think this may be true for most women, especially in America where we are constantly deluged with how we are supposed to look, I can trace the feelings of unhappiness with my body right back to the sexual harassment of these middle school experiences."

"Everything Revolved Around the Way You Looked"

Nicole, 49, is a professional person committed to helping children because, as she says, "adults don't tend to see that children need interventions." Nicole is a very attractive woman with kind eyes and a quick smile. She is not convinced this is true about herself. Nicole was sexually harassed by both peers and teachers at her school. Nicole shared,

"I was bullied and sexually harassed by a girl on a daily basis in 8th grade. This girl would stand outside my classrooms and constantly harass me. She thought I said something that I never did. It was embarrassing to hear her say things like 'I'm going to kick your ass,' 'F— you.' Adults must have seen this but they didn't do anything. I couldn't concentrate on my school work. She jumped on my back one day when I was walking down the hallway so we got into a fight and both got into trouble. This caused me to have a severe drop in grades from B's to F's. I developed a fear of going to school and began faking illnesses to get out of going. I had over 30 absences just in that one year. Looking back, I can see there was an enormous change in my behavior and personality."

She went on to say: "Years later, I saw this girl one day when I was working. She apologized to me and explained that her boyfriend at the time used to beat her. She stated 'I took it out on you and I'm just really sorry.' It helped that she said that because I didn't understand it and I just blamed myself."

Nicole also revealed, "If all of that wasn't enough, I have had my body parts grabbed by male students, my bra unhooked in front of everyone by male students, all of which took place in full view of teachers and all of which was never addressed by adults. I was insulted by teachers, embarrassed by teachers." Nicole became depressed and very anxious; this was diametrically opposed to her normal sunny outlook on life. At the time, she did not consider talking to the adults in her environment; they barely existed at the periphery of her young adolescent life. She felt certain that her parents cared about her, but the problem was they did not recognize what was going on with her. And, importantly, she believed they did not know how to recognize it or what to do about it. Nicole stated: "I was living two separate lives: the one my parents knew and the one my friends knew." Further, Nicole went on to say, "teachers at school did not seem to care and were not in charge." Several researchers and educators have written about the importance of the connection between teacher caring and bullying, between students' sense of safety at school and adults being in charge (Booren, Handy, & Power, 2011; deLara, 2008; Gaughan, Cerio, & Myers, 2001).

Nicole continued, "The school was very large and kids fell through the cracks. Violence occurred daily and drugs were rampant in school. Though it may seem like I am speaking of an inner-city school, my school was in the suburbs in a 'good' neighborhood, the kind of neighborhood parents move to so their children can have good lives!" Any issue was handled by punishment and suspension, no matter what the infraction or who started it. The students, it seemed, were running the school. In an earlier chapter, I discussed how schools as systems work. Nicole was reporting every aspect of a system that was broken.

I never felt 12 or 13. I felt sexualized already by then by the way men looked at us even at that age. We brought clothing on the bus that our parents didn't know about and changed before school. We always had to be cool. I tried pot at 12. I hated it; but it made me seem cool and grown up. It was always about the looks, how people see you. You always felt like people's eyes were on you, even the male teachers. Finally my girlfriends and I decided to walk down the hallways and do the ass-grabbing ourselves. It was the only way we had any power, or sense of power. My friends and I snuck into a bar one day. I was 16. One of our teachers was there and he bought me a drink. Then he kissed me! I was horrified and scared! Who do you tell?? If you told, the names you'd get called, it wouldn't be even worth it.

I can remember sexual harassment in the form of comments, touching and rumors from other kids, but the worst harassment came from teachers. In 8th grade, we had a teacher who was sexually harassing everyone. He said the most inappropriate things especially to the girls. He made them feel awful. I told my parents about it but they didn't believe it. This teacher really disliked the girls and he told this one girl who was tall and beautiful and so sweet, that she should "bend over the table and let the boys line up behind her" when she wore a short skirt one day. I will never forget the look on her face; she was embarrassed, humiliated and crushed. I of course, who was not so sweet, came to her defense and called him an "obnoxious pig," for which I was sent straight to the dean's office. I didn't care. He made me so angry I couldn't help myself. He sent me to the office every day, and I went gladly, relieved just to be away from him.

I fought with him every day. He always sent me to the Dean's office and the Dean said "Can't you just leave him alone?" The Dean said he knew the teacher was "weird" but that I should just behave. Of course I didn't and continued to call him names and get sent to the office. Rumors about him began to spread. Kids said that he was "doing things to boys." Sure enough, he eventually was arrested and fired for molesting boys. I remember seeing that teacher on the news in handcuffs and screaming to my parents with conviction "I told you so, I told you!'" Then, at least, they had to believe me. My parents were in shock . . . the teacher was fired . . . and the school never talked about it with the students.

Nicole's parents finally moved her to a new school. But because Nicole thought she was being punished for situations at school beyond her control, she ran away from home. From this ensued a great deal of turmoil for her and her family. Finally she came back home, got her life on track, and went back to school. At the new school, the system consisted of a tight-knit community and caring teachers where "problem resolution was handled through words and discussion, not random punishment." It is interesting that Nicole graduated a year early. She recounted: "By that point I had been moved back to a public school. "I wanted to get out of the atmosphere of bullying and I wanted to prove a point that I was smart."

Nicole knows she is one of the lucky ones whose parents had the financial means to move her to a better school environment when they did. It was a strain for the family, but she is grateful for it. It leaves her wondering, though, "What are the solutions for kids whose parents don't have the resources? Or who don't have the desire to move them from a hostile environment? Are they trapped in a hopeless situation?"

Impact Today

In terms of impact on her today, Nicole said:

My self-esteem is drastically affected. I think that many girls who may not be victims of "regular" bullying, and who people would never suspect are hurting, are in fact being sexually harassed. I would go as far as to say the majority of females over the age of 12 have been sexually harassed in some way. I was bullied so long and so consistently and at a time when I was so vulnerable in terms of my developing physical self that, to this day, I question if I am attractive enough to actually interest someone. Will they stay interested, will they want to stay with me in the long run? When you are bullied and sexually harassed every day, it just chips little pieces away from you every time. I still think about it. I wish my parents had understood what was going on at school. They didn't understand what was going on with me. Everything was blamed on me—the bad grades, the fighting at school, the fact that I ran away. They blamed me—they didn't understand the school circumstances. They didn't know that this girl was harassing me every day. But school adults and my parents should have suspected something when my grades went from being so good to F-. I was always good in school before that. I guess they thought I didn't need good grades thinking I was just going to get married and wouldn't need an education. I wish someone had intervened then because it wouldn't have taken me so long to get the degrees I have today. It took me a long time to get the confidence to say I could do something more with my life than be a bartender. I was a bartender for many years. When I think of the things that I allowed people to say to me over the years . . . it took me too long before I realized that there's something wrong with this. There's something wrong with going into a job where the dress code is: you have to wear a low-cut shirt, high heels,—to have people talk to you in a way that they would never talk to their mother or sister. That contributed to me being the way I am now. I let people say things to me that were disrespectful. I got to a point where it started to get to me. Some of the people at the bar I considered friends. But the second I got behind the bar, they started to talk to me in such a disrespectful way. I don't know why I changed all of a sudden but I did. The sexual harassment thing took a toll. This stuff affects us deeply!

To this day so many people think of me as a bitch. From the time I was in middle school, I had to be tough. I have to put it out there. It comes from a place of fear. I'm not very affectionate. Part of life is just having to put up with this. I'm known for having a thick-skin. Somehow you would never have known that being sexually harassed bothered me. I was so tough my entire life from feeling powerless, female, and being seen in a certain way. It goes back to everything.

I asked Nicole if it is difficult for her to share what she feels. She stated,

"On the inside it is so hard for me to let down the barrier to trust other people. There was no sharing of anything for many, many years. I still have trouble with that. There are only a couple I will share with. I have to make a joke to cover up for my feelings. I don't think I say the right things to others, either. I make jokes. I don't have a problem being empathic with strangers, but with people who are close to me—OMG! That's part of the impact for me. Keeping people at a distance. Everything is all surface. Because I had to be tough to take care of myself from the girl in 8th grade, from the boys, and from the teachers' bullying, I never cried. I never cried and as a young adult I couldn't cry. I am only now starting to be able to let myself cry when I need to. I didn't have that kind of emotion before. I didn't want anyone to think I was weak."

When I asked Nicole if there were any positives that came as a result of the sexual harassment she encountered, she had an interesting response. She said that when she saw someone getting bullied she was usually the one to stick up for that person and that was positive for her at the time. Nicole considers another positive outcome was when the girl who sexually harassed her explained her actions and apologized. She said that was "very eye-opening. It wasn't about me, it was her!" But in thinking about it as an adult, Nicole declared,

"There is nothing good that comes from sexual harassment, from girls seeing themselves that way (in the ways that they are being looked at, described, and called by others). Because of the inappropriate things by the kids and men teachers—it's dangerous. It made me a stronger person, but not in a good way. It cost me a lot, it cost me a lot of time doing things I wouldn't have done otherwise. I wouldn't have wasted so much time being a bartender. I had so much potential. I was talking before I was a year old. Nothing good comes from sexual harassment."

In terms of her intimate relationship, Nicole expanded:

"I am in a good relationship now but it only happened when I began to respect myself. When I think about my life now, I am so lucky. But I didn't get married until I was 30. I didn't want to marry anyone until then. My husband is a good, good person. He is my best friend. He's helped me with all of these issues. We have a good, close strong relationship. He is the only one I can say anything to. Is there anyone else I would be comfortable saying things to? Nobody. He is nice, nice, nice. He's big and burly and masculine—a gentle giant. He broke me down. I am only comfortable with him, not other people. It took someone who could genuinely show me love and respect. He is very respectful. Someone to heal with."

"Someone to heal with." These are such important words that perfectly sum up exactly what is needed for anyone who has been the victim of sexual harassment. This is especially true when it has been repeated and has involved more than one person. When there has been only one harasser or bully, you can try to say to yourself that it was "that guy" or "that girl" and their own unique problems. But when the bullying and harassment come at you from multiple kids, teachers, and adults, it is much more invasive and destructive. Nicole is very fortunate to have found in her husband, her best friend, and her healing partner.

Sexual harassment of girls and boys, of men and women is a worldwide problem that occurs in nearly every venue. However, recognizing that it begins in childhood and realizing that the consequences can be lifelong should provide an incentive to adults to take a closer look at this pernicious aspect of childhood bullying.

Considering everything thus far in the book, we may wonder about the kinds of decisions adults make who have been bullied as children. Do their decisions take them down positive pathways or toward something less healthy? We will investigate this in the next chapter on the effect of bullying on decisions.

CHAPTER 8
Does Bullying Affect Decisions?

"When you feel the force of being cornered time and again, the time comes when you
have nothing else left except to explode."

The Karmapa Lama, the Dalai Lama's putative successor

Decision-making for anyone is a complex mix of individual neurological and personality factors, family scripts and values, personal
moral development, community opportunities or the lack of them,
and societal mores. Neurologically, large-scale systems in the brain are
involved (Bechara, Damasio, & Damasio, 2000) and, given all of these
factors, there is a complicated relationship among emotions, thinking,
and a person's biochemistry. When it comes to bullying and decisions,
this, too, is a complicated question. For children it may be whether to
bully and harass others or not. But even that decision may be predicated
on whether a person has first been a victim, is in a retaliatory mood, or
believes in the justice of retaliation. In 1997, Ron Astor and William
Behre did an interesting study of 10- to 13-year-olds and their parents
who were all classified as aggressive. They found that in this group both
children and parents based their actions more strongly on the idea that
others shouldn't provoke them in the first place than they did on the
rightness or morality of retribution. Between 24% and 30% of the people in my study, over various grades in school, said they were both bullied and bullies. What is interesting is that much of this bullying was a
conscious decision. It not only was a means of retaliation but was often
considered a form of retributive justice. Retributive justice is exacted
as punishment for wrongdoing. It is not meant as vengeance but rather
as necessary to keep the scales of human interaction in balance (Rawls,

1971, 2009). Fatum and Hoyle (1996) looked at school violence from the students' perspective. What they found was even in secondary school morality still consists of black-and-white thinking and the students' credo is "disrespect deserves disrespect" (p. 29). Consequently, from their perspective, retaliation for acts of disrespect such as bullying is not violence; it is necessary.

In my study, approximately 24% of those who were bullied in elementary school were also bullies themselves. This compares with 26% of those who were both bullied and bullies in middle school. This figure jumped to 30% in high school. What can we make of this upward trend? We could surmise that, among other reasons, those who continued to bully into high school had learned this was an "effective" technique. How could it be effective when bullying others seems to fly in the face of what we consider appropriate interpersonal interactions? One answer: Bullying gets results. Children who bully feel powerful (Mishna, Cook, Gadalla, Daciuk, & Solomon, 2010) and they may not feel powerful in other ways or other areas of their lives.

There is the question of how bullying affects other decisions and actions once someone reaches adulthood. Interestingly, research supports a correlation between difficult life experiences and poor decision-making regardless of a person's demographic variables or cognitive abilities (Bruine de Bruin, Parker, & Fischhoff, 2007). Living through or in adverse life circumstances seems to push people toward poor decisions. They often do not have the skills necessary to sort out variables and often do not have positive decision-making models.

DO YOU THINK IT HAS AFFECTED YOUR DECISIONS?

Because many people still believe bullying is a rite of passage, is not of much consequence, and is something everyone outgrows, it is difficult for these same people to understand that bullying affects decisions. When I talked with one mother, she shared that her son was bullied mercilessly in middle school. When she and her husband figured out that the school was going to do nothing about it, they enrolled him in a nearby school district, where he made many friends immediately. However, damage to his self-esteem was done. She says about him now, "He has a good job and a lot of friends, but he is a constant name-dropper." She believes that the terrible treatment he got in middle school, when he was so vulnerable, has pushed him to try to convince others that he is worthwhile by saying, "See, I know this important person."

One of the questions I asked each participant was, "If you were bullied, do you think it has affected decisions you have made?" I found 41.6% thought it has affected decisions they have made, 31.7% thought it had no impact on decisions they have made, and 26.7% did not think the question was applicable to them or did not choose to answer the question. In the group of people who thought bullying had no impact on their decisions, some just plain said "no" to the question while others replied with a more thoughtful "not that I am aware of." This points out the fact that often we are not consciously aware of why we do the things we do or why we make the decisions we make. Of specific note, in terms of gender, there was no statistically significant difference between men and women on the question of impact on decisions that they made.

By race, 51% of biracial respondents of any racial background said that bullying has affected their decisions, compared with the following:

48% of both Asians and Asian Americans
40% of Caucasians
36% of Hispanic
33% of African Americans

As we can see, these figures reflect high percentages of people changing course or altering decisions in their lives based on childhood bullying.

ATTACHMENT, BULLYING, AND DECISIONS

The chapter on relationships and the chapter on health and mental health discuss the importance of attachment. What does attachment pattern have to do with childhood bullying and decisions? Children with insecure attachment tend to have developmental and adjustment problems. They are more likely than those who are securely attached to demonstrate poor social skills such as withdrawal, aggression, and impulsivity (Bowlby, 1969, 2008; Corvo & deLara, 2010; Johnson, 2006; Krieg & Dickie, 2013). These are the kinds of behaviors that result in children getting in trouble at school with adults and with their peers. One of the forms of trouble they display or encounter is bullying. As an example, some studies show children with insecure parental attachments are more likely to bully their peers or be bullied (Eliot & Cornell, 2009; Ireland & Power, 2004; Walden & Beran, 2010). Further, children who have less attachment to peers are more likely to be both bullies and victims of bullying (Burton, Florell, & Wygant, 2013; Nikiforou, Georgiou, & Stavrinides, 2013). Attachment to school, also, affects children in terms of peer mistreatment. Harel-Fisch et al. (2011) looked at 40 schools in European and North American countries involving over 250,000 children. Their investigation found that when students' attachment to their school was weak they were twice as likely to be involved with bullying as students with strong connections to school. As discussed in chapter 1, systems operate to maintain homeostasis or balance. How that translates for schools as systems is that they don't tolerate outliers well. When a child is acting out or acting as a loner or being different in any appreciable way, the child is typically subject to bullying and harassment. This action is not just meant to be mean but also meant to modify the child's behavior or manner of presentation to fit in with the majority (Garbarino & deLara, 2002; Pellegrini & Bartini, 2000; Sarason, 2001). As Dixon (2007) states, "ostracism enables the group to police uncooperative individuals to the benefit of the group as a whole," and "the first response by a group to nonconformity is the use of aversive behaviours which aim to coerce the individual to conform" (p. 5). Groups are apt to stigmatize individuals as a means of protection for the majority (Kurzban & Leary, 2001). Systems are willing to tolerate a degree of aggressive behavior in service to maintaining homeostasis (Garbarino & deLara, 2002) and ensuring compliance with social norms (Feinberg, Willer, & Schultz, 2014). Ethologists and anthropologists have witnessed the same form of behavior among other primates (Gruter & Masters, 1986; Nishida, Hosaka, Nakamura, & Hamai, 1995). From these studies, we can see that childhood attachment patterns evidenced at school can affect decisions about aggressive activities.

IMPACT OF BULLYING ON DECISIONS CHILDREN MAKE

As children and teenagers, the participants in the study made the best decisions they could to try to protect themselves from bullying, sexual harassment, and torment by their peers or school personnel. I asked each person, "If you were bullied, did it affect your decisions? If so, how?" The responses fell into these categories: decisions in general, decisions about appearance, decisions about extracurricular activities, decisions relating to moral development, and decisions about interpersonal relating.

Decisions in General

Children who are bullied, witness bullying, or hear about bullying at school make conscious decisions. These include how to walk the hallways, which corridors to avoid, and where to sit on the school bus (deLara, 2008; Garbarino & deLara, 2002). After being the target of bullying, some people in this study decided they needed to show they were "tough" to dodge further bullying. This decision, however, led to "getting in trouble" with parents, school personnel, and sometimes law enforcement. Decisions to relocate schools were also explored by participants when they were children. Although school is the workplace for children, they have relatively little flexibility or control compared with adults in theirs. For example, an adult who is bullied or sexually harassed at work can bring legal sanctions to bear against a perpetrator and against an employer if the harassment does not stop. Children do have protections under the law, but it is very difficult for them to effect these protections. Some children have the luxury of caring parents and parents who have the capability to transfer them to another school or school district. Several participants mentioned they were able to convince their parents to permit them to attend a different high school so they could make new friends and get away from the ones who had been tormenting them. One woman, age 25, said, "I needed to get away from people at my middle school. I decided to ask my parents if I could go to a new school when I started high school. I don't think they ever really fully understood my decision but they let me do it. It turned out to be the best thing."

Decisions About Appearance

Being tormented about appearance led to various choices and resolutions by the participants when they were children and adolescents. This is a typical response: "I really decided to lose weight to stop the bullying about how I looked. I make a conscious decision every day about what I eat. I will never be overweight again in my life. As a teen, I made it a lifelong resolution." Many of the respondents in the study talked about being bullied as kids because of their weight. One study by Puhl and Latner (2007) found that children were bullied by other children about their weight as early as age 3. They also faced biased attitudes by teachers from a very early age. Being bullied based on weight can have profound effects on children. These researchers found that children who experienced teasing, rejection, bullying, and other types of abuse because of their weight are two to three times more likely to report suicidal thoughts. Further, there is a link between the development of eating disorders and bullying or teasing in childhood (Jiang, Perry, & Hesser, 2010). Research points to the underlying concept of shame about body image that accompanies this kind of peer scrutiny (Sweetingham & Waller, 2008). Sometimes bullying based on appearance can happen based on something that may seem inconsequential to an adult, but to children difference is difficult to tolerate. One young woman said, "I was an outcast by the girls because I dressed differently than they did. They had a sort of uniform way of dressing, so I didn't fit in. My mother told me that if the girls didn't want to play with me, play with the boys. So that's what I did. That was a good decision. Today I feel very comfortable around men in my workplace."

Decisions About Extracurricular Activities

Research over the years has indicated that group membership can serve a protective function for children against being the target of bullying. While this is not always the case, children can be protected by their peers within a group context (Goldbaum, Craig, Pepler, & Connolly, 2003; Holt & Espelage, 2007; Kanetsuna, Smith, & Morita, 2006; Pellegrini & Bartini, 2000). One man in my study said, "It [being the target of bullying] moved me into playing sports because the athletes weren't bullied. So, to this day, I am still athletic and grateful for it." For others, who were teased for their lack of athletic prowess, they stopped believing in their abilities and quit sports entirely. We tend to think of adolescence as a time of experimentation—for the good and the bad. Teenagers are trying on different personas in an attempt to figure out who they are. They try new activities, such as dance or athletics, to see what fits with them, what they are good at. But when someone has been the brunt of laughter and bullying, this changes. While a small percentage of people (17%) said they decided to become more active in extracurricular activities in an attempt to find more or different friends, the majority of people had the opposite reaction—vigorously avoiding them. Scott, now 36, is a good example. He expressed how bullying affected the decisions he made when he was a kid. He said,

"In middle school I would get punched in the genitals while carrying my lunch tray. I was called names all the time and received threatening letters. I was framed by my 'friends' for all sorts of stuff. I attended small rural schools. In high school, I had a math teacher who would call me a 'moron' in front of the class. I was called names by older students. Some kids would try to start fights

with me by punching me or choking me. It led to me bullying my next youngest brother. I would beat him up and threaten him, calling him names all the
while. I had awful anxiety about going to school and threw up nearly every
single morning of my freshman year. I really had no idea that I was even smart
until I was a junior. It definitely affected decisions I made. One was to stay out
of all extracurricular activities so I could escape school. I also purposefully did
not participate in classes to avoid sticking my neck out."

This is a poignant example of physical, psychological, and emotional bullying. It represents a daily lack of safety and control over the environment
for Scott. Further, much of the harassment was committed by his so-called
friends. Where did he have to turn? I asked him if he told his parents. He
said that he didn't; he didn't think they could do anything to help and
they might do something that would make matters worse. The decision
not to tell parents about being mistreated at school is, unfortunately, all
too common (deLara, 2012; Mishna & Alaggia, 2005).

Decisions Related to Moral Development

Developmental psychologists Jean Piaget and Lawrence Kohlberg describe
the moral growth of children as moving from me-centered self-absorption
to interest in others and their opinions (Kohlberg, 1991, 2008; Piaget,
2007; Reimer, Paolitto, & Hersh, 1990). As earlier studies have found, children in early stages of moral development believe acting in an aggressive
manner is justified in many circumstances (Astor & Behre, 1997; Fatum &
Hoyle, 1996; Malti, Gasser, & Buchmann, 2009). They believe in retributive
justice—that the punishment should fit the crime (Rawls, 1971, 2009).
Even in secondary school, when adolescents are thought to be capable of
more advanced moral reasoning, they still may believe aggressive action
should result from disrespectful behavior and if adults do not provide justice, they will have to take matters into their own hands (Fatum & Hoyle,
1996). In my own previous work with adolescents, I have found that they
often express a sense of justification in bullying children on the autistic
spectrum because "they are so annoying, they bring it on themselves"
(deLara, 2002, p. 43). In this study, adults who commented on their sense
of moral development as children had a range of responses. There was a
wide spectrum, from "It [bullying] was what everybody did; I didn't feel
like I was doing anything wrong" to "I wish I could have stood up against
it" to "I knew it was wrong and tried to stop it whenever I could." Others
said, "When I was in high school, I tried to include everyone."

Decisions About Interpersonal Relating

As children, the study participants made some interesting decisions about relating to others. Many talked about "just wanting to fit in; just wanting to have a friend." Some decided to join "any group that would have me" or join the less popular kids to have a place to belong. One person, an athlete in secondary school, said he could not stop bullying others out of fear for his own safety. If he decided to stop, he would be the next target in line. Another man concurred, saying he didn't stop the bullying of others, and even participated, to avoid drawing attention to himself. Similarly many remained in their childhood groups because they believed to leave would be too risky. Often, the idea of looking for approval was voiced. Whether someone stayed in a group that bullied or decided to try to find another group, these children were looking for someone to affirm and approve of them.

Among the more serious decisions that children and adolescents made in reaction to bullying was to get involved in dangerous activities with others. A woman, age 30, revealed, "I certainly made poor decisions in high school from being bullied. I drank a lot, got into drugs, and sex. I wish I hadn't made those decisions." Smoking cigarettes, smoking weed, and using other drugs, both prescription and non-prescription, to blunt the pain from being targeted were not unusual responses. One person said, "Bullying contributed to my alcoholism." As discussed earlier, bullies are often victims. Therefore they, too, are in pain. Several studies support the findings from my research, stating bullies and bully/victims are more likely to self-medicate than other children (Bradshaw, Waasdorp, Goldweber, & Johnson, 2013; Farrington & Ttofi, 2011). Deciding to quit school and spend the day smoking marijuana contributed to one young man's struggle as an adult. He is not the only adolescent who has made the decision to leave school based on personal maltreatment there. In fact, as mentioned previously, thousands of kids skip school every day due to fears for the safety, which may influence their decision to quit school completely (Jozefowicz-Simbeni, 2008).

It seems clear that kids who are mistreated by their peers may end up doubting their own decision-making capabilities. They do not believe they can get things done, they do not believe they are capable and effective. They believe the opposite about themselves. And if they were not directly told they were ineffective, they surmise it or arrive at this conclusion based on the fact that they cannot change their circumstances. They have no power. They are unable to meet their general goals.

We have looked at how children make decisions in reaction to bullying and harassment in their lives. What is the impact on decision-making now as adults? A good portion of people reported being tentative in making any decisions today many years after the incidents of bullying. Ability to trust in themselves has been damaged. Victims don't trust their own judgments. One person said the ramifications on her decisions were simply too numerous to mention. The categories and stories that follow reflect the continuing repercussions in the lives and decisions of adults today. The decisions are separated into five categories: decisions in general, decisions about relocating, decisions about self, decisions related to moral development including criminality, and decisions on interpersonal relating.

Decisions in General

"Just in general, I waver a lot when I have to make a decision. I never feel sure of myself."

Female, age 34

How does childhood bullying affect adult decision-making? One woman, age 28, contends, "Being the brunt of bullying affects your thinking. I believe it has made me a more irrational person because I get upset easily if I think others are disrespecting me. Then I make decisions that are not in my best interest; they can be irrational. I react quickly, almost impulsively." She was not the only one who believed that decision-making was adversely affected. Participants cited feeling a great deal of anxiety when faced with having to make a decision and this anxiety contributed to what they considered illogical decisions. All ascribed this to bullying experiences in childhood. "I don't trust myself to make good decisions" was the sentiment stated by adults who said being the target of bullying makes them waver when it comes to making any decision at all. On the other hand, a small handful of people said being bullied made them more independent with respect to decision-making. They do not discuss what they think or what they are going to do with anyone. One woman was decisive as a child and continued on in the same fashion as an adult despite the adverse circumstances she encountered. She talked about bullying experiences on the school bus: "Did I observe any bullying on the school bus? All of the time from 7th to 12th grade. You had to sit in assigned seats. There was one guy who loved to be nasty. My sisters and I are half Native American and half African American, and he was nasty to us. Hitting us with his books.

So I talked to the bus driver and said we're not going to sit in assigned seats, we're sitting together from now on. I became and have continued to be a 'do what needs to get done' kind of person since then." For this young woman, decision-making does not appear to be problematic. If anything, she believes her abilities at decision-making were enhanced as a result of her struggles with peer bullying. Other adults supported this view. They said things like, "After being bullied, I decided to turn my life around, and it has propelled me to excel" and "Now, I carefully weigh everything before making a decision." However, being at either end of the continuum, struggling to make a decision or not talking decisions over with anyone, can lead to problems in relationships and in life in general.

Decisions About Relocating

Other types of decisions made by adults based on childhood bullying centered on where to live. A small portion has decided to move out of their current school district, city, state, or to another country in an attempt to shelter their children from bullying. While it is possible to protect children by relocating, bullying is a national and international phenomenon (Katensuna et al., 2006; Smith, Cowie, Olafsson, & Liefooghe, 2002; Smith, 2014). A parent may help a child escape being a target, but that child will likely still witness bullying in any school. I was surprised at the responses that indicated moving out of the United States altogether. A male college student, age 19, from abroad said, "I want to live in Sri Lanka when I am an adult and have my children grow up there." He decided this would be a safer environment for his future children. One young mother had been the victim of bullying when she was in school. She shared, "I've decided to move out of the US. I don't want my children to grow up in the kind of bullying atmosphere that our schools here have." Factoring importantly in her decision was her close attention to the news and to what is happening today for children at school. This is a very significant decision, with many implications for her and her family, based on the consequences and impacts of bullying.

Decisions about Self, Appearance, and Personality

"Yeah, I changed myself on purpose. I am not as willing to be goofy or have as much fun as I would like to. I am more withdrawn. The way I see myself has been molded from the way I felt I was seen, which has in return made me a lot harder on myself. I am much less likely to get out of my comfort zone now."

Male, age 24

While reluctance to move out of the "comfort zone" was mentioned as a common decision factor, there was another more insidious element associated with bullying and changes in a person's basic self. That has to do with personal motivation. Participants who had been victims of bullying said things like this: "I give up on things and people too easily. I am very fearful of being humiliated or embarrassed." This kind of attitude has enormous implications for someone's success in life. Personal success is dependent to some degree on the willingness to go after something that is prized. This has to be accompanied by a degree of belief in self and the willingness to risk rejection. However, if what was experienced in childhood was criticism and rejection, humiliation and shame, it would be extremely difficult to overcome this debilitated sense of self. In another chapter, the concept of resiliency and the factors that protect children from forming a degraded sense of themselves are discussed. All too often, children who are mistreated do not have the resiliency factors of a loving family or one caring adult in their lives to offset the impact of torment.

Worries over appearance have carried over from childhood for adults in the study. Being the target of bullying has produced a heightened sensitivity to body image that affects daily decisions about food, clothing, and exercise. One woman admitted to going to tanning salons even though she knows she is risking skin cancer. Her need to look good supersedes her concerns over her basic health. People mentioned body consciousness, the need to be thin, and eating disorders all resulting from bullying remarks. One woman, age 42, conveyed that she developed an eating disorder in which she made and continues to make poor eating decisions. There were many remarks about making poor eating decisions that began in childhood and are continuing. An African American woman, age 26, was called "fatty" in elementary and middle school. She had large stretch marks on her arms that the boys pointed out to everyone. She said, "I've tried starving myself, changing my looks, and being outgoing with boys so that no one can ever bully me again. I still second-guess myself all the time." Another, age 26, said she was bullied mercilessly from elementary school through high school by the same group of girls because she was a little chubby. Now she is 5'10" tall and weighs 135 pounds. While she knows she is not fat, she still remembers how badly she felt. This shows up in her decisions on whether to go out or not. She feels negatively about herself and is afraid that if she does decide to go somewhere no one will talk to her.

A Native American woman, age 31, said,

"I was ostracized based on how I looked, how my hair looked. I was raised around all white families. The duality of it was confusing for me. In high school, it was very confusing. When people started to sit by various racial tables at lunch, the Native American kids would say, 'Why aren't you sitting with us?' For a while I could float between tables. After a while I had to choose. Today I am hypervigilant about how I look. Now I am very aware of being different as a result of being bullied. I ostracize myself. I don't give people a complete chance. One decision I can see is I choose people who come from the same type of background as me."

Consequences and decisions based on bullying can be extremely harmful. One young woman, 25, said, "All the decisions I have made have been based on my concept of myself, which was affected by bullying. I try not to bully myself." Her self-esteem and self-concept were adversely affected by poor peer treatment and poor adult treatment. This has led to self-bullying that she attempts to overcome. For some, self-bullying comes in the form of negative self-talk such as "You're no good" or "You're a loser"—statements that were directed at them in their youth. For others, self-bullying comes in the form of self-harm, where adults are actively engaged in self-harming behavior such as cutting or hitting themselves. Self-harm is a coping mechanism for some who have experienced trauma. This correlation is widely seen among adolescents who are bullied (Fisher et al., 2012; Hay & Meldrum, 2010; McMahon, Reulbach, Keeley, Perry, & Arensman, 2012). Suicidal ideation is also connected with bullying. While this is present for children and adolescents (Hinduja & Patchin, 2010; Klomek et al., 2008; Klomek et al., 2011), suicidal ideation can also be seen in adults. A participant in the study said, "My self-esteem is so low from my bullying experiences that I have suicidal thoughts and engage in self-destructive behavior."

Concerns about appearance were not limited to women. Men also related insecurities left over from childhood bullying and sexual harassment. As children, they were "teased" for being too short, too tall, too thin, too fat, or for some other perceived defect in their appearance. For some, this affects decisions today about whether to date or not. Their basic self-esteem has been severely diminished.

Decisions Related to Moral Development

Being a part of bullying in any capacity seemed to make a particular impact on moral development. For children this may not be true. When bullied, children often believe that retaliation is justified. For adults, this can still be true if they have remained at the same level of moral development as a child (see Reimer, Paolitto, & Hersh, 1990). For most of the adults in my study however, bullying resulted in a fundamental shift in their moral development. People commented that seeing bullying or being the victim imbued them with a sense of empathy that they did not have before. The statement "I decided to treat others with respect" was very common. The vast majority of those who witnessed bullying or were bullied decided to be consciously more empathic, more considerate to others. These are a few examples:

> "I try to include everyone and go out of my way to be friendly and interact with everyone."
>
> "I will never participate in any activities that would hurt someone else."
>
> "I was never bullied, but I witnessed it at school. At the time, I didn't think anything of it, but now it makes me think twice about other people's feelings and how I choose to act."
>
> "I decided to never be a bully."

Criminality

"When you've been bullied you come home and you want to take your anger out on someone—parents, brothers, or sisters."

Female, age 27

"In grades 6 and 7, I was bullied terribly over my weight. I began eating far less, maybe a meal a day, most days not eating at all. I searched for any friends I could find leading to a group of friends that led me into robbery and vandalism. I was never caught or arrested but I easily could have been."

Male, age 41

How does someone end up deciding on violent behavior as an adult? It is generally accepted that there is considerable overlap between being a victim of violence and being a perpetrator of violence (Apel & Burrow, 2011; Cleary, 2000; Corvo & deLara, 2010; Duke, Pettingell, McMorris, & Borowsky, 2014). We see this is in the bully-victim-bully cycle as described in earlier chapters. Being a victim, or even vicarious victimization, can motivate people to engage in violent behavior as a means of "self-help." In other words, aggressive behavior, including aggravated assault, is conceptualized by the individual as a method of protection (Apel & Burrow, 2011).

> "I was pushed around constantly by awful kids to 'toughen me up.' This kind of childhood has made me violent as an adult. I was especially violent until

I was about 35 years old. Now less so, but the impulse is always there. I know I have to protect myself. It's just that I have less to protect myself against at this point."

Male, age 48

Sansone and colleagues (2013) discovered that when there is a history of being bullied, adults report a significant correlation of aggressive behaviors as adults compared with those who were not bullied as children. The longer bullying went on, the greater the number and type of aggressive behaviors. The adults in their study got into violent physical fights, deliberately broke things, and engaged in pushing or shoving a partner.

There is aggressive behavior resulting from bullying, and then there is the type of aggressive behavior that leads to a criminal record. Children who are bullies are twice as likely as nonbullies to be convicted of criminal offenses (Jiang, Walsh, & Augimeri, 2011). Wong and Schonlau (2013) wanted to explore the relationship between bully victimization prior to age 12 and ensuing delinquency. They looked at the National Longitudinal Survey of Youth (NLSY97), which involved almost 9,000 youth. Nineteen percent were victims of bullying. The findings, when measured over a 6-year period, indicated victimization was closely tied to delinquent behaviors such as vandalism, theft, and assault. But do childhood bullies run into trouble with the law as adults? Dan Olweus (2011) conducted a longitudinal study on the ramifications of being a bully on criminal activity in adulthood. He looked at adolescents and young adults over an 8-year period of time from age 16 to 24. He found that former bullies were greatly overrepresented in the criminal statistics in Sweden. Fifty-five percent had been convicted of one or more crimes, and 36% had been convicted of at least three crimes during the 8-year study period. The conclusion: Bullying in early adolescence strongly predicted later criminality. A young man, 28, in my study confirmed this kind of progression from bully to criminal. He said, "This psychopath found it funny to draw on my face and rub my face into the keyboard in music class. He ended up hospitalizing a kid and was sent to prison."

A study by Farrington and Ttofi (2011) lends further support to the connection between bullying and violent offending. They followed 411 boys from London, starting at age 8 to 10 for 40 years, using interviews and criminal records. They found "bullying at age 14 predicted violent convictions between ages 15 and 20, self-reported violence at age 15–18, low job status at age 18, drug use at age 27–32, and an unsuccessful life at age 48" (p. 90). Sourander and colleagues (2011) also found a strong association among Finnish males between being victimized and bullied in childhood that resulted in adult criminality.

Domestic violence is a form of aggression that is often hidden, but it can become known to law enforcement and result in incarceration. In a paper by Corvo and deLara (2010) this question is asked: Is bullying a precursor to later domestic violence? Certainly, witnessing violence in the home is correlated with both being a victim and being a bully at school (Baldry, 2003). Here we can invoke social learning theory and note that children are learning to handle interpersonal relationships by either being passive or being aggressive or both. Corvo and deLara point out that bullying may provide a developmental bridge between bullying and later adult domestic violence. Falb et al. (2011) corroborate this premise. Their research found that boys who bullied during school years were more likely to be perpetrators of intimate partner violence as adults.

Aggressive people are often excluded, but are excluded people aggressive? Social rejection can lead to aggression, but how does this happen? Experiments demonstrate that people who experience social exclusion are much more likely than others to have hostile cognitions. This is called hostile cognitive bias. In other words, even when something said is neutral or ambiguous, excluded people interpret it as antagonistic. As a result, their reactions are more likely to be aggressive (DeWall, Twenge, Gitter, & Baumeister, 2009; Perren, Ettekal, & Ladd, 2012). It is important to remember that when someone is violent, it is not always a decision, per se. Neurobiological factors and impulse control play a role. Low resting heart rate and low cortisol levels correlate with aggressive behavior (Farrington, 1998; Yu & Shi, 2009). Further, damage to the brain, particularly to the amygdala, can result in deficits in decision-making and greater impulsivity (Gupta, Koscik, Bechara, & Tranel, 2011). Consequently for some, impulse control to interrupt violent tendencies has to be learned.

Of course, bullying in all its forms is only one factor eventuating in criminal behavior. But among the worst decisions stemming from bullying were made by those in my study who said they did and continue to engage in illegal activities, including burglaries and violence toward others. They simply stated, "I am a violent person."

Decisions About Interpersonal Relating

"Now I choose things in which I can be alone."

Male, age 30

"If I hadn't been bullied, I think I would have made better relationship decisions. I think I would have been less willing to give everything I have to get nothing in return."

Female, age 27

"I am cautious and suspicious of new social environments."

Male, age 33

While the phrase "You have to let the barbs roll off you" was offered as a strategy, avoidance of others and restricting social contact were fundamental strategies used by people who had been bullied. As one young man conveyed, "I didn't try out for a lot of clubs and teams because I had already set it up in my head that I would fail based on what others said about me. I withdraw from social events now and I think this has limited the opportunities I might have had in my life." Similarly, a woman said she only participates in activities where she knows she is competent. She does not like to take risks and appear as if she doesn't know what she's doing. The downside is she feels she may have missed out on certain opportunities in life with this tactic. Loneliness can also be an unexpected outcome that proceeds from missed opportunities or using these interpersonal strategies. A woman who was mistreated by her peers confided,

> "I was bullied by my 'friends' starting rumors about me. I think that one important decision I have made due to this is to keep more things to myself. That way at least if anyone starts a rumor about me, it won't be based on anything even semi-factual. I've decided to be less social than what I could be simply because I don't want to run the risk that someone will use something they know about me against me. The only problem is, of course, it is a lonely decision."

I found it interesting that one man told me he avoids staring at people and tries to avoid making eye contact altogether with strangers as a result of experiences with violence and bullying when he was in school. I think this is an intriguing finding and wish I had asked more people about this idea. The notion of holding back with others was raised by a number of participants. This form of social retreat was put very plainly by one person: "Being bullied made me a less outgoing person and dissuaded me from approaching people and introducing myself." Many times this sentiment was expressed: "I'm cautious with people I meet now and I keep my distance from them. I am not as bold or outgoing." These are changes in personal relating. No one who talked about holding back described himself or herself as a shy person from childhood, but rather as changed due to mistreatment. Keeping to themselves rather than taking the risks associated with meeting new people and shutting down emotionally were decisions associated with bullying by peers or adults.

A soft-spoken biracial woman, age 23, told me, "All through elementary school, I was berated for my appearance. My mom started when I was 8 telling me I was fat and putting down how I looked. Today I find it hard to believe anyone would like me or find me attractive so I avoid close relationships for fear the other person will hurt me or hate me." Hopefully as she gets older she can overcome some of these terrible messages so she can make decisions to engage in healthy relationships.

While a minority of participants (19.8%) admitted to "picking on others" or being a bully, most of the participants involved in bullying said they were the recipients. A 41-year-old man described himself as a social outcast in high school. Before that, he was the butt of many jokes and "set-ups" in middle school about his clothes. Being victimized started as early as elementary school, where he was made fun of for being different, having an ethnic last name, and for not being any good at sports. He still has trouble in his relationships now, and attributes it to the damage done then. As a "social outcast" he never learned how to interact smoothly with other people and often decides to skip social occasions. We see that adults who were bullied as children can end up inhibited in their ability to share their innermost selves and feelings with others. Even superficial relating is problematic today for this man.

GROUP INCLUSION

Group inclusion is an essential human need. It is seen as primary for basic survival (Baumeister & Leary, 1995). When people are excluded, they experience anxiety, loneliness, depression, and actual physical pain (Leary, 1990; MacDonald & Leary, 2005). A young woman, age 25, disclosed that she was constantly tormented throughout her entire secondary school experience. A day did not pass when she was not called names, shoved, or when something was not thrown at her in the hallways or during class. This treatment resulted in severe depression and a bit of a sense of paranoia. When she walked into a room, if people were laughing she would think they might be laughing at her. As a young adult, she sees the influence on her decisions about friends, about how she handles conflict, and about men. She chooses her friends with extreme care, she takes on conflict but in an aggressive manner, and she "seeks affection from guys to comfort the pain." The sense of exclusion she felt as an adolescent has marked her adult experience thus far. It has impacted the deliberate nature with which she chooses close relationships and seems to have pushed her toward relationships with men that are primarily utilitarian. The fact that she handles conflict with aggression typically causes problems in most settings, such as work and in relationships. Group exclusion can be particularly cruel for lesbian, gay, bisexual, transgender, and questioning individuals. One man, age 31, shared, "I was always called 'gay' when I was in middle and high school. That made me too afraid to come out. So I decided that I had to wait—and I never did come out to anyone until I was 26. That decision left me lonely and always on the outside looking in."

Difference, whether due to race or sexual orientation or some other personal characteristic, can meet with group exclusion. Race-based bullying, as noted earlier, played a defining role in the lives of the people in this study. One woman, age 27, reported, "Since I was bullied based on my race, now I decide to avoid any inter-racial situations as best I can. If I have to contribute in a group project at work that is inter-racial, I'll do it, but I would prefer not to and my radar is always alert for possible intimidation." Even within racial groups subsets form over who is "in" and who is "out," often resulting in an even greater sense of rejection (Bernstein et al., 2010). This brand of bullying may push someone to protect themselves in a variety of ways.

"Shunned by all my peers, a forced isolate."

For most adolescents, being shunned or excluded from the company of peers is tantamount to being exiled in a foreign country. Beth, 54, a teacher in the public school system, escaped bullying or any form of sexual harassment throughout elementary school, but middle school was a different story. It began when the most popular boy in the school liked her and asked her to go steady. Beth described him as handsome and fearless. It felt like a pretty big deal for a 7th grade girl who had been known as a "kind kid" in elementary school. She said yes to going steady, but soon realized that meant going to "kissing parties." She described feeling terrified and said no to this activity. The boy broke up with her. But as painful as that was, it paled in comparison to what was ahead. At lunch she sat with the popular girls. When they heard that the boy broke up with her, all the girls turned away from Beth and made it clear she was no longer one of them. She was not emotionally equipped to deal with this level of rejection by anyone, much less by her friends. It got worse. No one would talk to her. She had clearly violated a group social norm, and that was not acceptable. Beth felt "scared, isolated, and lonely—something inside had been broken." One of her friends called to say, "Do you know how much everyone hates you?" Beth began to eat her lunch in a bathroom stall. What happened was precipitous and so unexpected. Beth was stymied by it and left to deal with her intense feelings alone. She did tell her parents what was going on, but "they were no match for this." Her dad advised her to stop answering the telephone. But she still had to face school every day. She had no skills to reach out to other people to try to make new friends. She felt terrified by the blatant exclusion and began to feel, "I can't take it." She tried as hard as she could to pretend that everything was alright. It is very clear that no one should have to undergo rejection of this type, but children particularly are not equal to the challenge. Beth related, "I wasn't ready for this kind of assault on my self-worth. It completely blind-sided me. I couldn't sleep. I felt stuck, I couldn't fix it, and I experienced a sense of freezing in place." At the same time, Beth was "unreasonably kind and forgiving" to the same people who were tormenting her hoping they would stop. Beth "didn't fight back; I just disappeared." But she describes it as the end of innocence.

By the time she got to high school, she had pretty much "figured out how to get invisible." She still feels ashamed that she began to "run with the pack and didn't do anything to oppose what was said" when someone was being bullied or tormented. She became a bystander. The analogy she used to describe witnessing bullying was, "It was like watching a shark circle. It was like tasting blood."

Beth has a learned response to conflict now that she wishes she did not have. She describes it as having "less emotional dexterity." Beth freezes in the face of conflict. She believes this is a direct result of the profound damage to her sense of self-confidence and the isolation she went through as a teenager. Today Beth does recognize the effects on her relationships and adult decisions. Attachment to friends and intimates is a priority for her. When she was a young adult she admits, "I delayed being myself" and paid too high a price to have a friend. She said her tolerance for the poor behavior of others was too high. Her friends now are a treasured part of her life. She confided, "When I attach, it's primary." Beth decided long ago, based on the incidents of peer mistreatment, to seek true friends as a high priority in life, to be involved at a deep level with no falsehood in the relationships. Being bullied made her value the gift of being a friend and having a friend. Understanding the concept of a true friend also led to another major decision in her life. Beth left her marriage of many years when she was unable to find in her husband the kind of friendship, even at a basic level, that she needed. Having the awareness of the value of sincere companionship gave her the courage to make the decision to leave him.

Because trust has been so severely affected due to bullying, one of the decisions people make is avoidance and keeping distance in their interpersonal relationships. The following statements are examples of this:

"I was threatened and hit by an older child when I was in elementary school. My decisions are affected to this day. I learned to be wary of other people and have remained so."

Male, *age 56*

"I am careful who I associate with and the first sign someone is not nice, I distance myself. I am much more picky about who I choose as friends."

Female, *age 23*

"I was bullied throughout all my school years by male friends. Now, the way I was treated, especially in high school, has really impacted how I attach in friendships with other men. I feel rejection and so I keep limits on friendships with them."

Male, *age 26*

Peter, 23, is a handsome and extremely articulate young man. He experienced numerous instances of bullying in his school years. He explained that he and his friends were always among the smallest in his grade. They were "nice and normal," and these factors made them easy to pick on. Often at lunchtime he would be berated and tormented with extremely negative names and language by one boy in particular. There was no peace. One day he finally yelled, "Man, leave me alone." As a result, the perpetrator tried to start a fistfight right there in the cafeteria. The bully was relentless and continued his terrible mistreatment of Peter. At the same time, Peter kept putting himself back into the same situations.

He depicted an appalling event that happened when he was in 9th grade involving the same boy from the lunch table whom Peter described as "intimidating" and "the perfect bully." On one occasion the boy brought what he said were really good chocolates to school and offered one to Peter. It was not at all typical for the other boy to be nice, but Peter wanted to fit into the group, so he took one. About 5 hours later his stomach didn't feel right and he still has "a horrifying memory of being in the bathroom, being sick, with this guy and my friends laughing and peering over the stall at me." He said, "I still have feelings about it now, to this day." As we were talking, Peter's voice was filled with sadness. He went on to say, "I wanted to fit in so badly. What bothers me most, all I really wanted was friends." He sometimes let himself be a victim just to get friends. He said, "I let myself go back. I could have sought out other friends but I put myself regularly in bullying situations. I felt constantly like a victim. I saw everything in my life as happening to me. Like I was helpless and had no control over anything. I never allowed myself the luxury of blaming other people."

Peter went on to explain that at the end of that school year, he ditched all of those old "friends." I asked if any of his friends stood up for him. He said none of his good friends from elementary school did but a friend from middle school tried on a random, once-in-a-while basis. Then the bullies would immediately turn on his defender. The main bully was "a benefit to the group." His parents allowed drinking at his house with no supervision. This made him very popular and everyone wanted to stay in his good graces.

There were instances of sexual harassment at school involving "games" that boys played in the hallways, in the locker rooms, and in other areas of the school. One game of sexual harassment was called "sac-tapping." It involved friends and other peers punching one another in the groin and was quite painful. It was a form of physical and sexual abuse, but it was always described as "just a joke." It happened from 8th grade throughout high school, but tapered off a bit once everyone was a senior. At that point, most decided it was "dumb." Prior to that, it was seen as normal. However, Peter shared, it could not help but generate anger. "You had to be on guard, figure out who might be ready to punch you, and be thinking about revenge. If you didn't retaliate, things would be much worse for you in terms of being victimized." According to Peter, conscious decisions of action had to be made, decisions about retaliation, to prevent being the target of escalated occurrences.

It is an unfortunate but true statement that so-called friends treat each other so badly. Much of the current research focuses on how often children are met with ridicule and torment by those they consider their friends (Daniels, Quigley, Menard, & Spence, 2010; Mishna et al., 2010; Pronk & Zimmer-Gembeck, 2010; Wei & Jonson-Reid, 2011). These tormentors are not merely random same-age peers, but rather people in their own cliques. A clear example comes from cyberbullying. One Canadian study of over 2,000 secondary school students found that most cyberbullying occurred among friends. After being the target of bullying, the children reported feeling angry, sad, and depressed. However, if they were the bully, they reported feeling "funny, popular, and powerful" (Mishna et al., 2010, p. 362).

This was the hardest time of his life, Peter explained, and it "spilled over to my parents." He described coming home from school and unleashing his pain there. He was angry, got into yelling and shouting matches with his parents, and would throw things. There were many consequences for Peter that resulted from his mistreatment by his peers. It made him feel that he must cut off empathy toward anybody else to survive in the world. He talked about other consequences that he believes are lifelong. He illustrated this point by sharing that he does not have many friends today. Making friends has been a problem because he has trouble trusting anyone. Peter said, "I don't even trust myself." By this he explained that he cannot always count on his ability to discern whether someone (a friend or potential girlfriend) is trustworthy. He tends to think they will hurt him—it's just a matter of time. He has learned not to rely on anyone except himself. In relationships with friends, he opens up much too quickly, then finds that he sabotages the friendship so he will not get hurt. Similarly, in relationships with girls that could lead to something substantial, he begins to feel helpless and powerless. So he compensates by trying to control the relationship. He said, "I begin to be manipulative." A feeling that the girl will end up hurting him begins to emerge so he starts to push her away before that can happen.

There are repercussions on decisions in Peter's life. He decided he needs to be "completely unreadable" to protect himself when he is around others. It has become second nature and is causing him a good deal of loneliness. He went on, "It's daunting going on a date and trying to let someone in and be vulnerable. You say in your head 'Don't give too much of yourself; you'll make it too serious.'" Further, he cuts people out of his life before that can even come close to happening.

In Peter's words:

"Bullying has affected my social decisions. I use my insight to determine who is most likely to hurt me. I see past the façade of the person and identify the special traits of who they are. I think my neurological pathways make unconscious decisions like 'No, this person isn't good. Run away.' This is definitely true with some girls if they begin to remind me of one girlfriend I had who was definitely a bully. I get a trigger that says, 'This is Christine all over again; run away.' In terms of professional decisions, I see that I am drawn towards helping people avoid pain or figure out how to cope with it. I've realized that I am a sensitive, intuitive person."

EDUCATIONAL AND PROFESSIONAL DECISIONS

"Being the target of bullying made me decide to become a doctor to show my peers that nothing they did could stop me."

Male, age 39

Being the target of bullying, sexual harassment, and hazing can leave an impressive imprint on adult decision-making about social, educational, and professional decisions. One woman, age 30, gave a particularly poignant response to the question about how her decisions may have been affected: "Since being bullied in high school, I am too fearful to stand on my own and to make my own decisions. I don't trust myself. As a result of the sexual harassment, I dropped out of school and obtained a GED. I regret it very much. I am not sexually graceful and I act inappropriate more often than I want. I think I didn't develop the social graces I needed or any of the developmental skills others have." As this woman explains, bullying can stunt someone's growth. While others are learning to make decisions, for the good or the bad, some targets of bullying are paralyzed in their ability to do so thinking instead, "I don't trust myself." The lack of trust comes directly from believing the hurtful words that have been said or absorbing the hurtful things that have been done to them as kids. Another result articulated by a man, age 33, was, "My confidence in myself was severely shaken from the bullying and now I don't pursue employment or educational opportunities that might be challenging. I think if I had more confidence I might have decided to possibly go after more difficult things."

On the other hand, bullying and harassment can push people to grow in more positive ways. One woman, age 49, decided to pursue a master's degree in English as soon as she could to "show those who bullied me that I wasn't stupid." A 24-year-old woman says of her educational goals and volunteer activities, "I always told my bullies that one day I'd be better than them and make something of myself. On a deep level, that may be part of what urges me on toward my PhD. Bullying also has led me to be involved with various youth groups as an adult to set a positive example for kids, girls especially."

A good many people in the study talked about the need to reach out to others. This was articulated by the following people:

"The hurt of being bullied moved me into a kind of Savior Complex. I can't stand seeing people unjustly accused, treated badly, or hurt emotionally. That's why I decided to pursue a profession where I could help other people."

Woman, *age 35*

"I have a strong sense of right and wrong and justice. I am drawn to human rights law as a primary professional interest. My mother calls this 'my super-hero complex.' I want to help people who can't help themselves."

Woman, age 24

One young woman, age 26, said that her interest in children is motivated by what she lived through in terms of bullying and sexual harassment. She has an interest in working with kids because she wants to be a voice for them when they might need someone to tell their story. She wants to make a difference in the lives of children and spends her time volunteering with kids. Colin, age 36, commented, "The bullying I experienced made me feel insignificant and definitely made an impact on my decisions. For one, I stayed out of extracurricular activities so I could escape school. I also purposely did not participate during classes to avoid sticking my neck out." We can see that these choices and decisions robbed Colin of opportunities. Who knows what skills he might have acquired or what he might have learned about himself if he had been involved in band, drama club, or another student organization? It makes sense that he did not sign up; he was doing what he could to protect himself. But we can only guess at what he missed as a result. On top of those at-the-time decisions to avoid extracurricular activities, Colin sees the impact on his adult decision-making. He works with kids in a professional capacity and believes that being bullied influenced that decision.

Sexual Harassment and Professional Decisions

Catherine is a dental hygienist who described what happened for her in middle school and the impact it had on decisions in her life:

"I can see where I was standing, in which classroom, where the boys were standing, what the teacher was doing—and not doing to interrupt it. I remember vividly the utter embarrassment and humiliation that I felt. It makes me grind my teeth to remember it. Maybe that's why I'm in the profession I'm in. [She laughs saying this.] I felt angry and helpless and trapped. It was in school, after all, and I was in a classroom so I couldn't just leave. Well, I guess technically I could if I was a different kind of student, but I was a good kid. The boys were relentless in their derogatory sexual comments to me because I was underdeveloped for our grade level. I had skipped a grade based on academic performance so I was really too young socially to be with these kids. They weren't really my peers in that sense. The boys called me all kinds of awful names. I did tell my mother but she just laughed it off. She thought they were funny and clever. She said: 'Don't take it seriously; they probably like you.' I didn't feel supported by her at all, by the teachers who just allowed it, and I didn't feel 'liked' by the boys who were doing this in each class. When I look back, I can see how it affected my development. I wanted to be an actress. I have really good auditory recall and a good memory. I thought I could be good at it. But my concept of myself as an even adequate person physically was changed forever. There was no way that I could envision myself as an actress if I would have to show any part of my body to do it. So much for that dream. I decided against even trying. I am 59 years old but I can still feel the scars from that time in my life. It has gotten in my way in terms of decisions about relationships for my whole life: who to date, whether to date, and whether to stay in relationships."

Lisa, age 29, described decisions in her sexual life that were impacted by being bullied and harassed. When she was in middle school, she was the brunt of many sexual rumors by two girls who said they were her friends. Her sense of herself as a sexual person, only just in early development, was dramatically disrupted. She reported this reaction: "Sexually, yes. I had some trouble sexually, being relaxed, until I was in my mid 20s. I still had boyfriends but no real physicality or intimacy in the relationships. When I finally had sex it was when I was really ready to because I was slow to get to know him (her boyfriend). I had a wall up . . . then he put in the extra effort to get to know me." Lisa also mentioned an impact on her professionally. She said, "When I first started out I was in an office full of women. So I said to myself, 'Watch the office dynamics before you open your mouth.' I know the horror of it; I know the dark side. I did start to get involved in gossip, then I really regretted it. I figured out how to back-peddle. I would always worry about the consequences. To this day, I am very careful, overly careful I think, about what I say and to whom." Lisa made decisions to be cautious in relating to others based on her bullying and sexual harassment as a young teenager. Among the people I talked with for the book, this was a common reaction. At first it may seem like having "a wall up" is not such a bad thing until there is the realization: This is in the way—and maybe in a very significant manner.

People made substantive choices and decisions based on their bullying experiences in childhood. One decision that stood out was to resist change—in terms of being less likely to move out of an established comfort zone. To do so exposes one to the possibility of ridicule by others. People had experienced this too many times to risk it again. Many cited the careful nature with which they choose friends now as adults as a result of bullying. Words such as "picky," "careful," and "selective" were used over and over. Making "snap judgments" and decisions based on someone looking like a past bully is now a defensive strategy. Another decision was to leave school as early as possible to escape bullying and sexual harassment. This had many ramifications in adult life. Each person who took this option did pursue a GED, but each also thought this limited professional and social opportunities. The opposite also occurred. There were those who felt pushed to achieve. They wanted to demonstrate their worth, to say to those who treated them with distain in the past "See, I am somebody." So they reached for higher educational and greater professional goals than they might have otherwise. Social avoidance—avoiding specific situations of harm, ridicule, and harassment, or the potential—was a prominent decision that resulted from bullying experiences in childhood. This was true for those who limited themselves professionally as well as those who may have overachieved. Social avoidance was perceived as imperative and effective. This often led to loneliness. Loneliness was articulated by many people who were bullied as children. They felt lonely then and they still experience loneliness now. Their sense of separateness as adults stems from decisions to protect themselves against potential bullying in adult friendships or intimate relationships. Deciding to skip social events or to keep up an emotional wall are protective mechanisms designed to never allow victimization again.

As we have seen in this chapter, those who were bullied as children and adolescents make decisions in their adult life based on their mistreatment in childhood. The decisions can be as far-ranging as those about appearance to decisions about relationships and employment. How does bullying come into play around family issues? The next chapter delves into this important aspect of each adult's life.

CHAPTER 9
It Comes Home to Roost

Bullying and the Family

"My youth an unripe plum, your teeth have left your marks on it; the tooth marks still vibrate, I remember always"

Thich Nhat Hahn, *The Heart of the Buddha's Teaching*

In the first chapter, systems theory was discussed along with the concept of homeostasis—the fact that all systems strive to maintain balance. Another systems concept that is pertinent is that of scapegoating. Scapegoating occurs in virtually all human systems that are dysfunctional. Often, systems will elect a scapegoat as a part of their homeostasis. Ethological studies of primate troupes show that they will use scapegoating to provide group cohesion and as a release of group tensions, through targeting one or more victims (de Waal, 2005; Gruter & Masters, 1986; Maxim, 1978, 1982). Without spoken language and more advanced conflict resolution skills, scapegoating is one of the only mechanisms left for these primates. Children and adults do the same by "picking on" or repudiating someone who is decidedly "other," someone who looks and acts different than the majority. Children who are maltreated by their parents or siblings may be the scapegoat in their family system. According to social learning theory (Bandura, 1976), they learn that bullying, violence, and scapegoating are acceptable forms of person-to-person interaction and an appropriate means of dealing with anger and conflict. Another example of learned bullying can be seen when an adult child must care for an elderly parent. Sometimes, this results in aggression toward the elder known as elder abuse. Of course this does not always happen, but when it does occur, it may be part of a continuing intergenerational cycle of scapegoating and violence (Doumas, Margolin, & John, 1994; Walsh et al., 2007). Ostensibly, human beings should be able to resolve conflicts and differences of opinion without resorting to scapegoating. When we see this happening, it is a systemic failure because it indicates that the system cannot mitigate conflicts in a more mature fashion.

PARENTS AS BULLIES

Bullying can start in the home where parents act in a bullying and intimidating fashion toward their children. Sometimes adults justify this as discipline; often it is an unjustified use of power over someone who is small or vulnerable. It is displaced anger and aggression in the form of scapegoating. A nationally representative sample of over 3,000 American parents found that 63% admitted to verbally abusing their children through swearing or insulting them. The study was conducted with children as young as preschool and those throughout high school age. Using the Conflict Tactic Scales, children who were verbally abused by their parents were found to exhibit "higher rates of physical aggression, delinquency, and interpersonal problems than other children" (Vissing, Straus, Gelles, & Harrop, 1991, p. 223). In another study, over 90% of parents demonstrated aggression toward children by age 17, with over 98% admitting to being psychologically aggressive toward their child by age 5 years. Forms of aggression included:

Shouting, yelling, screaming—74%
Threatening to spank—53.6%
Swearing or cursing at child—24.3%
Calling child dumb or lazy—17.5%
Threatening to send child away or kick child out of the house—6%
(Straus & Field, 2003).

There are numerous impacts on children due to parental mistreatment. Among them: Children who are maltreated by their parents and who witness violence at home are more likely to bully others (Centers for Disease Control and Prevention [CDC], 2011). They are also subject to depression and anxiety as a result (Baldry, 2003). Further, these children are more vulnerable to being bullied themselves (Baldry, 2003; CDC, 2011; Duncan, 2004; Hildyard & Wolfe, 2002). It is important to note that children and teens who may be outside the norm in sexual identity run into problems at home. Parents often have a great deal of difficulty accepting their children if they are not heteronormative (Diamond et al., 2012; Ryan, Russell, Huebner, Diaz, & Sanchez, 2010). Children and teens who identify as lesbian, gay, or bisexual receive "more psychological and physical abuse by parents or caretakers" compared with their siblings who are heterosexual (Balsam, Rothblum, & Beauchaine, 2005, p. 477). Without intervention, this may leave children who are bullied by parents due to sexual identity with fewer resources or diminished self-esteem as adults.

In my study, I posed this straightforward question to all participants: "Where you bullied at home?" Twenty-five percent said they were bullied at home, and these are some examples they offered:

- "My mother was emotionally abusive." (Female, age 23, Asian Korean)
- "My father would constantly verbally abuse and push me around." (Male, age 24)
- "My mother exerts control by name calling and so-called 'teasing.'" (Female, age 31)
- "I was made fun of by my parent for my appearance and race." (Female, age 28, race undisclosed)
- "My father was very verbally abusive to my family and he used to call my brother and I obscenities often when we were young." (Female, age 23, Asian/American)

One young man, age 25, explained,

"My father was my biggest bully. He would constantly put me down and still does if he gets the chance. I am better at defending myself now, but little children don't have much in the way of defenses. He would call me names and make me feel stupid. At the same time, I was expected to get excellent grades in school. When I got a "B" he would ask, 'Are you sure you did your best?' I was always afraid of failure, and I wanted desperately to make something of myself. I am still trying to get approval from others and I think it stems back from not getting this from my dad."

Sharon, age 53, told me,

"My mother was a bully and prided herself on it. She wanted me to be afraid of her. She said on numerous occasions 'Don't cross me; I am a formidable enemy.' This was a devastating thing to hear. I knew my friends had mothers they could count on, who were warm and caring. My mother made a habit of being aggressive in what she said to me and in her tone of voice. She threatened to harm me many times. It was psychological and emotional bullying. She achieved her overall goal. I was always afraid of her, and that feeling continued through most of my adult life. I was the scapegoat in the family and took the brunt of her unhappiness with my father. I think it has left me at a big disadvantage in terms of speaking up, and I am always on the lookout for anyone who might be aggressive toward me. I avoid confrontation at almost all costs. Her behaviors and attitudes left me feeling very unloved and unprotected. I have seen the negative outcomes from all of this, and I have been working on overcoming my fears for a very long time."

Research across the lifespan demonstrates that parental bullying can lead to numerous adverse effects. These include anxiety, depression, physical health problems, teen pregnancy, post-traumatic stress disorder, criminal activities, and homelessness (see Lamont, 2010). In addition, studies show alterations in brain structure as a result of parental bullying (Tomoda, 2011). Obviously changes in brain structures carry a lifelong impact.

Richard, age 43, talked about the effects of bullying by his mother. He said, "I definitely don't deal well with conflict. I look for relationships with people who are laid back. There was bullying at my house growing up. My mother wasn't in control of her temper a lot of the time. Regular kid things would set her off and she was physically threatening. If she caught me, there would be physical violence. I would run away in absolute fear."

SIBLINGS AS BULLIES

In the United States, sibling violence far exceeds other forms of family violence. It is four to five times more prevalent than parental child abuse and abuse between adult intimate partners. It can be inadvertently encouraged by parents who have favorites or who believe that sibling violence is "normal" and therefore do not intervene to stop it. Bullying by siblings may be verbal, psychological, sexual, or physical abuse and includes being punched, kicked, or bitten (Caffaro, 2013). It is not bound by gender, age, or culture and may include life-threatening assault. Further, both perpetrators and victims deem sibling assaults to be less dangerous than equivalent actions seen in dating violence situations (Khan & Rogers, 2015). Tanrikulu and Campbell (2014) studied over 450 children in grades 5 through 12. They found that 31.6% engaged in sibling bullying, while only 9.8% bullied peers. The siblings who bullied described complex forms of bullying perpetration both in vivo and via cybertechnology toward their siblings. All types of sibling bullying are associated with poor mental health outcomes. In a study of over 2,000 children ages 10–15, Wolke and Skew (2011) discovered that half of those with siblings were involved in bullying each other, while 12% were also victims at school. Those who were both bullies and victims with siblings and who were victimized at school were more likely than other children to show behavioral problems requiring some kind of clinical intervention. Research was conducted on this phenomenon by Tucker, Finkelhor, Turner, and Shattuck (2013) with 3,600 children up to age 17. Of this group, one-third had experienced victimization by either a sister or a brother in the past year. Results of the study demonstrated that these children measured higher on scores of depression, anxiety, and anger than children who were not bullied by a sibling. Bowes, Maughan, Caspi, Moffitt, and Arseneault (2014) found further issues associated with sibling bullying. They followed more than 6,900 children in the UK for 18 years and made assessments at ages 7, 8, 10, 12, and 18 years. Over the course of that time, 47.5% of the children said they were bullied by a sibling. The study indicated that verbal bullying was the most common form of sibling aggression reported by the children. Already by age 7, children who were bullied by siblings were more likely to show greater emotional and behavioral problems. The children who were subjected to sibling bullying were also more likely to be victimized by their peers. By age 18, 13% of the children reported depression, 19.3% reported self-harming behaviors, and 16% anxiety. The rate of depression and self-harming behaviors were twice that of children who were not bullied by their siblings. Unfortunately because sibling bullying is normalized (Hoetger, Hazen, & Brank, 2015), children can grow up believing that violence against a peer or victimization is normal and acceptable in a primary relationship.

Colin provided a good example of bullying at school that can lead to bullying of a sibling. Being bullied at school started for Colin as early as elementary school, when groups of other boys would chase him around the playground and sometimes try to beat him up. He was teased on the bus because of his curly, red hair and his name. Kids found creative ways of torturing him about it. In middle school, he was called names "all of the time" and would be punched in the genitals while carrying his lunch tray to the table to eat. He received threatening letters and was framed for all kinds of things by his so-called friends. Colin also had a math teacher in high school who regularly called him a moron in front of the rest of the class, so the name-calling by other students continued with the help of the example set by the math teacher. In high school, he was still being bullied physically, with kids punching him or choking him. Colin said he had "awful anxiety about going to school" and threw up nearly every single morning of his first year of high school. Due to the torment he had undergone for so many years from the kids and due to the math teacher's comments ("you're a moron"), he never even had an idea of how really bright he is until he was halfway through high school. Feeling sick and actually being sick before school is an example of a situation when parents are not putting two and two together to come up with "my child is being bullied at school."

Colin noted that all of this ended up spilling over to home. He began to bully his younger brother by beating him up, threatening him, and calling him names. Most of the time parents do not recognize bullying that is coming home from school. For Colin this was an important outgrowth of what he experienced day in and day out. Parents tend to think that sibling violence is "sibling rivalry" and is just a normal part of growing up. They fail to understand that kids can only tolerate so much demeaning before a "kick-the-dog" syndrome sets in. In other words, Colin had nowhere else to take his anger except to his sibling. I asked him if he thought about telling his parents to intervene. His response was very typical: "No, I didn't think they could do anything. I was also worried it might get worse. Also some of the bullies were my friends." This last sentence tends to perplex parents. Bullied by friends is a concept that does not seem to compute. However this is exactly what happened to Colin, and it happens to many kids.

Bullying by Sister

The following are some comments that were shared with me about sibling bullying:

- "My sister (she was my biggest conflict) constantly made fun of me, beat me up, always made me feel that I was bad and what I did, such as play the viola, was 'gay' and 'not cool.'" (Female, age 20)
- "My sister would put soap on my fruit and I couldn't reach the sink to wash it off. She tied me to chairs and then left the room. She pulled my arm out of the socket during 'play' wrestling." (Female, age 18)
- "My younger sister used to come up behind me when she was mad about something and tell me she was going to kill me in my sleep." (Female, age 64)

Carl, age 37, shared his experience of being victimized by his sibling:

"My sister is three years older than I am. The bullying by her was very calculated and methodical. It was both psychological and physical. I did try to fight back, but I was unsuccessful. My sister is very intelligent and got away with it for many years. She convinced my parents that the bad things that happened to me were my own fault. At first they didn't believe my denials. But they eventually caught on. She tortured me in very creative ways like by lulling me into a false sense of security for two weeks, then doing something I could never have been prepared for. She was very mischievous. I think she enjoyed the challenge of figuring out ways to torture me—forgivable childhood attributes. Though it was the most pervasive bullying I experienced in my childhood, I do forgive her. If I can forgive someone or not comes down to their motivation. The bullying by peers at school was mean-spirited. But I got many more bruises and scars from my sister than from anyone else. The psychological bullying ended when she went off to college. My sister has never apologized for it; she has no perception that she needs to or should. I think she was establishing and keeping a social hierarchy. So when I was able to compete with her everything ended."

In this case, there appears to be a positive outcome in the sense that he has forgiven his sister. It makes us wonder, however, about the impact that might still be there and show up for him in close adult relationships. What we learn about others and ourselves during formative years is our basis for adult friendships, interactions, and relationships.

Bullying by Brother

- "My brother would get into fights with me and often times put me in a physical position and make me say something that he wanted me to say." (Male, age 19, Asian Indian)
- "My brother was a football player who was very big, strong, and muscular. He used that power to exert control over me." (Female, age 19, African American/Nigerian)

I had the opportunity to interview Sean, age 23. He has just one sibling, a brother who is 4 years older. Sean was bullied mercilessly by teammates when he was in high school and is still asking himself the question, "Why me?" Some of the answer may lie in the answer to the question I asked: "Were you ever bullied by your brother?" Sean's response was: "Of course, he's my brother. But nothing more than from other brothers." During the interview regarding bullying by his peers and teammates, Sean was very forthcoming. In any further discussion regarding his brother and himself, however, Sean's facial expression changed from open and receptive to stony and guarded. His words were a bit more clipped and succinct than his other responses and his affect appeared guarded—where it did not during any other time in the interview. For Sean, it was a matter of, "Well there really wasn't much I could do [to protect himself from his brother]; he was always so much bigger than me." By high school, his brother was 6'5" tall and weighed well over 200 lbs. Sometimes it was to Sean's advantage to have a big brother; it stopped some percentage of kids from going after him, but not everyone, not his teammates. Sean is still left with a great deal of rage and with intrusive flashbacks to times he was bullied. It would seem from his response, that along with his past encounters with teammates, he may still have some things to work out with his brother.

CONSEQUENCES OF SIBLING BULLYING

How does bullying by a sibling relate to bullying at school? Does it set up kids to be victimized at school? Does it prepare them to be bullies at school? How does bullying at home or school contribute to intimate partner violence or domestic violence into adulthood? One young woman, age 29, stated,

> "My sister and I use to beat the crap out of each other. There was no parent in charge for hours after school. So we had a lot of hair-pulling, screaming, and verbal abuse. We'd shut our baby sister in the closet and leave her there. No one got hurt per se. We were just getting it all out there. I can see that it has an impact on me in terms of friendships. I start to keep a tally if people do something against me. I begin to think I shouldn't have this friendship anymore. If it's your family, that's different. But if it's just a friend, you have to really consider if it's worth it. Family will always be there. Friends may not always be there for you. Two different philosophies there."

This is an interesting example of the kind of sibling bullying that goes on in many households. It even happens when parents are present but believe "kids should work it out themselves." Children who are bullies and victims of peer bullying at school, it turns out, report the greatest amount of sibling bullying at home (see Duncan, 1999; Hoetger et al., 2015). We need to ask ourselves, what are some of the outcomes here? One is that young people are learning that verbal abuse and some forms of physical violence are normative in important intimate relationships. Corvo and deLara (2010) discussed the connections between bullying experienced in adolescence and later lifetime violence in personal relationships. Basically early mistreatment through bullying and harassment set someone up for a lifetime of maltreatment because it is experienced as de rigueur. The CDC (2010) says that dating violence often starts with name-calling, and unfortunately no one intervenes, thinking that this behavior is typical for adolescents. Many boys and girls believe it is acceptable to use threats and violence to get their way in relationships. Approximately 10% of high school students report being hit, slapped, or physically hurt on purpose by their boyfriend or girlfriend. Given this type of behavior and that people do not tend to interrupt it, it makes sense that some young people will carry over these forms of bullying interactions into their adult lives.

This is an area of research needing more investigation. Mackey, Fromuth, and Kelly (2010) did a small study with about 145 undergraduates asking about sibling bullying. Their results indicated that those who considered themselves to be bullied by a sibling when they were children continued to experience anxiety. There are questions that still must be addressed. When a child has been bullied by a sibling or more than one sibling, are there continuing effects into adulthood? The studies above indicate that children bullied by their siblings are more likely than those who have not been bullied to experience anxiety, depression, behavioral problems, and self-harming behaviors needing clinical intervention. Do these issues carry over to other stages of life? What happens to theses sibling relationships once they are adults? Is all forgotten or forgiven? Or is there always a sense of mistrust? Bowes et al. (2014) found that children who were bullied by their siblings were more likely to be bullied by peers and, as we have discussed in other sections of the book, the impact of peer bullying does last a lifetime. At this point in time, most people have figured out that peer bullying at school and in the community is not acceptable, but sibling bullying remains an arena where adults still take a hands-off attitude.

IMPACT ON THE FAMILY

What is the impact on families when their child is bullied? How does being the victim of bullying affect parenting? When a child is the target of bullying, it impacts the entire family. One young man shared, "I had many instances of this occur in my formative years, and it caused much stress, heartache, and pain for myself and my family."

Family members are typically not aware that their child or children are being subjected to bullying. This is because most children don't tell parents about what they are experiencing or witnessing at school in terms of victimization (deLara, 2012; Mishna & Alaggia, 2005). Once they are aware, parents often experience a sense of helplessness. I received the following e-mail from a distraught mother of a high school student asking for any help I could provide:

"My daughter is suffering devastating abuse at the hands of her teacher and coach, and this has been followed by more victimization by one of her classmates. This victimization involves horrific sexual harassment. Although I have provided written documentation to the school district of these instances towards my child and others, the school has continued to allow the teacher/coach to remain in her position. My daughter is depressed. She used to love school but now often she just doesn't want to go. I, personally, cannot sleep many nights. I consulted an attorney, but I was told that it is practically impossible to get a teacher removed. Can you suggest anything I can do to help my daughter? I am a single parent and don't know where to turn next."

In another e-mail, the mother of an elementary school student described the consequences to her little child:

"My daughter, a second grader, was complaining about a stomachache one morning before school last week. I could tell she wasn't really sick. But, my daughter is not the type to try to deceive me into allowing her to stay home from school, so it raised a little alarm. Kids don't answer a simple question like, 'did something happen at school yesterday?' They don't make the connection, because stuff happens at school every day. So, I tried a more direct question. I asked her, 'How are the other kids at school; are they nice to each other?' Wow, my daughter went on for twenty minutes about one little girl in her class who was being ripped apart by another little girl, behind the teacher's back. Even though she recounted that the bully never turned her attention onto my daughter, she still felt pain for this other little girl and wanted the abuse to stop. Now I know better than to simply tell my daughter to defend this little girl—that is a lot to ask of a seven-year-old who is not overly assertive to begin with. I asked my daughter if she wanted me to talk to her teacher; she said 'yes,' so I did. The teacher reported that she hadn't even been aware that this was happening. She said that she would try to pay special attention, and asked my daughter to come to her privately if there was anything she wanted her to know but wasn't comfortable saying in front of other students. Now she feels so much better that there is something she can do, that is on a comfortable level for her."

In this instance, there seems to have been a better resolution for the 7-year-old than for the high school student who was being tormented at school. However, it points out that parents do experience a broad range of feelings and reactions once they are cognizant of the facts—that their children are involved with bullying. One mother said that her eldest son was plagued at school by a group of kids. The children were led by one child in particular and they were "relentless." The mother continued,

> "I had no one to talk to or to help me. I called the school district for help and even went to the principal for help . . . I got nothing. They sent me to the school psychologist, who proceeded to want my son tested. I was very active in the school at the time as President of the PTO but I guess all my help in the school district and my knowledge of who's who wasn't any good. You see, the boy who headed up the attacks had a mom and dad in the district who were both teachers. But I did have the kid arrested and my son moved to another school district where he thrived and had tons of friends. He is successful now but has a constant habit of bragging about who he knows or what he knows and I feel it is because of this incident."

Other parents talked about the impact in terms of increasing their awareness and sensitivity toward those who are bullied. They talked about an increase in their levels of compassion for bullying victims. One parent said, "The experiences with my own child have heightened my awareness of the potential for harm associated with this kind of behavior and it has produced a different caution in my parenting as it relates to school and peer interactions."

HOW DOES CHILDHOOD BULLYING VICTIMIZATION AFFECT PARENTING?

"I believe that what I have seen of bullying has increased my awareness and sensitivity towards those who experience bullying and has created an increase in my compassion. As an adult, I have a heightened awareness of the potential harm associated with the behavior and caution in parenting as it relates to my children and their peer interactions."

Male, age 39

We met Beth in the chapter on decisions; she suffered rejection and exclusion by her friends that left her with many scars. Importantly, she did not fight back; she did not know how. When her son was going to start 6th grade, she decided to tell him her story in an attempt to help him figure out the concepts of true friendships and interpersonal respect. She worries that by telling him her story, she planted a seed about bullying and possibly about how to respond to it. He was bullied in middle school and he did not fight back. She wonders if she gave him that idea. Her son did the same thing that she did even though he had resources available to him in his parents. Beth desperately looked around for any support through her middle school ordeal, but did not find it anywhere—not even with her parents. Her son, though experiencing many of the same things, never turned to his parents. Beth found out later what he went through. Beth recalls thinking that even if an adult had known about her situation and told her she was okay, she would not have believed it. She felt she had evidence to the contrary. She couldn't be "okay", otherwise why was she being treated so poorly by her peers? Still, she feels badly that her son did not come to her when he was being bullied. She was prepared to be an advocate for him and often wonders what it means that he didn't.

One very dedicated mother, Cheryl, age 40, spoke of her fears after her daughter, Charlene, had witnessed bullying at school. She began to notice changes in her daughter's behavior, appetite, and sleep patterns. She was staying awake at night and started to complain of headaches. They went to the doctor for a check-up. While there, Charlene filled out a health questionnaire, which included the question, "Do you want any information on depression and suicide?" The doctor decided that Cheryl should discuss this at home with her daughter. She said, "That scared me; it was traumatic to hear that. I am very open with my kids, but I was scared. I stayed up all night. I found that I was constantly going to her bedroom to check on her." Finally Cheryl asked Charlene if she had a plan to kill herself or if she felt suicidal. Her daughter forthrightly answered, "It isn't me, Mom, it's a friend of mine." This mother experienced total relief until she realized that her daughter had not come to her with the burden she was carrying. She began to question the closeness and quality of the relationship with her daughter. All of a sudden she thought, maybe she's just saying that it is a friend but it's really her. They stayed up all night talking, and this resulted in an even stronger and more positive bond. It was traumatizing for Cheryl, however several good things have come out of this terrible experience. One: Charlene realized she could talk to her mother about anything; her mother was there for her. Two: Charlene and her mother promised each other not to keep secrets of this magnitude. Though her friend had made Charlene promise, she found out that this was not something she could handle by herself without adult assistance. Quickly, they talked to the bullied girl's mother and the girl started counseling. She also received medication for depression. Bullying can lead to suicidal thoughts. This young girl "didn't fit in" to the neighborhood and was picked on all of the time. I asked Cheryl if she thought this incident had affected her parenting. Her response was interesting. She said: "I was overprotective before, then I went overboard. I ended up sleeping with Charlene for many nights making sure she was okay. I became more protective because I wasn't sure how this was affecting her emotionally or how deeply. Was her friend still feeding her information that was affecting her? How was she managing? How much responsibility did she feel like she had?" Of course the friend felt betrayed when her mother was told. That is sometimes the price of saving a friend. Cheryl went on to say that she still looks for clues with her own daughter because the daughter is a caretaker and likes to solve problems for others. Cheryl also said it is important for people to know that if your child is involved with bullied, it affects the whole family. Everyone in the family made changes to monitor Charlene's behavior, to be cautious. The parents took shifts; when one was awake the other was asleep. She knows her daughter was angry because she thought there was no reason for doing this, but to this day, this incident still has a powerful emotional impact on Cheryl. She did not know, until she asked, that her daughter was struggling with such a profound issue—and the other mother had no clue that her daughter was actually suicidal.

Intergenerational Effects

We see another example of the effect on parenting offered by Grace, an extremely accomplished professional person. When she was young, she witnessed the impact of continual bullying on her brother. She related, "I am the oldest daughter of 5 children. My baby brother, Jeff, was born 6 years after me. Some of my earliest memories are of my other brothers' roughhousing in the living room. The middle brother, after having been wrestled to the ground by our eldest brother, would then try and grab Jeff to pull him into the fight. He would go limp, temper tantrum, and run into my mother's willing lap. This infuriated both brothers, who thought he was a spoiled brat." Two other family memories of importance stood out for Grace. Both demonstrate the emotional impact of bullying on Jeff as a child. Grace continued:

Purim is a Jewish holiday where children go to temple, dress up like Halloween, and basically run around the social hall. When directed, they play these loud harmonica-like instruments to drown out the name of the bad guy when his name is called. One Purim, when Jeff was 5, I was joyfully engaged with friends when I heard a blood curdling and desperate scream from somewhere far away in the social hall, and I knew it was my brother, Jeff. I ran to the noise and he was a decompensated mess, screaming and crying, curled into a fetal position with his hands over his face. The other children around him looked frightened and confused. The memory stands out for me, not because of Jeff's behavior, but because when I heard the scream, although I had never heard the scream before, I knew it was Jeff. I think now, no question, this was a reaction to the chaos and bullying at home by his brothers, and between my mother and father. It overwhelmed him. When Jeff was 8, he walked into my parent's bedroom one night and told them that he wanted to kill himself. My parents sent him to a psychiatrist twice a week (and Jeff has been in psychotherapy his entire life). One day I asked him what he talked about when he went to see Si (although that was not his name, it was short for psychiatrist and what my family called him). Jeff said, "I don't really talk to him about anything, I just go there and cry."

Jeff was bullied relentlessly in school. The ring leader was a boy named Damien. Damien lived four houses down from us with only his mother. Damien did and said awful things to Jeff, some of which I witnessed, some of which I heard about later from Jeff, and some of which I will never know. My parents and brothers always told Jeff to ignore him or to fight back, neither of which Jeff was capable of doing. My brothers sometimes tried to get Damien to stop, but it was halfhearted, since they sort of thought Jeff deserved it. I felt sorry for Jeff and tried really hard to be nice to him at home, as did my sister.

When I was 16, I got a summer job at McDonalds. One day, Damien came in to order something and stood in my line. When he reached me, I told him I was not going to take his order and made him go into another line. It was my first act of defiance and felt so incredibly empowering that I am convinced part of my professional identity was forged in that moment at the cash register. How did Jeff's experiences of bullying impact my parenting? I worried more than other mothers I was in direct contact with about my children's friendships. I was hypervigilant when I thought someone was being mean to my child and while sitting on a bench at a playground, watched hawkishly for danger from other children. I believe that it pained me so greatly to think about someone being mean to my children that I prevented some of them from actually sharing with me what they were really experiencing. I believe they did not think I could tolerate it and hold them when they needed support.

They have shared some of those experiences with me now and some will never be shared. Two of my children don't want to talk about middle and high school at all because it is too painful to remember. And we are a family who talks. I have one son who says now that he thinks we spent too much time talking about their experiences when they were living at home and should have spent more time talking about current events or politics. I was and am too worried and I acted in ways that are painful to re-experience. For example, when my oldest child was invited to a sleep over party by someone who had lots of friends, I was so overjoyed that I actually took him to the party (suitcase, sleeping bag, and all) a day early. When my 21-year-old son was left alone on New Year's Eve because the friend who was supposed to come over with a few of her friends, never texted him back, I actually said aloud, "I hope she has a good excuse, like that she was raped, or I will never allow her in my house again." Yes, these are not proud moments in my life but they are beyond doubt informed by my experiences with Damien. I see it all the time in my private practice. Adolescents are having horrendous experiences at school and in life, who are not sharing those experiences with their parents even though it seems as if, from an outside observer's perspective, the parents want to and are capable of offering emotional support to their hurting children. While I think, if I asked my young adult children now why they didn't share some of their experiences, they would find an excuse that had something to do with them, I blame Damien."

The impact on Grace's brother was obviously severe. It deeply affected Grace and filtered down to her children through her parenting. I have seen and heard of this same form of hypervigilance numerous times before, but it is not really known in the literature. Most of what is written to this point is about how much parents of bullied children know or do not know and why kids tell them or do not. Grace's story is a powerful indictment of childhood bullying and demonstrates the lasting intergenerational effects.

On Getting Help from a Parent

There is no question that parents can be helpful to a child who has been bullied and that the effects of parental support spill over as the child becomes an adult (Bowes et al., 2010). A'isha, age 24, shared that she was bullied but never felt the need to get any counseling for it. Why? Because of her parents. She said, "When I was sad, I went to my mother and I still do. Back then she told me 'those girls (who were bullying her), they just don't matter.' I would be worse off if I didn't have a strong family. My father was quietly helpful. That got me through. My relationship with my mother is wonderful. I can always count on her. For example, my last boyfriend drained the life out of me. If I'm acting like a fool, she'll tell me that too. I feel very secure because of them."

Chris, age 26, is very adamant that she could not have gotten through the bullying she endured without her parents. She considers them to be her best friends. They were her only support group during her school years; she had no friends. Talking with this very gregarious and lovely young woman, it is hard to image. Her bullying in elementary school was by both peers and teachers. She felt helpless, small, and intimidated. Her parents did everything in their power to intervene and change things for Chris. They were not really able to accomplish much in terms of any substantial change, but the warmth and support she received from her parents helped her overcome some of the toxic effects that bullying leaves behind by increasing her resilience. The research is very clear on this point: Parental support increases resilience in children (Bowes et al., 2010; Sapouna & Wolke, 2013). As an adult, she is a very determined young woman with numerous worthy goals and the personal fortitude and ability to reach them.

On Being a Parent After Being Bullied

"I am always asking my son questions to make sure he isn't being bullied."
Female, age 32

"I strive very hard to make sure that my kids don't bully others. Being a victim, I am sensitive to how it feels."
Male, age 42, African American

There are several consequences for those who were involved in bullying as they try to be good parents. One middle-aged man replied,

"The impact of bullying is very gradual especially if it gets established in elementary or junior high school. It's important for parents to know what's happening. It's a gradual impact. It affects everything about you. In terms of parenting, bullying has a profound effect on me. Being bullied and sexually harassed in high school made me look at what I valued: material things or people. I matured in my outlook. What I decided is that kindness is the most important thing to me. As an adult, I'm not shallow. I respect people who can't have the fanciest, trendiest clothes. I understand how they feel. I try to pass along this moral stance to my children. It is important to be kind. Being bullied taught me how not to be a mean person because I would never want anyone to feel like I did. I believe that what I have seen of bullying has increased my awareness and sensitivity towards those who experience bullying and has created an increase in my compassion. As an adult, I have a heightened awareness of the potential harm associated with the behavior and a caution in parenting as it relates to my children and their peer interactions. When I saw that people were cruel, I realized that I didn't like it and I didn't have to be that way in my life. Seeing the effects of bullying on my friends made me want to reach out to them to express sympathy. Today I am an empathic and sensitive person that others can come to with their problems. I think it started back with the bullying. It made me pretty morally conscious when it comes to talking about other people or any other kind of mean behavior. I try to pass this along to my children, and I hope I am."

A 43-year-old woman was bullied for about 3 years in grades 5 through 8. She was actively ostracized and excluded from the activities of the other girls. When I asked about how this may have affected any of her decisions she replied, "Yes, it affects me in how I raise my children. I want them to be kind and respectful. I want them to be protected from the kinds of experiences I had." As a result, her decision is to actively parent her children in a way that teaches them how to treat other people with kindness, consideration, and compassion.

Another woman shared about her involvement with bullying and how it affects her parenting now: "One of the worst aspects of getting bullied and ridiculed is that you end up so discouraged about yourself and your life. With my children I am very careful not to be discouraging but very motivating instead."

One 33-year-old African American father said:

"Because I was bullied, it is in the forefront of my mind. I'm very concerned about my kids and their educational settings. My wife and I talk about public versus private schools. I have a responsibility to shape who they are (my children) and I'm trusting the educational institution with my kids. There are certain settings in which kids are more prone to some damaging experiences than other settings. I think about how bad things can get at school for kids. It's hard for them to just be kids at school. I don't want to subject my kids to situations where bullying is amplified. My daughter has experienced racism at school and on the bus. I wasn't appreciative of the path the school took. They just said—'there's not anything we can really do.' Private schools tolerate problematic behavior a little less. There's a different approach that I've noticed. My son gives everyone the benefit of the doubt. He is a great kid. I don't want that tarnished by being the victim of bullying. I would like to avoid the 'you have to defend yourself' discussion with him. If he grows to be 6'4 or 6'5 he could really hurt someone someday."

Most parents who were involved in bullying had a heightened cognizance of their children's day-to-day activities at school. They were sure to ask questions about what is going on in their classes, on the bus, and with the other kids. They describe having an increased sensitivity and compassion due to the bullying they underwent when they were young. They believe that this has improved their parenting, not just in making sure that their children are not being subjected to bullying, but their sensitivity has enriched their parenting overall.

Parents Handling the Emotional Effects of Bullying

Of the participants in my study, 37% told their parents that they were bullied at school. Of that group, about half felt supported by their family whether or not the parent could do anything effective or not. The other half were met with a less than nurturing response. One example that stands out for its lack of compassion is shared by Shana. She was bullied throughout elementary and middle school. At the end of middle school, when she was feeling particularly low, she considered hurting herself. Her father found out about her solution and took her outside with a loaded shot gun. He showed her how to commit suicide by kneeling down, putting the gun under her chin, and pulling the trigger. He very forcefully told her that if that was the route she wanted to take she should do it right then and there. Fortunately, Shana did not follow her father's suggestion. Whether Shana's father behaved in this way out of ignorance or his own fears, we don't know. What we do know is that children who feel connected to and supported by close relationships with family members fare much better at overcoming bullying and developing a sense of resilience that lasts a lifetime (Bowes et al., 2010; Hong & Espelage, 2012; Levin, 2011; Resnick et al., 1997).

In my study, almost 40% were bullied at school in elementary and middle school, 22% were bullied in high school, while 25% reported they were bullied at home. As noted above, other studies demonstrate a correlation between being bullied at home and bullying at school. We might ask: Are kids set up to expect mistreatment from others if they are first mistreated at home? Are they desperately looking for someone to like them? If a child is bullied by his father, is he desperately searching for male friends and companionship? Similarly for girls and mothers? Or is the reverse more likely to be the case? On the other hand, when a child is bullied at school, some participants confided that they brought their anger home and visited it on their siblings and parents, thus effectively becoming a bully in the home.

Parents and caregivers are our first teachers. Siblings, too, model ways of behaving and of settling conflicts. They help or harm our psychological and social development. In terms of bullying, they can be bullies themselves. Parents can allow or fail to interrupt sibling bullying, or they can teach respectful family interactions and be a child's best advocate. All of these choices carry immediate and long-term consequences. When there has been psychological injury, people may forgive but they rarely forget. There are lifelong reverberations.

As we have noticed in this chapter, there are numerous ways that childhood bullying affects the family and then carries forward into adult thinking and behaviors. Being the victim of childhood bullying or even just having the awareness that it exists informs parenting practices for many of the people in this study. Sibling bullying is another important and often overlooked form of bullying with which children contend. The impacts are significant and need further study. In the next chapter, we look at what the participants of the study said about any unexpected outcomes of the bullying and harassment they experienced.

CHAPTER 10

Is There Anything Positive?

Unexpected Outcomes of Bullying and Harassment

"Thank you to the bullies and the coaches who taunted us, who rejected us . . . without you we never would have gone into comedy."

Steven Levitan, accepting the 2013 Emmy Award for Best Comedy
Program of the Year

It is only since the 1980s that mental health professionals have acknowledged the fact that trauma can result from abuse and violence other than that experienced in war or horrific circumstances (Barrett, 2010). Children can be traumatized from abuse, neglect, and from many forms of bullying. Victims of bullying score significantly higher on the Trauma Symptom Checklist for Children than those who have not been victimized (Nilsson, Gustafsson, & Svedin, 2012).

Trauma from childhood bullying can result in numerous adverse impacts in adulthood including psychotic symptomatology (Bentall, Wickham, Shevlin, & Varese., 2012; Cohen, 2011). While we know this to be true, I was interested in finding out whether anything positive could be the result of bullying and harassment, so I asked each of the participants in my study about this. Approximately 47% of adults reported what they considered to be a positive impact resulting from their own childhood bullying. I was frankly quite surprised at this finding. These are some of the positive effects participants mentioned:

- They had a greater sense of empathy for others.
- It enhanced their moral development; they made an internal commitment to never treat anyone as badly as they were treated.

- Being bullied provided an incentive for goal attainment; they wanted to "show" that they were okay.

Among the 47% who reported anything positive from being involved with bullying, the following categories were mentioned:

> Resiliency/Independence—14% said bullying made them "stronger," "more resilient," more "independent" (less dependent on the opinions or approval of others), more "self-reliant" and more "confident."
>
> Empathy—11% expressed a positive effect in that it increased their sense of empathy toward others.
>
> Moral Development—11% were certain it made them more "morally conscious" and helped them figure out how to treat others with respect.
>
> Goal Attainment—7% said bullying had affected them in a positive way toward goal attainment, toward specific professions, and wanting to "make something of myself."

A good example of this can be seen in the life of Erika Harold. When she was 16 years old she was bullied at school for being part African American and part Native American. Her peers talked about buying a gun to shoot her. As a result, she went from being an outgoing, high-achieving, happy teen to someone who was shy and reclusive. She no longer wanted to go to school, she stayed in her room as much as possible, and her grades plummeted. Her parents did not attribute this dramatic change to "normal adolescence." They took action, tried to address it with the school, and eventually moved her to a nearby high school, where she was not taunted or bullied any longer. She went on to become Miss America an advocate for children, and her platform addressed childhood bullying.

The concept that great growth can come from great pain is axiomatic in the early writings of Greek philosophers and in the teachings of some of the great religions such as Christianity, Buddhism, Islam, and Hinduism. Suffering can be transformative, for the positive or for the negative, depending on several factors associated with each individual. Are there positive outcomes from bullying? Especially when the bullying has resulted in trauma? When you ask children, "Is there anything good about bullying?" The universal response is "No!" But what about when that same question is posed to adults who have survived childhood (and sometimes college) peer or teacher mistreatment? I heard this kind of response numerous times from adults: "There was nothing good about it, it just created a lot of trauma in my life and hurt me a lot." But then there were the 47% who said there were some positives. We take a close look at this idea in this chapter.

POST-TRAUMATIC GROWTH

Although we tend to hear a great deal about post-traumatic stress disorder (PTSD) and its impacts on development, we hear less about post-traumatic growth. This is an interesting concept, the idea that you could grow as a result of trauma. We know that as human beings we are resilient, but how resilient and under what circumstances are still questions psychologists are trying to quantify. Researchers are investigating how resilience and growth from trauma can occur. People who experience trauma seem to fall into three categories: those who survive the trauma but do not quite return to their original baseline functioning, those who recover from the trauma, and those who actually grow and exceed prior functioning as a result of the trauma they have overcome (Bonanno, Galea, Bucciarelli, & Vlahov, 2007). Tedeschi and Calhoun (2004) discovered the following indicators of post-traumatic growth in adults who had overcome trauma:

A greater appreciation for life in general
A greater appreciation for relationships
A sense of increased personal strength
Changes in personal priorities
A richer spiritual life

Cognitive processing has also been suggested as an important element in the advancement of post-traumatic growth. In other words, how a person thinks about and contemplates events leads to ensuing feelings about what has happened. So if you survive what you consider to be a terrible event and your take on it is "Boy, am I lucky," you have a greater chance for post-traumatic growth than if you ruminate on "Why did this happen to me?"

Cognitive Growth

One man, age 36, was the target of bullying and he was also a bystander to bullying in his middle school. He was a member of band and, being bright, he was in accelerated classes throughout his educational years. The bullying that he received and that he witnessed had to do with his musical talent and his academic prowess. His comment on any positive aspect of bullying was: "You come to the realization that no one should ever generalize about anything. There are always multiple viewpoints on every matter." This is definitely a mature understanding to result from his experiences. Typically, one has to grow into this level of comprehension about why bullying may occur and how to use it for your own growth instead of keeping it as a resentment.

The post-traumatic growth studies discussed above are with adults—traumatic events that occurred when someone was already an adult. The resilience of children who have been traumatized as a result of bullying and sexual harassment by peers and school personnel is an important question. Recent research is probing the relationships among genes, environment, and resiliency to traumatic events in children (see Beaver, Mancini, DeLisi, & Vaughn 2011). An interesting study was conducted investigating the resiliency of identical twins who had been exposed to bullying at school and compared it to the amount of maternal warmth each received. Predictably, the twin who obtained the most warmth was found to be more resilient to bullying at school and demonstrated fewer post-bullying behavioral problems (Bowes, Maughan, Caspi, Moffitt, & Arseneault, 2010).

Resilience has been described as a positive disposition despite adverse circumstances. Resilience is also described as the capacity to keep moving forward in a positive way despite difficult conditions (Newman & Newman, 2014). We often hear the phrase, "Children are resilient." When I hear that, I think of the resilient quality of a rubber band. If you stretch it out of shape, it will snap back to its original shape. Children may indeed be resilient, but we need not fool ourselves that they can return to their original form and characteristics after they have been overly stressed. They do not. They make an adaptation to stressful events and interpersonal interactions in their lives. It is important to remember that some children are more resilient than others. Consequently whatever adaptations they do or do not make follow them into adulthood.

We consider those who have the tendency to cope with stress and adversity in a positive manner to be demonstrating resiliency. The field of psychology debates whether resilience is an individual trait or is acquired as a result of a process that a person undergoes. Bronfenbrenner (1979), one of the fathers of developmental and ecological psychology, stressed that children interact with their environment and it is the outcome of this interaction, along with their risk and protective factors, that produces resilience or not.

Resiliency in children and adolescents is influenced by a number of things. Here are a few:

1. genetic and neurobiological factors
2. environmental and developmental factors
3. an individual's bio-psycho-social-spiritual factors (Aisenberg & Herrenkohl, 2008; Beaver et al., 2011; Bowes et al., 2010; Feder, Nestler, & Charney, 2009)

Can children who have been bullied, hazed, and received other forms of harassment arrive at a positive outcome as a result of these experiences? Certainly there are those whose research supports the idea that there can be some positives associated with bullying for the bullies themselves. It appears that the dominance and sexual goals of bullies are promoted by their actions (Volk, Camilleri, Dane, & Marini, 2012).

In what other ways does resiliency fit with issues of bullying? Research on resiliency has found that the lack of adult involvement and caring signals weaker community bonds and is correlated with youth violence such as bullying, hazing, and harassment. At the same time, children who handle bullying "well" seem to have numerous protective factors. One is consistently positive peer support. This equals acceptance. Bullying is so damaging to a child because it means rejection and exclusion. Resilient children also have supportive adults in their lives either at school or at home, optimally in both places (Greeff & Van den Berg, 2013). They have a sense of some kind of connection to school. They have a sense of purpose, they engage in meaningful activities, and they feel a sense of empowerment to speak to adults. Last but not least, children who manage bullying with the best results employ individual cognitive mechanisms that enable them to "consider the source" of the harassment. In other words, they do not take to heart what is said or done to them because they tell themselves such things about the bully as "He's a loser," "He's going nowhere in life," or "She doesn't know what she's talking about" (deLara, 2008).

ARE THERE ANY POSITIVE CONSEQUENCES?

To this question many adults replied, "Bullying is simply bad. It's not cool and there is no positive outcome from it." One person said outright, "Nothing positive. I am very damaged." Other adults had intriguing responses to the question, "If you were bullied, please explain any positive consequences." For those who thought there were positives in their lives associated with bullying, a universal theme emerged. They believed you become more aware of other people's feelings, you are more sensitive to others, while at the same time becoming a bit tougher yourself. If you are lucky, you develop a "thick skin" to cope with it. You become stronger—eventually. And you are far less likely to act as a bully yourself. One middle-aged man said of his experiences, "Was there anything positive about being bullied for me? Sure. I learned to stop taking everything so seriously in life. I developed a tougher view and that's not always bad, since the world isn't always a friendly, perfect place. You figure out the realities of life and it teaches you a lot about human behavior." Another man in his mid-30s revealed,

> "My experience with being a victim of bullying has produced within me a real
> sensitivity to the fact that adolescence can be a very challenging period in an
> individual's life. In addition to that, I also strive to always be a 'present' audi-
> ence for young men and women as they share the obstacles and challenges of
> their lives. My professional goal is to be a motivational speaker for children
> and young adults with the hope of combating some of the damage that bully-
> ing and harassment has caused today's youth and young adults."

PROVING THEM WRONG: "I'M SOMEBODY"

A fair number of people in the study spoke English as a second or even third language. When they came to the United States, they were often teased and bullied mercilessly over their mispronunciations and misuse of words. Those who thought they had a positive outcome as a result of the bullying had a commitment to prove something. One woman from China described her determination to master English as rapidly as she could. She wanted to demonstrate that she was competent and capable and smart. When her English was flawed, kids called her stupid.

Even without having to conquer a new language, many who had been bullied for their differences wanted to excel to disprove all of the ugly things that had been said about them. "Loser" is a term that is used extensively, unfortunately, in our schools and in our culture. Kids who are bullied hear this hurled at them repeatedly. For some, the positive outcome is that they make an early decision to overcome this label by making a success of their lives. In other research I found that children who have high social-emotional intelligence can more readily rid themselves of the tyranny of nasty epithets through their own cognitive abilities (deLara, 2008).

There is a different outcome for children without high social-emotional intelligence and who may, instead, have come to view social interactions in a negative manner. Social exclusion and rejection can lead to violence and revenge. This is counterintuitive in that it would seem to make more sense to act in a socially acceptable manner to be included by others. However, there are many examples, such as in school shootings, where people who were shunned by their peers reacted with violence (Vossekuil, Reddy, & Fein, 2000). Some research attributes this kind of aggressive reaction to hostile attribution bias (DeWall, Twenge, Gitter, & Baumeister, 2009). In other words, how the excluded person interprets rejection is what contributes to his violent reaction. This is, at its basis, social cognitive theory. However, hostile attribution bias suggests that those who respond with violence to social rejection are prone to expect aggression in interactions with others, even interactions that others would judge as neutral. Consequently, these individuals' responses in many situations are biased toward aggression (see DeWall et al., 2009).

Hostile attribution bias is an explanation for the actual physical violence that may occur as a result of experiencing social rejection. But we may infer that hostile cognitions, or hostile thoughts toward peers who reject you, are natural. We do know that, as stated previously, some children and teenagers are able to prevent themselves from reacting aggressively by virtue of their level of moral development or social-emotional intelligence. What contributes to a high level of social-emotional intelligence? Children with high social-emotional intelligence have learned to develop good skills for self-management and self-control. Social-emotional learning also improves relationships at all levels of the school community and reduces conflict among students. Advocates for social-emotional learning (SEL), among them most schoolteachers, believe that high levels of SEL and intelligence contribute to many areas of success in adult life. While promoting positive academic and relational outcomes, SEL programs can actually help prevent bullying (casel.org, n.d.).

Fitting well with the idea of social-emotional intelligence is the theory of the "optimistic child" (Seligman, 2007). Martin Seligman has written a great deal over the years about how to build optimism and resilience in children. He carefully documents the difference in child outcomes between one who is pessimistic and one who is optimistic. His book *The Optimistic Child* specifically describes how parents, teachers, and coaches can help build this capacity in all children to help prevent depression and other poor outcomes. An optimistic person is one who is resilient and positive in the face of life's challenges. Perhaps this quality is present for adults who find something positive in their experiences of being bullied as children.

The adults in this research project who decided to take a positive approach moved purposefully in their lives toward accomplishments to show that the bullies were wrong. As adults they wanted to be able to declare, "I'm somebody. You were wrong about me."

SUCCESS

Notable luminaries have had to contend with bullying when they were young. One example is the enormously successful actor, Tom Cruise, born Thomas Cruise Mapother IV in Syracuse, New York, on July 3, 1962. He is best known for starring roles in *Top Gun*, and the Mission Impossible series. Tom Cruise was bullied at home by his father and bullied regularly in the 15 different schools he attended in 12 years. He was dyslexic and short. These qualities made him different and resulted in unwelcome attention. In one media interview about his early life, Cruise gave a graphic description:

> "So many times the big bully comes up, pushes me. Your heart's pounding, you sweat, and you feel like you're going to vomit. I'm not the biggest guy, I never liked hitting someone, but I know if I don't hit that guy hard he's going to pick on me all year. I go, 'You better fight.' I just laid it down. I don't like bullies."
>
> Boston.com, *2006; Mizell, 2006*

He has made a success of his life despite how badly he was treated as a kid. In the majority of his movies, he plays a tough and no-nonsense hero. I can't help wondering how his history of bullying plays a part in his interest and abilities in these kinds of roles. People who have been bullied often feel like they have a lot to overcome, a lot to prove to themselves and other people.

Others whom we consider extremely successful were also the targets of bullying when they were children. Even future presidents do not escape. President Barack Obama was bullied by classmates in school. In a White House Press Conference on bullying, President Obama shared, "I have to say that with big ears and the name that I have, I was not immune. I did not emerge unscathed." He was overweight as a child, and when he chose to keep his birth name instead of the name that his family used for him, Barry Soetoro, he was in for more abuse. The president concluded, "Sometimes we overlook the real damage that bullying can do, especially when young people face harassment day after day, week after week" (Warren, 2011). It is sobering to think that the president of the United States says of the impact of bullying that he "did not emerge unscathed." That is a remark to consider.

Former President Bill Clinton, too, was bullied as a child. He was overweight, a member of the band, and unpopular with the other kids. He discusses some of the incidents he endured in his autobiography, *My Life*. These are just a few examples of people with iconic status in our society who have made significant contributions despite their childhood backgrounds of bullying and harassment. There are many more examples that could be included. The people I interviewed might be considered "everyday people," and so I was interested in their will to succeed despite maltreatment by their peers.

Numerous people responded that being the target of bullying or any kind of harassment motivated them to succeed in life. One young man, age 28, said, "I was the target of sexual harassment at my school for years. It made me aware of other people's feelings and I became determined to succeed in life. I dedicated myself to school as a way to find self-satisfaction and feel good about myself. I decided to excel in sports and academics, and now I have a great career." Chris, a PhD student, confided that the bullying she experienced for so many years pushed her to become her best. She wanted to "show" all of her peers that she would succeed. She wanted everyone to know; she wanted to be on TV. They called her a "loser" for so long. She remembers thinking, even at a young age, "One day you'll know my name and I'll be famous."

MORALITY

Whether or not children engage in traditional bullying or cyberbullying is strongly related to their current level of moral development. Perren and Gutwiller-Helfenfinger (2013) approach their research from an integrative moral developmental perspective. They interviewed students between ages 12 and 19 and found cyberbullying was predicted by a lack of moral values and emotions. They also discovered that students who came up with morally disengaged justifications for their behaviors were more likely to engage in traditional bullying. Children tend to believe that anything that is not illegal is also not immoral. Stricter antibullying laws may help with this, but if we are to understand why kids bully, we have to understand both the systemic problems in the environment as well as the moral development of individuals and groups.

Gini, Pozzoli, and Hauser (2011) looked at differences in moral compe-tence in a large study of children ages 9 to 13 who were grouped as bullies, victims, and bystanders. They found that the bullies and bystanders had a higher level of moral competence than the victims. In other words, they were more competent at knowing that their behaviors were either right or wrong. Victims showed delayed development in the area of moral compe-tence. Although the study did not speculate about this, my opinion is that this confusion about whether the behavior directed at victims is right or wrong may have to do with the fact that victims begin to believe that it is something bad or offensive about themselves that draws peer mistreat-ment to them. The study further concluded that bullies showed deficits in moral compassion compared with both victims and bystanders and that this kind of deficit is reminiscent of what is seen in adult psychopaths.

In terms of moral stance, people can experience a sense of gratification that their tormentors are getting what they deserve in life, but they can also have a different reaction. When asked about any positive outcome of being bullied, hundreds of people in the study gave responses like these: "I'll never do the kinds of cruel things that were done to me." "I want to help others." "I have great empathy for others who feel ugly or different or flawed."

Jane, 37, was bullied relentlessly as a child when she was in elementary school. She came from a poor family, her clothes were not the latest style and often they were dirty. She can remember feeling sad, helpless, and ashamed even as a little child. When I asked her if there was anything posi-tive that she could think of that came from this bad treatment, she did not hesitate. She said, "Oh yes, I am self-conscious about my actions and how they affect others. I try to be kind so that I don't hurt anyone. I grew up watching kids get bullied and I tried to defend them. Mostly the kids who were bullied were considered different in some way. All of this had a big impact on me. I still defend people who are being bullied at my workplace."

Steven, 41, was the target of bullying in high school and also witnessed a fair amount of sexual harassment. His comments were,

"When I saw that people were cruel, I realized that I didn't like it and I didn't have to be that way in my life. Seeing the effects of bullying on my friends made me want to reach out to them to express sympathy. Today I am an empathic and sensitive person that others can come to with their problems. I think it started back with the bullying. Bullying made me pretty morally conscious, and as a result it has helped me to make the right decisions now when it comes to talking about people or any other kind of mean behavior."

As I listened, I was surprised to discover that person after person described a positive impact on their individual moral development. One young woman, age 25, reflected, "I was a relatively sensitive child, so it [being bullied] made me very aware of myself, others, and my environment; especially how I fit into the whole picture. Now as an adult, I understand it gave me a perspective that helped me to see the way people feel when they are teased or tormented. I made a decision to never do anything like that because I know how terrible it feels." Another woman, age 34, shared, "Being bullied and sexually harassed in high school made me look at what I valued: material things or people. As an adult, I'm not shallow. I respect people who can't have the fanciest, trendiest clothes. I understand how they feel. I matured in my outlook. What I decided is that kindness is the most important thing to me."

EDUCATORS CAN CONTRIBUTE TO THE PROBLEM

Those who become teachers enter a noble profession, and most uphold the sacred trust the public places in them. However, educator bullying and sexual harassment are a persistent problem in our schools. When children attend school, they look to teachers and other school personnel to protect them and serve as role models in the absence of their parents. Unfortunately adults at school can behave in ways that are as bad as or worse than the students (James et al., 2008; Shakeshaft, 2004). Of course this is a total abuse of their power. Stuart Twemlow, Fonagy, Sacco, and Brethour (2006) did a study of teachers' perceptions of bullying in their schools. Of the 116 teachers who participated from seven elementary schools, 45% admitted to bullying a child. For the purposes of their study, bullying was defined as using power to punish, manipulate, or disparage a student beyond what would be a reasonable disciplinary procedure. Similar to peer bullying, bullying by teachers or other school personnel serves to humiliate and degrade the child who is targeted. Research also indicates that the vast majority of school personnel who engage in bullying or harassment of children meet with no disciplinary action of any kind (McEvoy, 2005; Shakeshaft, 2004).

What is the result of this kind of educator abuse? What are the outcomes once a child, subjected to adult mistreatment at school, becomes an adult himself? Adam, age 37, shares his story:

When I was in middle and high school, I had two teachers who were masters at the art of bullying. They were also coaches. Sadly, both men also had an incredible bullying streak that bordered on sadism, as they were masters of selecting the weak from their classes and exposing them to vicious abuse. Both coaches had a similar technique for their bullying. Coach S., who taught Earth Science, would heap praise on the athletes in his classroom, and pick out the less popular or 'different' kids for abuse. His most common technique was to call out one student to come to the front of his classroom, usually twisting the student's last name in an unflattering and mocking way. Then he would stand up, adjust his belt and slowly walk over to the student, who would be standing in front of the class. Coach S. would then approach the student from behind, grip the student's neck with a big thick hand, and grab it like a mother dog would grab the scruff of a newborn puppy. He would slowly squeeze your neck from behind, while you attempted to maintain composure. Coach S. would then ask you some sort of class-related question. Whether you got it right or wrong, you were in for some physical abuse. If we answered his questions incorrectly, he would kick us in the behind and send us back to our seat. If we answered them right, we were spared the kick, and were allowed to return to our seat with just a sore neck. Day after day, this process would repeat itself. I think everyone in that classroom except Coach S. knew this bullying behavior was wrong, but we were smart enough to know we would only suffer worse consequences by complaining to anyone. We all knew, even at that young age, that Coach S. was at our school because of his football coaching skills, and sports trumped concerns over bullying, much like it does in most schools and universities.

Our sole resistance to his bullying was in small private groups. We would sit during lunch or break time discussing our frustration at how much of a jerk he was. We would curse him and wish him ill will, but we never brought our concerns to any higher authorities out of fear of reprisals. In hindsight, the lessons I learned from these middle school bullying events were more about survival than about fixing the problem. We learned how to behave in ways that would decrease our chances of being targeted. An example is seating in the classroom—the further away from the "center mass" of desks, the less chance he would see you and call you up to the front. We also jockeyed to be identified as friends with the popular athletic students, because Coach S. seemed to shield them from his abuse. He preyed on the weak and ostracized, so we did what we could to not be perceived that way.

When I went on to high school, I thought I had left behind this traumatic adult bullying. Coach S. was literally the first and only example of an adult bully I had experienced in my life up to that point, and I was willing to chalk it up as an aberration. But, lo and behold, I was quick to learn that while Coach S. was a junior varsity bully, my high school coach, Coach C., brought his bullying finesse to a higher level that incorporated overt racism, homophobia, and greater levels of public ridicule. Coach C. looked the part of the stereotypical high school gym coach; high and tight military haircut, whistle always at the ready, shorts and sports jacket, and a stern face that never seemed to express happiness. For reasons I do not know, he was extremely racist against Asian students, many of whom were recent immigrants and spoke little English. While I was never the primary target of his abuse (there were always plenty of Asian kids for him to pick on), I still got a regular peppering of Coach C. harassment. I was targeted because I dressed, acted, and identified with the "drama-fag"-"punk rock"-"weirdo" clan. While I did play sports, during the day I identified as a countercultural type, which Coach C. did not approve of.

I had developed a strong interest in leftist politics, and had developed a strong social justice conscience. I began to understand bullying as a means of oppression, and I decided to work to foster revolt and rebellion against those who perpetrated this tactic. Coach C. was an easy target for returning fire against his abuse. I was part of a small covert campaign against his polished reputation as a coach, highlighting his racism and bullying to fellow students and teachers who seemed willing to listen. I drew graffiti mocking him as a tin-pot Hitler-esque character. And on occasion, I would heckle him while he was harassing some poor unfortunate Asian student. I knew I would get flack for this from him, but I was quick on my feet in verbal sparring, had allies among the teaching cadre and administrators, and felt it was important to set an example of protest against his bullying.

Fortunately for everyone, the era of Coach C's bullying came to an abrupt end during my senior year. I was sitting in physics class when the news came over the loud speaker that Coach C. had dropped dead in the middle of gym class from a massive heart attack. I am not ashamed to say at that very moment, I looked at my fellow "weirdo" friends, and we all shared a big smile. We would have spontaneously cheered his demise, but discretion won out and instead we limited our relief to private smiles at the passing of a man who had bullied and mocked us for years.

Looking back on my experiences with bullying, I feel that the lessons they taught me are mostly positive. In the cases where I was the victim, I learned how to manage anxiety and angst, and frankly I feel that I am more resilient and street smart as a result. There is a saying that 'damaged people are dangerous because they know they can survive,' which I think fits the bill here. For me, my victimization through bullying was never severe, and as a result my scars were not so deep that they impaired me. To the contrary, they appear to have taught me good lessons and toughened me up for the future scars of life that inevitably occur as we walk through the minefield of life. Witnessing the bullying of others, and the strong emotion it engendered in me to support the victim and work to undermine the bully, planted a seed in my young mind that eventually grew into my strong commitment to social justice. I have worked many hours for many organizations locally, nationally, and internationally in support of social justice movements and campaigns. In many of the causes I was involved, one could say I was always fighting the bully, be it the United States bullying revolutionary Nicaragua, or chemical companies bullying poor minority neighborhoods in Baton Rouge, where I worked to help organize and demand environmental protections. Either way, Coach C. was the first bully I felt motivated to fight back against, and as a result was perhaps the first example of my decision to "fight the power." I can't say for certain that bullying is the sole reason for my left-leaning politics and two-decade history of social activism on behalf of the downtrodden, but it seems logical that it played a large part in my worldview development. The fact that I feel the same gut feeling that inspires my activism as I did witnessing bullying, and that I got the same satisfaction from leading various social justice organizations over the years as I did standing up to Coach C., makes me feel that there was at least a positive out-product of these negative experiences.

Adam describes what happened for him as "a traumatic example" of adult behavior. At the same time, in recounting his experiences, he is clearly able to see a positive outcome on his overall development and worldview. Adam is an example of resiliency in the face of difficult circumstances for a child. His willingness or propensity to fight back displays this positive aspect of his personality. While Adam does not directly talk about the negative impact of his encounters with these two teacher/coaches, and indeed concentrates his focus on the positive, we are left to wonder what, if any, negative consequences there were for him. Certainly for others there would be. Given the research and what has been presented previously in the book, we know what some of the consequences probably are for the children, now adults, who were more seriously targeted by the coaches. Among the immediate effects for children who are bullied by educators are skipping classes, missing school, and avoiding classes taught by those teachers.

In general, those who gained lessons contributing to their developing sense of morality confided that they learned how *not* to treat people. The distinctions between right and wrong conduct in interpersonal relationships became very obvious with this moral take-away. Far from imitating the same objectionable behavior, once adults, they decided to behave with tact and consideration for others—even toward those they did not particularly like.

IT MADE ME STRONG: "I CAN STAND UP FOR MYSELF WITH ANYBODY"

Though it was "rough at the time," many participants came to the conclusion as adults that the bullies were of little consequence and now they are stronger people as a result of the bullying. They said they were much less likely to be "walked over" because of what they suffered as children. Being bullied provided the impetus to want to be strong so that they would be able to protect the people they care about—family and friends. These are sentiments expressed about the idea of being assertive and strong:

> "I wish that kids hadn't made my life so miserable, but then I know that 'what doesn't kill you, makes you stronger.' So I guess that's true in my case."
>
> "I slowly began to realize, after being bullied by people older than me, that age is not a good reason to be intimidated by anybody. I began to stand up for myself and I see that this has continued into adulthood for me."
>
> "Once I learned how to deal with the confrontations, the experiences restored my sense of confidence to stand up for myself when provoked by other bullies."

Many of the respondents in the study said a positive outcome of bullying for them was that they learned how to deal with conflict and to deal with many kinds of people. One woman encapsulated what others said: "You learn how to be assertive, how to stand up for yourself with difficult people. You become a more mature person. You learn how to become more self-sufficient and less likely to let someone take advantage of you."

However, there seems to be a spectrum of responses that could be considered more or less positive. For instance, one woman in the study said: "I decided never to be friends with shallow people. You have to select and trust friends more carefully." Yet another person's comment was, "Yes, I think that I learned to be more independent and not to rely on anyone." In terms of healthy development and community participation, we would like to think that young people are learning to be interdependent, not that they are learning to rely solely on themselves. Another person who could be considered on the more-or-less positive outcome scale is A'isha, 24. In her interview she shared, "I'm not as naïve as I was. I'm more alert or aware of surroundings than I was before. Having a wall up can be a positive thing. I have to be sure I can trust people before letting them in."

When asked about any positive impact of being bullied, Lisa, 29, answered, "I had a wake-up call. Now I slow down my process in trusting people. I was overly naïve then. I believed in the goodness of everyone. Now, I believe it's ok to slowly share information about yourself. It's ok to gauge someone first. I see it as a blessing. Maybe you don't tell everyone about all sides of yourself, for example your spiritual side. First you have to determine if they will accept it or not."

Also along the continuum of more or less positive responses were these:

"After being the brunt of bullying for so long, I became tougher and now I have my guard up. I think this can be considered a good thing, a positive outcome."

"It made me tough and I realized my anger potential."

"It made me realize that I'm not going to get along with everyone and not get all disturbed if I get into a fight."

"I've learned to be suspicious of people who, at first, seem like they are your friend."

On the other hand, one person said, "I became tougher and I looked at the aspects of myself that people were ridiculing. I decided they were right and changed those things about myself. I improved myself. That's positive, isn't it?" Having a shield to protect themselves and being suspicious of people may not seem like a positive outcome of being bullied, but perhaps it is, especially for those who tend to share too much too soon. Having the courage to look at the things people were saying and changing those aspects is a remarkable response. I was impressed by the number of people who simply said, "The bullying I experienced made me who I am today: a strong person."

POSITIVES IN RELATIONSHIPS

Being bullied by males led to a thought-provoking outcome for one man, age 28. He commented, "I was bullied exclusively by my male peers. As a result, my friends were all female when I was in school. I got to know what they thought was important in a guy. So I think now I am more personal, attentive, and romantic in my relationships with women than other guys my age." While some people who were bullied tended to become more hesitant to seek out friendships, others described becoming more proactive in finding the "right" kinds of friends and groups to join.

These comments are other examples of how people have seen the silver lining in the mistreatment they received as a result of bullying:

"After middle school, the guy who used to bully me became my best friend. Now he is like my brother, and this has given me a sense of hope I carry with me today."

"Bullying gives you a reality check; people don't behave rationally. This is a good thing to learn young because you need it throughout your lifetime."

"I was judged harshly on my appearance when I was in secondary school. Now I am more aware of the physical differences between people and how most differences shouldn't be significant when you decide to be friends. So I've learned not to judge people on their looks."

INDEPENDENCE

Many people commented that being bullied or harassed made them into a more independent person, not wanting to rely on others. In our culture, we prize independence. However, we want people to stay within certain limits, for example not heading off to Montana to become the next unibomber. In my study, there were definitely those who talked about not trusting others, not allowing themselves to rely on anyone, staying distant, and keeping up a wall. This was a direct result of the bullying, sexual harassment, or hazing they experienced.

One man said, "Now I am an independent person. I had to move away from friends and peers who were constantly putting me down and calling me names. I also moved toward more independent and self-centered activities, like individual-type sports and hobbies. I don't discuss my decisions with anyone." We can see how being independent is valuable and also how it might be an impediment in intimate relationships where the partner is hoping for the kind of closeness that brings with it sharing of thoughts before making major decisions. Self-reliance and independence were two frequently mentioned outcomes of the incidents of bullying experienced as children.

SELF-ACCEPTANCE AND SELF-WORTH

Self-acceptance and a feeling of self-worth are two qualities that we hope people acquire as adults. The ability to mature into a true sense of self-acceptance may be seen as a fully positive outcome for some people who sustain bullying and harassment as kids. One man I interviewed commented, "As a result of being bullied, I began to appreciate that my differences from others made me unique. I stood out from others and I eventually saw this as a very good thing." Self-worth may be a characteristic that has to be developed over time for those who have been bullied and believed their tormentors. People discussed building a sense of self-worth and self-esteem, saying,

> "It took a while but I finally developed a greater sense of self-worth. I realized that I don't deserve to be treated poorly and I don't desire to treat other people poorly in order to make myself feel better. In retrospect, it's made me realize that despite the bullying I endured I have adjusted pretty well to adult life compared with others I know."
>
> "Although I have been affected by bullying, I have been able to work past a lot of my insecurities from those days. I view my progress now very positively."
>
> "At first it had an adverse effect on my self-concept, but now, I have regained a good self-esteem and the bullying I experienced helps me to deal with aggressive people."

A greater sense of empathy, enhanced moral development, and incentive for goal attainment were all outcomes discussed as something affirming from bullying. When I first engaged in this study, I did not anticipate hearing much in terms of what can be considered positive from the experiences of childhood bullying. Many participants surprised me. Their statements demonstrate a good deal of self-reflection and maturity. They exhibit post-traumatic growth. As we have seen, many other people do not come to this kind of resolution. To say that there are some positive outcomes as a result of childhood bullying is not to endorse bullying. On the whole, there appear to be many more negative outcomes than positive ones. The ability to come to a positive resolution after peer and sometimes educator mistreatment is a testament to many individual, family, and community factors. Growing into adulthood, resiliency, basic optimism, a supportive, nurturing family, and a community or organization that intervenes where there is bullying are all critical to the power to achieve a positive outcome from childhood bullying.

The last chapter briefly recaps of some of the themes in the book that we have investigated. It also discusses interventions that can be implemented to prevent childhood bullying and steps adults can take now to deal with the aftermath of bullying in their lives.

Conclusion

"The first principle of non-violent action is that of non-cooperation with everything humiliating."

Mahatma Gandhi

Though childhood sobriquets or so-called teasing may seem harmless, being a victim, a witness, a bully, or all of these can result in several detrimental outcomes for adults. Bullying feels like rejection to children and adolescents and has been described as "a psychological malignancy" (Rohner, 1975, 1986). Throughout the book, we have seen numerous examples that led to this kind of outcome. Disturbing memories of being involved with bullying and harassment came immediately to mind for participants as they described issues they contend with still. Their emotional and mental well-being is compromised as they struggle with various forms of anxiety and depression. Children who were bullied have grown up with a diminished sense of self. Their self-image and self-esteem are tarnished. As adults they have to work to try to achieve an accurate sense of self-worth.

It is important to be aware of the continued damage people take with them from childhood pain into many aspects of adult life and relationships. There are several areas in which damage can result. The decisions that are made in adult life after childhood bullying reflect the problems associated with self-esteem. Through the voices of those in the book, we heard about choices to misuse and abuse substances, to participate in violent activities, to cling to others or refrain from relationships altogether. The decision-making process of those involved in bullying is altered by their experiences of mistreatment. Interestingly, some decisions indicated growth in moral development. For example, people purposefully decided to treat others with respect. Decisions were made signifying the importance of being helpful to others. These decisions sometimes led to service-oriented careers.

Relationships with friends and intimate partners seem to bear the brunt of the impact of childhood bullying for those most affected. Trust in others is severely affected. Adults expect to be betrayed and, indeed, find themselves in relationships where that is exactly what happens. From a developmental and a systems perspective we would say that these adults are repeating patterns they know, they are repeating configurations they are "comfortable" with merely because they are the familiar.

BULLYING INCIDENCE

There are numerous studies on the incidence of bullying, however the data are competing. This is complicated by differing definitions used by researchers (Carbone-Lopez, Esbensen, & Brick, 2010) and by the fact that children may use a definition for bullying not adhered to by adults (Cheng, Chen, Ho, & Cheng, 2011; Cuadrado-Gordillo, 2011; deLara, 2008, 2012; Garbarino & deLara, 2002). This was elucidated in the first chapter. Calculating incidence trends is further compromised by children not reporting bullying when they are asked either in person or via survey (deLara, 2012; Mishna, 2005). In my research, 38.7% of the over 800 participants were bullied in elementary school, 39.8% were bullied in middle or junior high schools, and 22% were bullied in high school. A quarter of the participants said they were bullied at home. About 20% admitted to being a bully at some point in their school years. Also, 24% to 30% of the people in my study admitted to being *both* a bully and a victim, confirming the bully-victim-bully cycle and further confounding the definition debate.

BEING DIFFERENT

Being different in any way is the main reason that a child is selected for mistreatment (Annerback, Sahlqvist, & Wingren, 2014; Swearer, Turner, Givens, & Pollack, 2008). For example, adolescents prize conformity and therefore will bully someone who looks or behaves outside the norm (deLara, 2002; Garbarino & deLara, 2002). Even at the adult level, most organizations find orthodoxy important and will promote it (Scott, 1995).

Viewed from a systems theory perspective, conformity is useful for any organization or system because it enhances predictability of behavior. It is a component of the homeostasis or balance of the system (deLara, 2002; Von Bertalanffy, 1973).

The participants in the study spoke eloquently of their experiences with bullying as a result of some sort of difference from others—or perceived difference—and also discussed the lifelong impacts. The differences may seem minute or unworthy of consideration to most adults, but being discriminated against as a child is a very powerful experience. Childhood bullying can be as a result of being too tall, too short, too fat, too thin, too white, too black. A child may cry easily. And these bullying incidents can be perpetrated by adults on children, not just by one peer on another. Those subjected to bullying by people with authority over them, such as parents or teachers, may suffer with issues of authority for their entire lives. They may find it difficult to trust bosses or others holding power (see Johnson, 2011).

BULLYING IMPACT IN ADULTHOOD

Of those bullied as children, 63% said they noticed an impact in their adult lives. The consequences were in various areas but included their personal sense of well-being, their relationships to others, and their decisions. This finding is similar to that of Schafer et al. (2004), who found that self-esteem and relationship quality in adult life suffered as a result of childhood bullying victimization. Interestingly, among those in my study who were *not* bullied as children, fully 42% of those who witnessed bullying in elementary and middle school and 53% of those who did in high school claimed an impact in their lives now just as a result of observing acts of violence and torment against other children. My research indicates those consequences seem to be in the area of moral development and decisions about how to treat other people.

GENDER TRENDS

As Children

Over the last several years, research trends have held steady regarding bullying and gender. Boys tend to be involved in physical bullying more often than girls, and girls tend to be indicated in relational bullying more often than boys (Carbone-Lopez, Esbensen, & Brick, 2010). However, although these trends and tendencies exist, both boys and girls participate in all forms of bullying. Consequently, the impacts from all forms show up in adulthood for both men and women (Sourander et al., 2007; Sourander et al., 2009). I have seen this trend in my research as well, particularly the fact that boys will engage in relational aggression and girls will participate in physical bullying. However, all types of bullying were recounted by both men and women. Without identifying a specific type of bullying, the following statistics represent the experiences of those in my study:

Were You Bullied in Elementary School?
40.8% of boys and 38% of girls
Were You Bullied in Middle or Junior High School?
48.2% of boys and 37.5% of girls
Were You Bullied in High School?
21.1% of boys and 22.1% of girls
Were You Bullied at Home?
24% of boys and 25.3% of girls

As Adults

On the question of general impact from childhood bullying, male respondents claimed they experienced impact in their adult lives about as frequently as females. There was no statistically significant difference between them on this score. In survey information and in discussions, men and women appeared to face the same issues in relationships, decision-making, and basic self-concept. On the question of the impact on decisions, there was no statistically significant difference between men and women. Similarly, on the question of positive consequences as a result of bullying, there was no statistically significant difference seen. A significant difference did show up in response to the question, "Do you see an impact on your relationships?" Male respondents were much less likely to experience this or to see an impact, compared with females in the study (30% v. 40%).

HEALTH AND MENTAL HEALTH

There were consequences in terms of health and mental health for those who were victimized as children. Among them were eating disorders, anxiety disorders, and depression. There were those whose lives were changed forever due to acting-out and violence. For some, substance use was an outcome that carried over to abuse in adult life. Other research finds long-term impacts on health and mental health for those bullied as children (Biebl, DiLalla, Davis, Lynch, & Shinn, 2011; Copeland, Wolke, Lereya, Shanahan, Worthman, & Costello, 2014; Monsvold, Bendixen, Hagen, & Helvik, 2011; Teicher, Samson, Sheu, Polcari, & McGreenery, 2010). There are a number of studies indicating a correlation between bullying victim-ization and anxiety in adults (Gladstone, Parker, & Malhi, 2006; Schafer et al., 2004; Sourander et al., 2007). There is also a significant correla-tion between bullying, depression, violence, and substance use (Copeland, Wolke, Angold, & Costello, 2013; Kim, Catalano, Haggerty, & Abbott, 2011; Renda, Vassallo, & Edwards, 2011). As we have seen, bullying and harassment are psychological malignancies in a variety of ways. Survivors in my study experience anxiety and depression, substance misuse prob-lems, and self-image issues that haunt them from the time they were first subjected to bullying into adulthood.

CONSEQUENCES IN RELATIONSHIPS

Adults were divided in terms of consequences in relationships per se. Of the respondents, 35.6% claimed no consequences in their relationships, while 37.6% responded saying there were definite effects. The other par-ticipants did not choose to answer the question. Interesting trends were present. On the survey data, women did indicate a greater impact on their relationships than men, however in focus groups and individual interviews no significant difference was seen. This may be due to the fact that once engaged in a verbal interview, people have the chance to think through an issue in greater depth. Those affected by bullying described difficulty in friendship and intimate partner relationships. They cited problems trusting others, expecting betrayal, wanting to be accepted, and becom-ing "people-pleasers" to have or keep someone in relationship with them. This resulted in what they deemed a lack of genuineness in relating. Other research does find consequences in adult relationships similar to my own findings. These include problems with trust, problems with attachment, and issues of insecurity in friendships and intimate relationships (Schafer et al., 2004). Other studies also find bullying leads to social and emotional problems in adult relationships (Almquist & Brännström, 2014; Boulton, 2013; Jantzer, Hoover, & Narloch, 2006). So far, we have seen that there are consequences in adult relationships for those involved with bullying as children. Still further research is indicated in this important area.

SEXUAL HARASSMENT

The 2011 study by the American Association of University Women reported an incidence of about 50% of both boys and girls involved with sexual harassment by peers (Hill & Kearl, 2011). During my focus groups and individual interviews, almost half of all participants reported encountering sexual harassment in childhood or adolescence as victims or bystanders. Those who did described significant impacts on their self-esteem and development. It is important to note some studies find more adverse health outcomes from sexual harassment than from any other form of bullying (Gruber & Fineran, 2008; Keeshin, Cronholm, & Strawn, 2012). In the focus groups and individual interviews, more women than men admitted to being sexually harassed. Typically, sexual harassment is a cultural construct that we most often apply to the lives of women and girls. One important question might be asked: How many men consider any or all of the sexual encounters they endure, such as games of "sac-tapping," to be sexual harassment?

EFFECT ON DECISIONS

When asked about adult decision-making, 41.6% said being bullied affected their decisions now, while 31.7% saw no effect on their decisions as adults. The other participants did not respond to this question. As stated earlier, I found no statistically significant difference between men and women on this score. An example of an effect on decision-making can be seen in the ongoing struggle with low self-esteem and confidence that promotes decisions to stay in unhealthy relationships. People conclude, "Who else will want me?" Other consequences on decision-making are in the realm of jobs or professions to pursue and extending trust in friendships. The impact or consequences on adult decision-making as a result of childhood bullying is an area in need of further research.

IMPACT ON FAMILIES

A quarter of those in the study said they were targets of bullying in their own homes. All types of bullying were mentioned, including verbal abuse, sexual harassment, and physical abuse. There can be a considerable impact for families when children are bullied at home or at school. In earlier chapters, we read about those who were bullied at school who then brought their rage home to visit upon family members. We have read accounts of children who were bullied at home and also bullied at school. Perhaps children accept peer mistreatment because they come to expect being treated disrespectfully in all environments. The impact can even extend intergenerationally as adults come to terms with what has happened to them or as they attempt to protect their own children from peer mistreatment. Some parents become overly zealous and cautious in their parenting approach. Parents who have witnessed or participated in bullying in any way feel an intense need to shelter their children from any similar harm.

Being bullied by a sibling leaves its own brand of injuries. While sometimes a sibling can be supportive, other times siblings torment one another, saying and doing the worst they can think of at the time. This kind of behavior flourishes in families where parents don't expect anything different and don't intervene to stop it. In most systems, adults believe kids will be kids and this means treating each other badly at times. The end result in this family is that children, even when they are grown, believe that sibling bullying is just the way it is—an acceptable form of interaction. Of course this sets the stage for later interpersonal adult relationships and behavior. People learn as children how to act, either with respect toward everyone or not. Some families cultivate respectful behaviors by example, by family rules, and by interrupting poor behavior. Other families do not see this as a priority; they do not know the consequences for the future of their children's relationships with one another or of their children's sense of themselves in the world as adults.

Sibling bullying is a form of peer bullying and should be considered as such. Long-lasting effects from sibling bullying include mistrust in significant relationships in adulthood and a permanent disruption in the sibling relationship. Further, when siblings bully one another this becomes an acceptable, learned behavior that is then carried over to adult interactions with same-age intimates. Bullying has been learned as the means to negotiate interpersonal interactions.

For many, the passage of time seems to take care of the effects of bullying in the family. However, for others, the bullying and/or harassment were too severe or too chronic and have left too many unresolved remnants. Relating as an adult is strained, at best, or even impossible. If family members want to come to a resolution so they can move forward, family therapy is recommended. In this case, it is imperative to find a mental health practitioner who is trained as a family systems therapist. That person will have a true understanding of how family systems work and the dynamics that helped to support the bullying that took place. Without a systems-trained person, there is a danger that one member of the family will be blamed for all of the bullying that took place. He or she will be scapegoated and will be victimized again. That would not be a therapeutic outcome.

UNEXPECTED OR POSITIVE OUTCOMES

In my research, 47.2% of all adults reported what they described as a positive impact resulting from childhood bullying, while 17.5% said there were no positive effects. The rest were unsure or did not answer the question. This means that though struggling to deal with the aftermath, almost half were able to not only overcome some of the poor influences of bullying but also find something positive. This finding contrasts sharply with research on children and bullying. When children and teens are asked, "Is there anything positive about bullying?", they universally reply, "No." However, the adult responses from my study are in line with research findings on post-traumatic growth (Calhoun & Tedeschi, 2014; Tedeschi & Calhoun, 2004).

ADULT POST-BULLYING SYNDROME

At this point in our history, no one contends that post-traumatic stress exists. Much is known about its etiology, its symptoms, and its poor outcomes. However, for hundreds of years those suffering with PTSD faced ridicule. They were considered mentally weak or cowardly for what were normal reactions and behavior after experiencing trauma. The trauma of war is the best-known example.

The noted developmental psychologist Bessel Van der Kolk (2005) has written about post-traumatic stress disorder:

> The PTSD diagnosis does not capture the developmental effects of childhood trauma: the complex disruptions of affect regulation; the disturbed attachment patterns; the rapid behavioral regressions and shifts in emotional states; the loss of autonomous strivings; the aggressive behavior against self and others; the failure to achieve developmental competencies; the loss of bodily regulation in the areas of sleep, food, and self-care; the altered schemas of the world; the anticipatory behavior and traumatic expectations; the multiple somatic problems, from gastrointestinal distress to headaches; the apparent lack of awareness of danger and resulting self-endangering behaviors; the self-hatred and self-blame; and the chronic feelings of ineffectiveness. (p. 406)

This diagnosis may not capture the effects on development of trauma in childhood, but Van der Kolk's assessment does describe many of the elements and impacts on development that are common for those suffering from adult post-bullying syndrome (APBS) brought on by the traumas they experienced in childhood. It is evident from their stories that people live with and experience APBS. They demonstrate the indicators of this syndrome as outlined in the chapter describing it. While APBS does not tend to be associated with threats of death or serious harm as PTSD does, there are some instances in which a person does experience death threats and serious harm as a component of the bullying they endure. Researchers are beginning to uncover the extent of the impact of bullying into adulthood. Its trauma cannot and should not be written off as weakness as we once did with PTSD. It needs to be fully recognized for what it is: Adult Post-Bullying Syndrome. Some people who encounter childhood bullying will end up with this syndrome. They need understanding, not scorn. The consequences need consideration, not disregard. In some cases, people with APBS will need to and want to seek professional help to overcome traumatic memories and their effects. We have seen all too clearly how these memories can cripple. It is essential for mental health practitioners to increase their awareness of the aftereffects of bullying in people's lives and to become aware that there are ongoing consequences. The first place to start is by asking clients about any bullying they experienced as children. This question is not commonly asked by health or mental health providers at this time. It needs to be. We don't tend to ask children and we don't ask adults. From their responses, practitioners can formulate a treatment plan that will address the issues raised by a client or a family. As adults report depression and anxiety stemming from childhood bullying, medication may be indicated in some cases. Typically for anxiety and depression that impair, research demonstrates that the most effective treatment is a combination of some form of psychotherapy along with appropriate medications (Young, Klap, Sherbourne, & Wells, 2001).

WHAT CAN BE DONE?

Adults in the study commented that passive kids are targeted for bullying. I often heard the suggestion that children should be taught to be assertive, not aggressive, and that martial arts programs could be beneficial for children who lack confidence and do not know how to stand up for themselves. While some schools do offer martial arts classes (see Twemlow et al., 2008), there are recognized intervention strategies that can be employed in the school setting. Where bullying has become established in a school, a systemic approach to interrupt or decrease incidents is required.

Programs Meeting with Some Success and Using a Systemic Approach

The Olweus Bullying Prevention Program is a whole-school approach for children grades K-12 and has the greatest research base of all programs currently in use. It has been found to reduce bullying among children, improve the social climate of classrooms, and reduce antisocial behaviors (Olweus & Limber, 2010). For more information on how this program is implemented in the schools and possible difficulties, please consult Espelage, (2013), Olweus (2007).

Steps to Respect provides training about bullying to the full staff of the school including bus drivers, teachers, and cafeteria workers. It is aimed at grades K-8. Its results demonstrate a decrease in bullying behaviors, an increase in bystander interventions, and an overall increase in positive school climate (Brown, Low, Smith, & Haggerty, 2011; Committee for Children, 2015).

PeaceBuilders is a K-12 program that includes students, staff, and parents. The values of the program include praising others, giving up the use of put-downs, encouragement to seek wise people when you are faced with an interpersonal dilemma, noticing if someone is hurt, righting wrongs, and helping others. Results have shown decreased aggression and increased social competence (Vazsonyi, Belliston, & Flannery, 2004).

The *Resolving Conflicts Creatively Program* is research-based and intended for K-12 students. It is focused on social-emotional learning and is one of the longest-running programs in the United States on conflict resolution. It attempts to create caring environments, and the program's strategies are continuous over several years (De Jong, 1993; Selfridge, 2004).

KiVa is an evidence-based program originating in Finland and now being used globally. It is demonstrating good results in curbing bullying in school settings. KiVa is effective because it takes a systemic perspective involving the students, counselors, teachers, and parents. Along with intensive training of adults as well as students, the program accounts for the need for reconciliation between those who have been involved in a disrespectful encounter.

Restorative Justice programs are based on the premise that bullies and victims need to enter into reconciliation to prevent future bullying and to enhance a safe school environment. It focuses on the impact of interpersonal actions and the associated shame (Ahmed & Braithwaite, 2012). Restorative justice supports the idea of engaging multiple stakeholders in the school over the long term to build a positive community atmosphere (Wong, Cheng, Ngan, & Ma, 2011).

In general, readers are encouraged to review the work of Maria Ttofi and David P. Farrington on bullying prevention programs and their impact on reduction, shame, and later criminal offending. Further, Peter K. Smith's book *Understanding School Bullying: Its Nature and Prevention Strategies* (2014) provides some invaluable information.

Programs Showing Promise

Roots of Empathy is a program that helps very young elementary school children build empathy for others and social-emotional competence by using a developmental approach. Children become acquainted with an infant who visits their classroom on a regular basis over a substantial period of time. The children begin to understand the baby's growing strengths and limitations. In this way, they start to develop a sense of empathy and compassion for another person (Schonert-Reichl, Smith, Zaidman-Zait, & Hertzman, 2012). Growing empathy for others is thought to be an important aspect of moral development and a stepping-stone in bullying reduction.

The goal of *CASEL (Collaborative for Academic, Social, and Emotional Learning)* is to make social-emotional learning a critical part of education for children from preschool through high school. As mentioned earlier, promoting social-emotional intelligence is one way that schools and organizations can address respectful behavior among children. Emotional intelligence was a concept first developed by psychologists John Mayer and Peter Salovey. The idea was elucidated by psychologist Daniel Goleman (1996, 2006). He wrote, further, on social intelligence. Social-emotional intelligence then is the combination of these ideas. It describes how we deal with our impulses and our abilities to succeed in interpersonal relationships. Social intelligence and emotional intelligence are concepts beyond what we think of as a person's IQ. Children with high social-emotional IQs seem to have a built-in barrier against the ravages of bullying. They exercise certain cognitive-behavioral strategies that assist them when they are bullied by their peers (deLara, 2008). They say such things to themselves as, "They don't know who I am." "He's [the bully] going nowhere." "I'm going to make something of my life. For them, high school is all they have." These cognitions or inner speech serve to keep a child's dignity and a sense of self intact. Fortunately, social-emotional intelligence and cognitive-behavioral strategies can be taught. At this point, some schools have classes that focus on building a child's social-emotional IQ. To learn more about this, visit the Collaborative for Academic, Social and Emotional Learning at http://www.casel.org/. The website states, "Social and emotional learning (SEL) is the process through which children and adults acquire and effectively apply the knowledge, attitudes and skills necessary to understand and manage emotions, set and achieve positive goals, feel and show empathy for others, establish and maintain positive relationships, and make responsible decisions" (CASEL).

Programs that are helpful specifically for lesbian, gay, bisexual, transgender, and queer or questioning (LGBTQ) students are the *Gay-Straight Alliance*, a program bringing gay and heterosexual students together in schools to support one another, and *GLSEN*, the Gay, Lesbian, Straight Education Network. Another organization specifically for the support, education, and advocacy of gay children and adults is *PFLAG*, the largest of its kind in the country uniting parents, families, friends, and allies of lesbian, gay, bisexual, queer, and transgender people.

TREATMENT: ADULTS COPING WITH THE AFTERMATH OF CHILDHOOD BULLYING

What we have seen from the stories presented is that many of those affected by bullying have to build or rebuild a basic sense of self. Their self-esteem and self-worth have been severely diminished. Much effort, as an adult, goes into claiming an individual sense of dignity. Further, childhood maltreatment, including bullying, changes the brain (Edmiston et al., 2011). It impacts development and influences all aspects of a person's behavior in relationships. Schor reminds us that "the concept of trauma . . . is by definition psychobiological" and is "a bridge between the domains of both mind and body" (2003, p. 109). Schor indicates further that when children are exposed to stress early in life, this produces neurobiological changes that continue through adulthood. These changes can manifest as a dysregulation in the brain's "fight or flight" centers—one being intense rage, one expressing as intense terror. Anyone, child or adult, struggling to get past the damage done by others can seek help from mental health professionals trained in cognitive therapy or cognitive-behavioral therapy (CBT). Both are effective in terms of establishing a new, more helpful, and more appropriate way of thinking about themselves and past events

(Beck, 1979; Beck, Rush, Shaw, & Emery, 1979). Without treatment or at least some insight into residual pain, adults and children may lash out against others or turn the pain inward in the form of poor treatment toward themselves. A practitioner trained in trauma treatment is essential. There are several ways to approach the treatment of the anxiety, depression, or trauma associated with bullying. It is important to look for interventions that are evidence-based in terms of their effectiveness. The cognitive-behavioral therapies have proven efficacy (Courtois & Ford, 2009; Silverman et al., 2008). This holds true for a wide range of ages and with different populations of people. Cognitive-behavioral therapy is beneficial because it addresses the thoughts or cognitions that a person is telling him or herself. It exposes the essential elements that are continuing to support a negative self-image and works to change that. A very specific form of CBT for anxiety, depression, and trauma is trauma-focused cognitive-behavioral therapy (TF-CBT) (Foa, Keane, Friedman, & Cohen, 2008; Silverman et al., 2008). A hybrid model for treating trauma, TF-CBT integrates cognitive-behavior principles, family therapy, empowerment therapy, attachment therapy, humanistic therapy, trauma sensitive interventions, and knowledge of developmental neurobiology. Consequently it addresses cognitive problems, relationships problems, family problems, difficulty with affect, somatic concerns, and behavior problems stemming from trauma (Mannarino, Cohen, & Deblinger, 2014). Another form of CBT to address these concerns is mindfulness-based CBT. Popularized by Jon Kabat-Zinn for stress reduction and positive well-being, it is based on conscious mindful awareness (Davidson et al., 2003; Evans et al., 2008; Kabat-Zinn & Hahn, 2009; Segal, Williams, & Teasdale, 2012). Victims with severe trauma alter their awareness and consciousness to make trauma more tolerable. Consequently, to minimize the possibility of retraumatization, a phase-oriented approach is suggested in clinical practice for addressing the effects of trauma, including when PTSD has been diagnosed (Cloitre et al., 2011; Leenarts, Diehle, Doreleijers, Jansma, & Lindauer, 2013; Resick, Suvak, Johnides, Mitchell, & Iverson, 2012). For clinicians looking to determine whether a client is, indeed, experiencing PTSD, the PTSD Checklist—Civilian Version (PCL-C) is an effective tool. It can be completed by a client prior to any session and should take no more than 10 minutes (Weathers, Litz, Herman, Huska, & Keane, 1991). The interpretation of the checklist is completed by the clinician, but it provides a vehicle for discussion with the client once this has been done (Weathers et al., 1991).

Developed by Francine Shapiro (1998, 2013), eye movement desensitization and reprocessing (EMDR) therapy uses proven methods to reduce the emotions surrounding traumatic memories. As a result, this is a very effective therapy to consider for those enduring the pain of past events including bullying (Forbes et al., 2007). It is critical, however, to find a practitioner who has had this specialized training.

There are other evidence-based treatments for those who have been exposed to trauma and violence including multidimensional family therapy and multisystemic family therapy. Multidimensional family therapy is a developmentally focused therapy targeting violence and delinquency with the goal of promoting successful adolescent and family growth. This family therapy is successful with children and adults from diverse ethnic, racial, and socioeconomic groups (Liddle, 2010; Rowe & Liddle, 2008). Multisystemic family therapy is a blend of cognitive-behavioral therapy, behavior management training, family therapies, and community psychology. Its strength is that it acknowledges that families, communities, friends, and schools all impact a child. From that perspective, practitioners of multisystemic family therapy aid children and families with the traumas they have experienced (Carr, 2000, 2009; Stratton, 2011).

The collaborative change model (CCM) (Barrett & Stone Fish, 2014) is a clinically evaluated model that helps individuals and families move from traumatic mind-states to a hopeful and meaningful vision of the future. The model has three stages that eventuate in individuals acting from engaged states of mind to regulate their affect, cognitions, behaviors, and relationships. Clients in this model are active members of their treatment as their strengths and resources are integrated into the creation of the interventions that will help them recover. The model was developed from many years of working with individuals and families who experienced complex trauma. In this case, complex trauma is defined as "a pervasive mindset that often develops from historical and ongoing relationships of abuse, neglect, and violation." Aspects of trauma resilience and mindfulness are incorporated into this effective intervention.

POST-TRAUMATIC GROWTH AND RESILIENCY

Researchers have been writing about the possibilities of individual growth after trauma for over 20 years (Calhoun & Tedeschi, 1998; Tedeschi & Calhoun, 1995). It is evident that there can be growth for some individuals after a traumatic event. Bonanno, Galea, Bucciarelli, and Vlahov (2007) found that for a portion of those exposed to trauma, the aftereffects included post-traumatic growth. Their growth was measured to exceed their prior functioning. Others recovered to their previous baseline of functioning, while still others were categorized as being in the merely surviving group. They did not return to normal functioning after the traumatic event. Certainly people who have experienced trauma and loss can be encouraged through various community-based interventions and through therapy to find a portion of resiliency (Boss, 2006). Resilience is a construct attributed to the "positive psychology" field. Resilience "focuses on identifying strengths ... rather than weaknesses ... and is generally considered a multidimensional construct consisting of behaviors, thoughts, and actions, which can be learned overtime" (White, Driver, & Warren, 2008, p. 9). Further, there is some research that depicts neural changes in the brain reflecting resilience to trauma (Feder, Nestler, & Charney, 2009). Consequently, one means of growing after trauma is to increase resiliency, which can be accomplished with the help of practitioners who are trained to identify strengths and positives in individuals and families. Clinicians should review Calhoun and Tedeschi's book (2014) for numerous chapters on clinical applications in this area.

ALTERNATIVE TREATMENTS

As we have seen, bullying and other forms of maltreatment of children have been linked to the development of poor health and mental health outcomes including psychosis in adult life (Allison, Roeger, & Reinfeld-Kirkman, 2009; Bebbington, 2011; Cohen, 2011; Wolke, Copeland, Angold, & Costello, 2013). The fear response in the brain of a maltreated child is under constant stimulation. This means that other regions of the brain, such as those for complex thought, are less activated. The brain becomes focused on survival at the expense of other aspects of healthy development. Additionally, there is a permanent alteration in the brain's use of serotonin, a chemical needed to promote a sense of well-being (Healy, 2004; Perry, 2009). Other research demonstrates changes in the brain's hypothalamic-pituitary-adrenal (HPA) axis that result from bullying (see Cicchetti & Rogosch; Vaillancourt et al., 2008). Chronic stress or repeated traumas can result in a number of biological reactions, including a persistent fear state (Perry, 2009). In other words, the brain learns to be on the lookout and fearful. Consequently because the brain sustains substantial changes, employing alternative therapies such as yoga, mindfulness, acupuncture, and massage can be effective in quieting the autonomic nervous system (Agelink et al., 2003; Diego & Field, 2009; Streeter, Gerbarg, Saper, Ciraulo, & Brown, 2012). Trauma is jarring to the nervous system. Trauma throws us off, out of balance. After experiencing trauma, people need to do a variety of things to reset their nervous systems to try to feel okay. Some people seem to have instinctual abilities along these lines. They "shake it off" figuratively or literally, as singer Taylor Swift enjoins. However, when the nervous system is overwhelmed or overloaded from trauma, a somatic experiencing (SE) practitioner can help restore equilibrium. According to the theory behind SE, trauma can result from a wide variety of stressors and its symptoms are a result of dysregulation of the autonomic nervous system. However, an event does not cause trauma per se. The theory behind SE postulates trauma is the outgrowth of an inability of the body, the mind, and the nervous system to deal with adverse occurrences (Levine, 2010).

An interesting new study finds that painful memories may be dissipated or changed during sleep. In an experiment conducted at Northwestern University, volunteers were shown a face connected with an unpleasant odor then paired with a shock. The volunteers learned to anticipate the shock when they encountered the face and odor again. Then during a nap, the volunteers experienced the odor again but without the shock. After they woke up, they no longer associated the face–odor combination with anticipating a shock. It appears that as a result of the aromatherapy, neural changes had occurred in the hippocampus and the amygdala. They had overridden the bad memory. Brain scans revealed these changes had indeed occurred (Hauner, Howard, Zelano, & Gottfried, 2013). While this is similar to exposure therapy, it has the advantage of being easier for the participant who is not confronted with painful memories or images while awake. It has promise for those who suffer with various forms of PTSD and for those whose distressing memories were formed during childhood bullying. People with adult post-bullying syndrome may benefit from this intervention. It is important to point out that, at this time, neither SE or aromatherapy have substantive evidence-based research backing. Consequently, they should be thought of as alternatives to consider in the healing process.

IN SUMMARY

Bullying, harassment, and hazing by peers or by adults can have serious and lifelong implications. Much of the time, adults want to deny that this is a possibility and cloak any discomfort about it under euphemisms. As research piles up on the adverse effects of this phenomenon, we cannot allow ourselves to be in denial. We cannot rely on the belief that anything untoward that occurred during school years is left behind at graduation.

Despite the efforts of adults, bullying, harassment, and hazing continue to be widespread problems in our nation's schools. Virtually all students are involved as victims, bullies, bully/victims, or witnesses. With severe impacts on lifelong development and mental health, finding a way to prevent bullying is a major public health concern. Far more prevalent than we once believed, bullying occurs in our schools and via cyberspace on an around-the-clock basis. There are long-term costs that haunt those involved, and these consequences are not solely carried by the victims. Bullies are more likely than the general population to become workplace bullies (Matthiesen & Einarsen, 2007; Zapf & Einersan, 2011) or to end up involved with the criminal justice system (Apel & Burrow, 2011; Carter, 2012). As noted earlier, research establishes that both bullies and victims can experience lifelong depression, anxiety, difficulties in relationships, and an inability to trust others. Because bullying is traumatic, it can result in post-traumatic stress disorder.

Schools and grassroots movements attempt to curtail bullying by involving children who witness peer-on-peer violence. While it is commendable to engage students to stop bullying, it is simply not enough. Bullying and hazing flourish in organizations where they are inadvertently enabled, tacitly permitted, or worse, openly sanctioned by the behavior of adults. Parents know that children are great imitators. Children watch their parents, and their moral development is based on what they see within the family. Children watch their teachers and other school personnel, and this contributes to their growing moral compass. Yet research informs us that 45% of teachers have admitted to bullying children (Twemlow et al., 2006). When this happens, bullying is a systemic problem and becomes almost intractable as part of the school or organizational culture. While adults admonish children to stop bullying each other, there is an adult moral code witnessed in their behavior that allows for—and promotes—bullying and revenge. Consequently, we have to realize that children do not have enough power to change it and it is not their responsibility. Prevention of this pervasive phenomenon is the direct responsibility of adults. Adults at school and in the community need to make the commitment to examine and change their own behavior if they hope to diminish bullying among children.

Parents, educators, and policy makers must see the serious long-term consequences of bullying. Only in this way will there be a concerted and ongoing effort to interrupt bullying at first signs in childhood. We can no longer afford the attitude that says, "Bullying is just a rite of passage" or "Bullying happens; you get over it." Clearly this is not the case. The adults in this study and in other research prove otherwise. Health and mental health practitioners need a comprehensive vision of the effects of bullying on both children and adults. With the understanding that bullying and harassment may lead to a lifetime of poor decisions, of relationship problems, and of mental health issues, practitioners can begin to regularly ask about current or past bullying episodes. Doing so will provide a key to unlocking the history behind problems clients are experiencing and will offer a direction for treatment. This is a call to parents, educators, all health practitioners, and policy makers to stand up and make a difference so that a childhood of bullying does not turn into an adult life full of its aftermath. Bullying scars.

REFERENCES

INTRODUCTION

Bellis, M. A., Hughes, K., Jones, A., Perkins, C., & McHale, P. (2013). Childhood happiness and violence: A retrospective study of their impacts on adult well-being. *BMJ Open, 3,* e003427.

Biebl, S. J., DiLalla, L. F., Davis, E. K., Lynch, K. A., & Shinn, S. O. (2011). Longitudinal associations among peer victimization and physical and mental health problems. *Journal of Pediatric Psychology, 36,* 868–877.

Corbin, J., & Strauss, A. (2014). *Basics of qualitative research: Techniques and procedures for developing grounded theory.* Thousand Oaks, CA: Sage.

Glaser, B., & Strauss, A. (1967). *The discovery of grounded theory: Strategies for qualitative inquiry.* London, England: Wiedenfeld and Nicholson.

Greene, J. C., & Caracelli, V. J. (1997). Defining and describing the paradigm issue in mixed-method evaluation. *New Directions for Evaluation, 74,* 5–17.

Lincoln, Y. S., & Guba, E. G. (1988). *Naturalistic inquiry.* Thousand Oaks, CA: Sage.

Meltzer, H., Vostanis, P., Ford, T., Bebbington, P., & Dennis, M. S. (2011). Victims of bullying in childhood and suicide attempts in adulthood. *European Psychiatry, 26,* 498–503.

Scott, W. R. (1995). *Institutions and organizations.* Thousand Oaks, CA: Sage.

Strauss, A., & Corbin, J. (1998). *Basics of qualitative research.* Thousand Oaks, CA: Sage.

Templeton, J. F. (1994). *Focus groups: A guide for marketing and advertising professionals* (Rev. ed.). Burr Ridge, IL: Irwin.

Ttofi, M. M., Farrington, D. P., Lösel, F., & Loeber, R. (2011). The predictive efficiency of school bullying versus later offending: A systematic/meta-analytic review of longitudinal studies. *Criminal Behaviour and Mental Health, 21,* 80–89.

Von Bertalanffy, L. (1973). *General system theory: Foundations, development, applications* (Rev. ed.). New York, NY: George Braziller.

CHAPTER 1: BULLYING: THE PARAMETERS OF THE PROBLEM INTO ADULTHOOD

Adams, L., & Russakoff, D. (1999, June 13). High schools' "cult of the athlete" under scrutiny. *Washington Post,* p. 1ff.

Boren, C. (2014). NFL report finds Richie Incognito, other Dolphins, harassed Jonathan Martin. *Washington Post.* Retrieved from http://www.washingtonpost.com/blogs/early-lead/wp/2014/02/14/nfl-report-finds-richie-incognito-other-dolphins-harassed-jonathan-martin/

Bowes, L., Wolke, D., Joinson, C., Lereya, S. T., & Lewis, G. (2014). Sibling bullying and risk of depression, anxiety, and self-harm: A prospective cohort study. *Pediatrics, 134,* e1032–e1039.

Cassidy, W, Brown, K., & Jackson, M. (2012). "Under the radar"™: Educators and cyberbullying in schools. *School Psychology International, 33*(5), 520–532.

Centers for Disease Control and Prevention (CDC). (2011). Bullying among middle school and high school students—Massachusetts, 2009. *Morbidity and Mortality Weekly Report, 60,* 465–471.

Connolly, J., Josephson, W., Schnoll, J., Simkins-Strong, E., Pepler, D., MacPherson, A., . . . Jiang, D. (2015). Evaluation of a youth-led program for preventing bullying, sexual harassment, and dating aggression in middle schools. *Journal of Early Adolescence, 35,* 403–434.

Connolly, J., Pepler, D., Craig, W., & Taradash, A. (2000). Dating experiences of bullies in early adolescence. *Child Maltreatment, 5,* 299–310.

Daniels, T., Quigley, D., Menard, L., & Spence, L. (2010). "My best friend always did and still does betray me constantly": Examining relational and physical victimization within a dyadic friendship context. *Canadian Journal of School Psychology, 25,* 70–83.

Davis, S., & Nixon, C. L. (2013). *Youth voice project: Student insights into bullying and peer mistreatment.* Champaign, IL: Research Press.

Debnam, K. J., Johnson, S. L., & Bradshaw, C. P. (2014). Examining the association between bullying and adolescent concerns about teen dating violence. *Journal of School Health, 84,* 421–428.

Deery, S., Walsh, J., & Guest, D. (2011). Workplace aggression: The effects of harassment on job burnout and turnover intentions. *Work, Employment and Society, 25,* 742–759.

deLara, E. W. (2006). Bullying and violence in American schools. In N. E. Dowd, D. G. Singer, & R. F. Wilson (Eds.), *Children, culture and violence* (pp. 333–353). Thousand Oaks, CA: Sage.

deLara, E. W. (2012). Why adolescents don't disclose incidents of bullying and harassment to adults. *Journal of School Violence, 11,* 288–305.

DeVoe, J., & Murphy, C. (2011). Student Reports of Bullying and Cyber-Bullying: Results from the 2009 School Crime Supplement to the National Crime Victimization Survey. Web Tables. NCES 2011-336. *National Center for Education Statistics.*

Einarsen, S., Hoel, H., Zapf, D., & Cooper, C. L. (Eds.). (2011). The concept of bullying and harassment at work: The European tradition. *Bullying and harassment in the workplace: Developments in theory, research, and practice* (pp. 3–39). Boca Raton, FL: CRC Press.

Garbarino, J., & deLara, E. W. (2002). And words can hurt forever: How to protect adolescents from bullying, harassment, and emotional violence. New York, NY: The Free Press.

Ghosh, R., Jacobs, J. L., & Reio, T. G. (2011). The toxic continuum from incivility to violence: What can HRD do? *Advances in Developing Human Resources, 13,* 3–9.

Gibbs, N., & Roche, T. (1999). The Columbine tapes. *Time Magazine, 154,* 40–51.

Gladden, R. M., Vivolo-Kantor, A. M., Hamburger, M. E., & Lumpkin, C. D. (2014). *Bullying surveillance among youths: Uniform definitions for public health and recommended data elements, Version 1.0.* Atlanta, GA: National Center for Injury Prevention and Control, Centers for Disease Control and Prevention and US Department of Education.

Hauge, L. J., Skogstad, A., & Einarsen, S. (2009). Individual and situational predictors of workplace bullying: Why do perpetrators engage in the bullying of others? *Work and Stress, 23*, 349–358.

Hauge, L. J., Skogstad, A., & Einarsen, S. (2010). The relative impact of workplace bullying as a social stressor at work. *Scandinavian Journal of Psychology, 51*, 426–433.

Hauge, L. J., Skogstad, A., & Einarsen, S. (2011). Role stressors and exposure to workplace bullying: Causes or consequences of what and why? *European Journal of Work and Organizational Psychology, 20*, 610–630.

Hinduja, S., & Patchin, J. W. (2014). *Bullying beyond the schoolyard: Preventing and responding to cyberbullying.* Thousand Oaks, CA: Corwin Press.

Hoetger, L. A., Hazen, K. P., & Brank, E. M. (2015). All in the family: A retrospective study comparing sibling bullying and peer bullying. *Journal of Family Violence, 30*, 103–111.

Johnson, S. L. (2011). An ecological model of workplace bullying: A guide for intervention and research. *Nursing Forum, 46*, 55–63.

Kosciw, J. G., Greytak, E. A., Bartkiewicz, M. J., Boesen, M. J., & Palmer, N. A. (2012). *The 2011 National School Climate Survey: The Experiences of Lesbian, Gay, Bisexual and Transgender Youth in Our Nation's Schools.* Gay, Lesbian and Straight Education Network (GLSEN). 121 West 27th Street Suite 804, New York, NY 10001.

Kowalski, R. M., Limber, S. P., & Agatston, P. W. (2008). *Cyberbullying: Bullying in the digital age.* Malden, MA: Blackwell.

Kowalski, R. M., Morgan, C. A., & Limber, S. P. (2012). Traditional bullying as a potential warning sign of cyberbullying. *School Psychology International, 33*, 505–519.

Lahelma, E., Lallukka, T., Laaksonen, M., Saastamoinen, P., & Rahkonen, O. (2012). Workplace bullying and common mental disorders: A follow-up study. *Journal of Epidemiology and Community Health, 66*, e3–e3. doi:10.1136/jech.2010.115212

Lallukka, T., Rahkonen, O., & Lahelma, E. (2011). Workplace bullying and subsequent sleep problems—the Helsinki Health Study. *Scandinavian Journal of Work, Environment and Health, 37*, 204–212.

Leland, J. (2001). Zero tolerance changes life at one school. *NY Times:* Sec 9, p. 1, p. 6.

McWilliams, K., Goodman, G. S., Raskauskas, J., & Cordon, I. M. (2014). Child maltreatment and bullying. In G. B. Melton, A. Ben-Arieh, J. Cashmore, G. S. Goodman, & N. K. Worley (Eds.), *The SAGE handbook of child research* (pp. 300–315). London, England: SAGE.

Menesini, E., Camodeca, M., & Nocentini, A. (2010). Bullying among siblings: The role of personality and relational variables. *British Journal of Developmental Psychology, 28*, 921–939.

Milam, A. C., Spitzmueller, C., & Penney, L. M. (2009). Investigating individual differences among targets of workplace incivility. *Journal of Occupational Health Psychology, 14*, 58.

Mishna, F., Cook, C., Gadalla, T., Daciuk, J., & Solomon, S. (2010). Cyber bullying behaviors among middle and high school students. *American Journal of Orthopsychiatry, 80*(3), 362–374.

Nansel, T. R., Overpeck, M., Pilla, R. S., Ruan, W. J., Simons-Morton, B., & Scheidt, P. (2001). Bullying behaviors among US youth: Prevalence and association with psychosocial adjustment. *JAMA, 285*, 2094–2100.

Olweus, D. (1978). *Aggression in the schools: Bullies and whipping boys*. London, England: Hemisphere.

Olweus, D. (1993). *Bullying at school: What we know and what we can do*. Malden, MA: Blackwell.

Pomeroy, E. C. (2013). The bully at work: What social workers can do. *Social Work*, *58*, 5–8.

Posner, B. Z., & Schmidt, W. H. (1993). Values congruence and differences between the interplay of personal and organizational value systems. *Journal of Business Ethics*, *12*, 341–347.

Pronk, R. E., & Zimmer-Gembeck, M. J. (2010). It's "mean," but what does it mean to adolescents? Relational aggression described by victims, aggressors, and their peers. *Journal of Adolescent Research*, *25*, 175–204.

Salin, D., & Hoel, H. (2011). Organisational causes of workplace bullying. In S. Einarsen, H. Hole, D. Zapf, & C. L. Cooper (Eds.), *Bullying and harassment in the workplace: Developments in theory, research, and practice* (pp. 227–243). Boca Raton, FL: CRC Press.

Scott, W. R. (2000). *Institutions and organizations* (2nd ed.). New York, NY: Sage.

Shakeshaft, C. (2004). *Educator sexual misconduct: A synthesis of existing literature (PPSS 2004–09)*. Washington, D.C.: US Department of Education, Office of the Undersecretary.

Shetgiri, R., Espelage, D. L., & Carroll, L. (2015). Bullying trends, correlates, consequences, and characteristics. In A. P. Giardino (Ed.), *Practical strategies for clinical management of bullying* (pp. 3–11). Cham, Switzerland: Springer International.

Smith, P. K., & Sharp, S. (Eds.). (1994). *School bullying: Insights and perspectives*. London, England: Routledge.

Sypher, B. D. (2004). Reclaiming civil discourse in the workplace. *Southern Journal of Communication*, *69*, 257–269.

Thomas, M. (2012, February 29). Tragedy in Ohio: When the bullied strike back. *Huffington Post*. Retrieved from http://www.huffingtonpost.com/marlo-thomas/bullying-marlo-thomas_b_1305325.html

Twale, D. J., & De Luca, B. M. (2008). *Faculty incivility: The rise of the academic bully culture and what to do about it*. Hoboken, NJ: Jossey-Bass.

van Heugten, K. (2013). Resilience as an underexplored outcome of workplace bullying. *Qualitative Health Research*, *23*, 291–301.

Vaillancourt, T., McDougall, P., Hymel, S., Krygsman, A., Miller, J., Stiver, K., & Davis, C. (2008). Bullying: Are researchers and children/youth talking about the same thing?. *International Journal of Behavioral Development*, *32*(6), 486–495.

Volk, A. A., & Lagzdins, L. (2009). Bullying and victimization among adolescent girl athletes. *Athletic Insight*, *11*, 12–25.

Von Bertalanffy, L. (1968). *General systems theory: Foundations, development, applications*. New York, NY: George Braziller.

Wang, J., Iannotti, R. J., & Nansel, T. R. (2009). School bullying among adolescents in the United States: Physical, verbal, relational, and cyber. *Journal of Adolescent Health*, *45*, 368–375.

Wei, H. S., & Jonson-Reid, M. (2011). Friends can hurt you: Examining the coexistence of friendship and bullying among early adolescents. *School Psychology International*, *32*, 244–262.

CHAPTER 2: ADULT POST-BULLYING SYNDROME

American Psychiatric Association. (2013). *Diagnostic and statistical manual of mental disorders* (5th ed.). Arlington, VA: Author. *DSM-5*.

Anda, R. F., Felitti, V. J., Bremner, J. D., Walker, J. D., Whitfield, C. H., Perry, B. D., . . . Giles, W. H. (2006). The enduring effects of abuse and related adverse experiences in childhood. *European Archives of Psychiatry and Clinical Neuroscience, 256,* 174–186.

Biebl, S. J., DiLalla, L. F., Davis, E. K., Lynch, K. A., & Shinn, S. O. (2011). Longitudinal associations among peer victimization and physical and mental health problems. *Journal of Pediatric Psychology, 36,* 868–877.

Burstow, B. (2005). A critique of posttraumatic stress disorder and the DSM. *Journal of Humanistic Psychology, 45,* 429–445.

Carlisle, N., & Rofes, E. (2007). School bullying: Do adult survivors perceive long-term effects? *Traumatology: An International Journal, 13,* 16–26.

Copeland, W. E., Wolke, D., Angold, A., & Costello, E. J. (2013). Adult psychiatric outcomes of bullying and being bullied by peers in childhood and adolescence. *Journal of American Medical Association Psychiatry, 70,* 419–426.

Crockett, M. J., Apergis-Schoute, A., Herrmann, B., Lieberman, M. D., Müller, U., Robbins, T. W., & Clark, L. (2013). Serotonin modulates striatal responses to fairness and retaliation in humans. *Journal of Neuroscience, 33,* 3505–3513.

Edmiston, E. E., Wang, F., Mazure, C. M., Guiney, J., Sinha, R., Mayes, L. C., & Blumberg, H. P. (2011). Corticostriatal-limbic gray matter morphology in adolescents with self-reported exposure to childhood maltreatment. *Archives of Pediatrics and Adolescent Medicine, 165,* 1069–1077.

Fallon, J. (2013). *The psychopath inside: A neuroscientist's personal journey into the dark side of the brain.* New York, N.Y.: Penguin.

Farrington, D., & Ttofi, M. (2011). Bullying as a predictor of offending, violence and later life outcomes. *Criminal Behaviour and Mental Health, 21,* 90–98.

Garbarino, J. (2013). *Children exposed to violence* [lecture]. Department of Marriage and Family Therapy, Syracuse University, Syracuse, NY.

Gilbert, P. (2009). Introducing compassion-focused therapy. *Advances in Psychiatric Treatment, 15,* 199–208.

Higgins, G. E., Khey, D. N., Dawson-Edwards, B. C., & Marcum, C. D. (2012). Examining the link between being a victim of bullying and delinquency trajectories among an African American sample. *International Criminal Justice Review, 22,* 110–122. doi:1057567712443965.

Hostinar, C. E., & Gunnar, M. R. (2013). The developmental effects of early life stress: An overview of current theoretical frameworks. *Current Directions in Psychological Science, 22,* 400–406.

Idsoe, T., Dyregrov, A., & Idsoe, E. C. (2012). Bullying and PTSD symptoms. *Journal of Abnormal Child Psychology, 40,* 901–911.

Kim, M. J., Catalano, R. F., Haggerty, K. P., & Abbott, R. D. (2011). Bullying at elementary school and problem behaviour in young adulthood: A study of bullying, violence and substance use from age 11 to age 21. *Criminal Behaviour and Mental Health, 21,* 136–144.

Kolts, R. L., Robinson, A. M., & Tracy, J. J. (2004). The relationship of sociotropy and autonomy to posttraumatic cognitions and PTSD symptomatology in trauma survivors. *Journal of Clinical Psychology, 60,* 53–63.

Knack, J. M., Jensen-Campbell, L. A., & Baum, A. (2011). Worse than sticks and stones? Bullying is associated with altered HPA axis functioning and poorer health. *Brain and Cognition, 77*, 183–190.

Kubiak, S. P. (2005). Trauma and cumulative adversity in women of a disadvantaged social location. *American Journal of Orthopsychiatry, 75*, 451.

Lemos-Miller, A., & Kearney, C. A. (2006). Depression and ethnicity as intermediary variables among dissociation, trauma-related cognitions, and PTSD symptomatology in youths. *Journal of Nervous and Mental Disease, 194*, 584–590.

Luk, J. W., Wang, J., & Simons-Morton, B. G. (2010). Bullying victimization and substance use among US adolescents: Mediation by depression. *Prevention Science, 11*, 355–359.

Moser, J. S., Hajcak, G., Simons, R. F., & Foa, E. B. (2007). Posttraumatic stress disorder symptoms in trauma-exposed college students: The role of trauma-related cognitions, gender, and negative affect. *Journal of Anxiety Disorders, 21*, 1039–1049.

Rivers, I. (2004). Recollections of bullying and their long term implications for lesbians, gay men, and bisexuals. *Crisis: The Journal of Crisis Intervention and Suicide Prevention, 25*, 169–175.

Schaller, M., & Duncan, L. A. (2011). The behavioral immune system: Its evolution and social psychological implications. In J. P. Forgas, M. G. Haselton, & W. Hippel (Eds.), *Evolution and the social mind: Evolutionary psychology and social cognition* (pp. 293–307). Hove, United Kingdom: Psychology Press.

Smokowski, P. R., & Kopasz, K. H. (2005). Bullying in school: An overview of types, effects, family characteristics, and intervention strategies. *Childrenand Schools, 27*, 101–110.

Sourander, A., Jensen, P., Rönning, J. A., Niemelä, S., Helenius, H., Sillanmäki, L., . . . Almqvist, F. (2007). What is the early adulthood outcome of boys who bully or are bullied in childhood? The Finnish "From a Boy to a Man" study. *Pediatrics, 120*, 397–404.

Teicher, M. H., Samson, J. A., Sheu, Y. S., Polcari, A., & McGreenery, C. E. (2010). Hurtful words: Association of exposure to peer verbal abuse with elevated psychiatric symptom scores and corpus callosum abnormalities. *American Journal of Psychiatry, 167*, 1464–1471.

Van der Kolk, B. A. (1988). The trauma spectrum: The interaction of biological and social events in the genesis of the trauma response. *Journal of Traumatic Stress, 1*, 273–290.

van der Kolk, B. A. (2003). The neurobiology of childhood trauma and abuse. *Child and Adolescent Psychiatric Clinics of North America, 12*, 293–317.

CHAPTER 3: BEING DIFFERENT: THE TRACES THAT DIFFERENCE LEAVES BEHIND

Ahmed, E., & Braithwaite, J. (2005). Forgiveness, shaming, shame and bullying. *Australian and New Zealand Journal of Criminology, 38*, 298–323.

Aslund, C., Leppert, J., Starrin, B., & Nilsson, K. W. (2009). Subjective social status and shaming experiences in relation to adolescent depression. *Archives of Pediatric and Adolescent Medicine, 163*, 55–60.

Berlan, E. D., Corliss, H. L., Field, A. E., Goodman, E., & Bryn Austin, S. (2010). Sexual orientation and bullying among adolescents in the growing up today study. *Journal of Adolescent Health, 46*, 366–371.

Brixval, C. S., Rayce, S. L., Rasmussen, M., Holstein, B. E., & Due, P. (2012). Overweight, body image and bullying—an epidemiological study of 11-to 15-years olds. *The European Journal of Public Health, 22,* 126–130.

Butterfield, F. (1995). *All God's children: The Bosket family and the American tradition of violence.* New York, Avon Books.

Carlisle, N., & Rofes, E. (2007). School bullying: Do adult survivors perceive long-term effects? *Traumatology, 13,* 16–26.

Chappell, C. A. (2004). Post-secondary correctional education and recidivism: A meta-analysis of research conducted 1990–1999. *Journal of Correctional Education, 55,* 148–169.

Coggan, C., Bennett, S., Hooper, R., & Dickinson, P. (2003). Association between bullying and mental health status in New Zealand adolescents. *International Journal of Mental Health Promotion, 5,* 16–22.

Cunningham, N. J., Taylor, M., Whitten, M. E., Hardesty, P. H., Eder, K., & DeLaney, N. (2010). The relationship between self-perception of physical attractiveness and sexual bullying in early adolescence. *Aggressive Behavior, 36,* 271–281.

deLara, E. W. (2002). Peer predictability: An adolescent strategy for enhancing a sense of safety at school. *Journal of School Violence, 1,* 31–56.

deLara, E. W. (2008). Bullying and aggression on the school bus: School bus drivers' observations and suggestions. *Journal of School Violence, 7,* 48–70.

Eamon, M. K. (2001). The effects of poverty on children's socioemotional development: An ecological systems analysis. *Social Work, 46,* 256–266.

Eisenberg, M. E., Neumark-Sztainer, D., & Story, M. (2003). Associations of weight-based teasing and emotional well-being among adolescents. *Archives of Pediatric and Adolescent Medicine, 157,* 733–738. doi:10.1001/archpedi.157.8.733

Farmer, T. W., Petrin, R., Brooks, D. S., Hamm, J. V., Lambert, K., & Gravelle, M. (2012). Bullying involvement and the school adjustment of rural students with and without disabilities. *Journal of Emotional and Behavioral Disorders, 20,* 19–37.

Fast, J. (in press). *Beyond bullying: How to break the cycle of shame, bullying, and violence.* New York, NY: Oxford University Press.

Fox, C. L., & Farrow, C. V. (2009). Global and physical self-esteem and body dissatisfaction as mediators of the relationship between weight status and being a victim of bullying. *Journal of Adolescence, 32,* 1287–1301.

GLSEN. (2005). *From teasing to torment: School climate in America.* Retrieved from www.glsen.org

Glumbić, N., & Žunić-Pavlović, V. (2010). Bullying behavior in children with intellectual disability. *Procedia-Social and Behavioral Sciences, 2,* 2784–2788.

Gilligan, J. (1996). *Violence: Our deadly epidemic and its causes.* New York: G.P. Putnam.

Goldweber, A., Waasdorp, T. E., & Bradshaw, C. P. (2013). Examining associations between race, urbanicity, and patterns of bullying involvement. *Journal of youth and adolescence, 42,* 206–219.

Goodall, J. (1988). *The chimpanzees of Gombe.* Boston, MA: Belknap Press of Harvard University Press.

Huffington Post. (2012, February 21). Christina Hendricks talks high school days, being bullied. *Huffington Post.* Retrieved from http://www.huffingtonpost.com/2012/02/21/christina-hendricks-talks-childhood-being-bullied-high-school_n_1291650.html

Hugh-Jones, S., & Smith, P. K. (1999). Self-reports of short-and long-term effects of bullying on children who stammer. *British Journal of Educational Psychology, 69*, 141–158.

Jansen, P. W., Verlinden, M., Dommisse-van Berkel, A., Mieloo, C. L., Raat, H., Hofman, A., . . . Tiemeier, H. (2014). Teacher and peer reports of overweight and bullying among young primary school children. *Pediatrics, 134*, 473–480.

Kanetsuna, T., Smith, P. K., & Morita, Y. (2006). Coping with bullying at school: children's recommended strategies and attitudes to school-based interventions in England and Japan. *Aggressive Behavior, 32*, 570–580.

Larochette, A. C., Murphy, A. N., & Craig, W. M. (2010). Racial bullying and victimization in Canadian school-aged children individual and school level effects. *School Psychology International, 31*, 389–408.

Lumeng, J. C., Forrest, P., Appugliese, D. P., Kaciroti, N., Corwyn, R. F., & Bradley, R. H. (2010). Weight status as a predictor of being bullied in third through sixth grades. *Pediatrics, 125*, e1301–e1307.

Matos, M., & Pinto-Gouveia, J. (2010). Shame as a traumatic memory. *Clinical Psychology and Psychotherapy, 17*, 299–312.

Meyer, D. (2015). "One Day I'm Going to Be Really Successful": The social class politics of videos made for the "It Gets Better" Anti-Gay Bullying Project. *Critical Sociology*, 0896920515571761.

Mishna, F. (2012). *Bullying: A guide to research, intervention, and prevention*. New York, NY: Oxford University Press.

Morrison, A. P. (2014). *Shame: The underside of narcissism*. Abingdon, Oxford: Routledge.

Nelson, T. D., Jensen, C. D., & Steele, R. G. (2011). Weight-related criticism and self-perceptions among preadolescents. *Journal of Pediatric Psychology, 36*, 106–115.

Perren, S., Gutzwiller-Helfenfinger, E., Malti, T., & Hymel, S. (2012). Moral reasoning and emotion attributions of adolescent bullies, victims, and bully-victims. *British Journal of Developmental Psychology, 30*, 511–530.

Pittet, I., Berchtold, A., Akré, C., Michaud, P. A., & Suris, J. C. (2010). Are adolescents with chronic conditions particularly at risk for bullying? *Archives of Disease in Childhood, 95*, 711–716.

Puhl, R. M., & Latner, J. D. (2007). Stigma, obesity, and the health of the nation's children. *Psychological Bulletin, 133*, 557–580. doi: 10.1037/0033-2909.133.4.557

Robinson, J. P., & Espelage, D. L. (2012). Bullying Explains Only Part of LGBTQ–Heterosexual Risk Disparities Implications for Policy and Practice. *Educational Researcher, 41*, 309–319.

Ryan, C., & Futterman, D. (2001). Lesbian and gay adolescents: Identity development. *Prevention Researcher, 8*, 1–16.

Schaller, M., & Duncan, L. A. (2011). The behavioral immune system: Its evolution and social psychological implications. In Forgas, J. P., Haselton, M. G., & von Hippel, W. (Eds.), *Evolution and the social mind: Evolutionary psychology and social cognition* (pp. 293–307). Hove, United Kingdom: Psychology Press.

Schaller, M., & Park, J. H. (2011). The behavioral immune system (and why it matters). *Current Directions in Psychological Science, 20*, 99–103.

Sentenac, M., Arnaud, C., Gavin, A., Molcho, M., Gabhainn, S. N., & Godeau, E. (2012). Peer victimization among school-aged children with chronic conditions. *Epidemiologic Reviews, 34*, 120–128.

Shakeshaft, C. (2004). Educator Sexual Misconduct: A Synthesis of Existing Literature PPSS 2004-09. *US Department of Education*.

Shetgiri, R., Lin, H., Avila, R. M., & Flores, G. (2012). Parental characteristics associated with bullying perpetration in US children aged 10 to 17 years. *American Journal of Public Health, 102*, 2280–2286.

Sreckovic, M. A., Brunsting, N. C., & Able, H. (2014). Victimization of students with autism spectrum disorder: A review of prevalence and risk factors. *Research in Autism Spectrum Disorders, 8*, 1155–1172.

Stevens, T., Morash, M., & Park, S. (2011). Late-adolescent delinquency risks and resilience for girls differing in risk at the start of adolescence. *Youth and Society, 43*, 1433–1458.

Stuewig, J., Tangney, J. P., Heigel, C., Harty, L., & McCloskey, L. (2010). Shaming, blaming, and maiming: Functional links among the moral emotions, externalization of blame, and aggression. *Journal of Research in Personality, 44*, 91–102.

Stuewig, J., Tangney, J. P., Kendall, S., Folk, J. B., Meyer, C. R., & Dearing, R. L. (2014). Children's proneness to shame and guilt predict risky and illegal behaviors in young adulthood. *Child Psychiatry and Human Development, 1–11.* doi:10.1007/s10578–014–0467–1

Sweeting, H., & West, P. (2001). Being different: Correlates of the experience of teasing and bullying at age 11. *Research Papers in Education, 16*, 225–246.

Tangney, J. P., & Dearing, R. L. (2003). *Shame and guilt.* New York, NY: Guilford Press.

Vacca, J. S. (2004). Educated prisoners are less likely to return to prison. *Journal of Correctional Education, 55*, 297–305.

Yoon, E., Funk, R. S., & Kropf, N. P. (2010). Sexual harassment experiences and their psychological correlates among a diverse sample of college women. *Affilia, 25*, 8–18.

CHAPTER 4: PEOPLE-PLEASING VERSUS REVENGE: CONSEQUENCES ON DEVELOPMENT OF BEING BULLIED

Apel, R., & Burrow, J. D. (2011). Adolescent victimization and violent self-help. *Youth Violence and Juvenile Justice, 9*, 112–133.

Bentall, R. P., Wickham, S., Shevlin, M., & Varese, F. (2012). Do specific early-life adversities lead to specific symptoms of psychosis? A study from the 2007 Adult Psychiatric Morbidity Survey. *Schizophrenia Bulletin, 38*, 734–740.

Black, S., Weinles, D., & Washington, E. (2010). Victim strategies to stop bullying. *Youth Violence and Juvenile Justice, 8*, 138–147.

Bloom, S. L. (2001). Commentary: Reflections on the desire for revenge. *Journal of Emotional Abuse, 2*, 61–94.

Boulton, M. J. (2013). Associations between adults' recalled childhood bullying victimization, current social anxiety, coping, and self-blame: Evidence for moderation and indirect effects. *Anxiety, Stress and Coping, 26*, 270–292.

Brown, S., & Taylor, K. (2008). Bullying, education and earnings: Evidence from the National Child Development Study. *Economics of Education Review, 27*, 387–401.

Centers for Disease Control and Prevention (CDC). (2009). *Helping your child feel connected to school.* Retrieved from http://www.cdc.gov/healthyyouth/protective/pdf/connectedness_parents.pdf

Cloke, K. (1993). Revenge, forgiveness, and the magic of mediation. *Conflict Resolution Quarterly, 11*, 67–78.

Copeland, W. E., Wolke, D., Lereya, S. T., Shanahan, L., Worthman, C., & Costello, E. J. (2014). Childhood bullying involvement predicts low-grade systemic inflammation into adulthood. *Proceedings of the National Academy of Sciences, 111*, 7570–7575.

Due, P., Krølner, R., Rasmussen, M., Andersen, A., Damsgaard, M. T., Graham, H., & Holstein, B. E. (2011). Pathways and mechanisms in adolescence contribute to adult health inequalities. *Scandinavian Journal of Public Health, 39*(6 suppl), 62–78.

Emberton, O. (2013, October 2). What are bullies like as adults? *Quora*. Retrieved from http://www.quora.com/Psychology/What-are-bullied-children-like-as-adults/answer/Oliver-Emberton?share=16-12-13

Fisher, H. L., Moffitt, T. E., Houts, R. M., Belsky, D. W., Arseneault, L., & Caspi, A. (2012). Bullying victimisation and risk of self harm in early adolescence: Longitudinal cohort study. *BMJ: British Medical Journal, 344*, e2683.

Gaughan, E., Cerio, J. D., & Myers, R. A. (2001). *Lethal violence in schools: A national survey final report*. Alfred, NY: Alfred University.

Herman, J. (1992). *Trauma and recovery*. New York: NY: Basic Books.

Kim, M. J., Catalano, R. F., Haggerty, K. P., & Abbott, R. D. (2011). Bullying at elementary school and problem behaviour in young adulthood: A study of bullying, violence and substance use from age 11 to age 21. *Criminal Behaviour and Mental Health, 21*, 136–144.

Kohlberg, L. (1991). *The philosophy of moral development: Moral stages and the idea of justice*. New York, NY: Harper Row.

Kohlberg, L. (2008). The development of children's orientations toward a moral order. *Human Development, 51*, 8–20.

Melzer, S. (2013). Ritual violence in a two-car garage. *Contexts, 12*, 26–31.

Moffitt, T. E., Arseneault, L., Belsky, D., Dickson, N., Hancox, R. J., Harrington, H., . . . Caspi, A. (2011). A gradient of childhood self-control predicts health, wealth, and public safety. *Proceedings of the National Academy of Sciences, 108*, 2693–2698, 201010076.

O'Keeffe, G. S., & Clarke-Pearson, K. (2011). The impact of social media on children, adolescents, and families. *Pediatrics, 127*, 800–804.

Prior, M., Smart, D., Sanson, A., & Oberklaid, F. (2000). Does shy-inhibited temperament in childhood lead to anxiety problems in adolescence? *Journal of the American Academy of Child and Adolescent Psychiatry, 39*, 461–468.

Sanson, A., Hemphill, S. A., & Smart, D. (2004). Connections between temperament and social development: A review. *Social Development, 13*, 142–170.

Sansone, R. A., Leung, J. S., & Wiederman, M. W. (2012). Self-reported bullying in childhood: Relationships with employment in adulthood. *International Journal of Psychiatry in Clinical Practice, 17*, 64–68.

Seton, P. H. (2001). On the importance of getting even: A study of the origins and intention of revenge. *Smith College Studies in Social Work, 72*, 77–97.

Shonkoff, J. P., Garner, A. S., Siegel, B. S., Dobbins, M. I., Earls, M. F., Garner, A. S., . . . Wood, D. L. (2012). The lifelong effects of early childhood adversity and toxic stress. *Pediatrics, 129*, e232–e246.

Stein, M. B., & Stein, D. J. (2008). Social anxiety disorder. *Lancet, 371*, 1115–1125.

Varhama, L. M., & Bjorkqvist, K. (2005). Relation between school bullying during adolescence and subsequent long-term unemployment in adulthood in a Finnish sample. *Psychological Reports, 96*, 269–272.

Whitlock, J., Eckenrode, J., & Silverman, D. (2006). Self-injurious behaviors in a college population. *Pediatrics, 117*, 1939–1948.

CHAPTER 5: CONSEQUENCES IN RELATIONSHIPS

Ainsworth, M. S., & Bowlby, J. (1991). An ethological approach to personality development. *American Psychologist, 46,* 333.

Bartholomew, K., & Horowitz, L. M. (1991). Attachment styles among young adults: A test of a four-category model. *Journal of Personality and Social Psychology, 61,* 226–244.

Bellis, M. A., Hughes, K., Jones, A., Perkins, C., & McHale, P. (2013). Childhood happiness and violence: A retrospective study of their impacts on adult well-being. *BMJ Open, 3,* e003427.

Bandura, A. (1991). Social cognitive theory of moral thought and action. In W. M. Kurtines & J. L. Gewirtz (Eds.), *Handbook of moral behavior and development: Volume 1. Theory.* (pp. 45–103). Hillsdale, NJ: Erlbaum.

Barchia, K., & Bussey, K. (2011). Predictors of student defenders of peer aggression victims: Empathy and social cognitive factors. *International Journal of Behavioral Development, 35,* 289–297.

Baumeister, R. F., & Leary, M. R. (1995). The need to belong: Desire for interpersonal attachments as a fundamental human motivation. *Psychological Bulletin, 117,* 497–529.

Bellis, M. A., Hughes, K., Jones, A., Perkins, C., & McHale, P. (2013). Childhood happiness and violence: A retrospective study of their impacts on adult well-being. *BMJ Open, 3,* e003427.

Boulton, M. J. (2013). Associations between adults' recalled childhood bullying victimization, current social anxiety, coping, and self-blame: Evidence for moderation and indirect effects. *Anxiety, Stress and Coping, 26,* 270–292.

Bowes, L., Maughan, B., Caspi, A., Moffitt, T. E., & Arseneault, L. (2010). Families promote emotional and behavioural resilience to bullying: Evidence of an environmental effect. *Journal of Child Psychology and Psychiatry, 51,* 809–817.

Bowlby, J. (1969). *Attachment and loss: Vol. 1. Attachment.* New York, NY: Basic Books.

Cappadocia, M. C., Pepler, D., Cummings, J. G., & Craig, W. (2012). Individual motivations and characteristics associated with bystander intervention during bullying episodes among children and youth. *Canadian Journal of School Psychology, 27,* 201–216.

Centers for Disease Control and Prevention (CDC). (2010). *Teen dating violence.* Retrieved from http://www.cdc.gov/ViolencePrevention/intimatepartnerviolence/teen_dating_violence.html

CNN. (2008). Survey reveals abuse in teen relationships. *CNN.* Retrieved from http://www.cnn.com/2008/LIVING/personal/07/08/teen.dating.abuse/index.html

Collins, W. A., Welsh, D. P., & Furman, W. (2009). Adolescent romantic relationships. *Annual Review of Psychology, 60,* 631–652.

Corvo, K., & deLara, E. W. (2010). Towards an integrated theory of relational violence: Is bullying a risk factor for domestic violence? *Aggression and Violent Behavior, 15,* 181–190.

deLara, E. W. (2008a). Bullying and aggression on the school bus: School bus drivers' observations and their suggestions. *Journal of School Violence, 7,* 48–70.

deLara, E. W. (2008b). Developing a philosophy about bullying and sexual harassment: Cognitive coping strategies among secondary school students. *Journal of School Violence, 7,* 72–96.

deLara, E. W. (2012). Why adolescents don't disclose incidents of bullying and harassment to adults. *Journal of School Violence, 11,* 288–305.

DeWall, C. N., Twenge, J. M., Gitter, S. A., & Baumeister, R. F. (2009). It's the thought that counts: The role of hostile cognition in shaping aggressive responses to social exclusion. *Journal of Personality and Social Psychology, 96*, 45–59.

Dixon, R. (2007). Ostracism: One of the many causes of bullying in groups? *Journal of School Violence, 6*, 3–26.

Ellis, W. E., & Wolfe, D. A. (2014). Bullying predicts reported dating violence and observed qualities in adolescent dating relationships. *Journal of Interpersonal Violence, 1–22.* doi: 10.1177/0886260514554428

Falb, K. L., McCauley, H. L., Decker, M. R., Gupta, J., Raj, A., & Silverman, J. G. (2011). School bullying perpetration and other childhood risk factors as predictors of adult intimate partner violence perpetration. *Archives of Pediatrics and Adolescent Medicine, 165*, 890–894.

Feinberg, M., Willer, R., & Schultz, M. (2014). Gossip and ostracism promote cooperation in groups. *Psychological Science, 25*, 656–664.

Fish, J. N., Pavkov, T. W., Wetchler, J. L., & Bercik, J. (2012). Characteristics of those who participate in infidelity: The role of adult attachment and differentiation in extradyadic experiences. *American Journal of Family Therapy, 40*, 214–229.

Foshee, V. A., Reyes, H. L. M., Vivolo-Kantor, A. M., Basile, K. C., Chang, L. Y., Faris, R., & Ennett, S. T. (2014). Bullying as a longitudinal predictor of adolescent dating violence. *Journal of Adolescent Health, 55*, 439–444.

Frisén, A., Hasselblad, T., & Holmqvist, K. (2012). What actually makes bullying stop? Reports from former victims. *Journal of Adolescence, 35*, 981–990.

Garbarino, J., & deLara, E. W. (2002). *And words can hurt forever: How to protect adolescents from bullying, harassment, and emotional violence.* New York, NY: Free Press.

Gibbs, N., & Roche, T. (1999). The Columbine tapes. *Time Magazine, 154*, 40–51.

Gilmartin, B. G. (1987). Peer group antecedents of severe love-shyness in males. *Journal of Personality, 55*(3), 467–489.

Hazan, C., & Shaver, P. (1987). Romantic love conceptualized as an attachment process. *Journal of Personality and Social Psychology, 52*, 511–524. doi:10.1037/0022-3514.52.3.511

Hazan, C., & Shaver, P. R. (1994). Attachment as an organizational framework for research on close relationships. *Psychological Inquiry, 5*, 1–22.

Hong, J. S., Cho, H., Allen-Meares, P., & Espelage, D. L. (2011). The social ecology of the Columbine High School shootings. *Children and Youth Services Review, 33*, 861–868.

Josephson, W. L., & Pepler, D. (2012). Bullying: A stepping stone to dating aggression? *International Journal of Adolescent Medicine and Health, 24*, 37–47.

Kurzban & Leary, (2001). Evolutionary origins of stigmatization: The functions of social exclusion. *Psychological Bulletin, 127*, 187–208.

Leary, M. R., Twenge, J. M., & Quinlivan, E. (2006). Interpersonal rejection as a determinant of anger and aggression. *Personality and Social Psychology Review, 10*, 111–132.

Mikulincer, M., & Shaver, P. R. (2003). The attachment behavioral system in adulthood: Activation, psychodynamics, and interpersonal processes. In M. P. Zanna (Ed.), *Advances in experimental social psychology* (Vol. 35, pp. 53–152). San Diego, CA: Elsevier Academic Press.

Mishna, F., & Alaggia, R. (2005). Weighing the risks: A child's decision to disclose peer victimization. *Children and Schools, 27*, 217–226.

Newman, B. M., & Newman, P. R. (2014). *Development through life: A psychosocial approach* (12th ed.). Stamford, CT: Cengage Learning.

Onugha, N. N., & Finlay, F. (2012). 444 Sexting, fraping and hyper-tweeting: What should paediatricians be doing to help? *Archives of Disease in Childhood, 97*(Suppl 2), A130–A130.

Perren, S., Ettekal, I., & Ladd, G. (2012). The impact of peer victimization on later maladjustment: Mediating and moderating effects of hostile and self-blaming attributions. *Journal of Child Psychology and Psychiatry, 54*, 46–55.

Perren, S., Gutzwiller-Helfenfinger, E., Malti, T., & Hymel, S. (2012). Moral reasoning and emotion attributions of adolescent bullies, victims, and bully-victims. *British Journal of Developmental Psychology, 30*, 511–530.

Powell, M. D., & Ladd, L. D. (2010). Bullying: A review of literature and implications for family therapists. *American Journal of Family Therapy, 38*, 189–206.

Rohner, R. P. (2004). The parental "acceptance-rejection syndrome": Universal correlates of perceived rejection. *American Psychologist, 59*, 830.

Ryan, L., & Mulholland, J. (2014). "Wives are the route to social life": An analysis of family life and networking amongst highly skilled migrants in London. *Sociology, 48*, 251–267.

Schäfer, M., Korn, S., Smith, P. K., Hunter, S. C., Mora-Merchán, J. A., Singer, M. M., & Meulen, K. (2004). Lonely in the crowd: Recollections of bullying. *British Journal of Developmental Psychology, 22*, 379–394.

Schaps, E., Battistich, V., & Solomon, D. (2004). Community in school as key to student growth: Findings from the Child Development Project. In J. E. Zins, R. P. Weissberg, M. C. Wang, H. J. Walberg, J. E. Zins, R. P. Weissberg, . . . H. J. Walberg (Eds.), *Building academic success on social and emotional learning: What does the research say?* (pp. 189–205). New York, NY: Teachers College Press.

Seibert, A., & Kerns, K. (2015). Early mother–child attachment: Longitudinal prediction to the quality of peer relationships in middle childhood. *International Journal of Behavioral Development, 39*, 130–138.

Silverman, J. G., Raj, A., Mucci, L. A., & Hathaway, J. E. (2001). Dating violence against adolescent girls and associated substance use, unhealthy weight control, sexual risk behavior, pregnancy, and suicidality. *JAMA, 286*, 572–579.

Stroud, S. R. (2014). The dark side of the online self: A pragmatist critique of the growing plague of revenge porn. *Journal of Mass Media Ethics, 29*, 168–183.

The National Campaign to Prevent Teen and Unplanned Pregnancy. (2008, December). *Sex and tech: Results from a survey of teens and young adults.* Retrieved from http://www.thenationalcampaign.org/sextech/pdf/sextech_summary.pdf

Vaillancourt, T., Brittain, H., Bennett, L., Arnocky, S., McDougall, P., Hymel, S., . . . Cunningham, L. (2010). Places to avoid: Population-based study of student reports of unsafe and high bullying areas at school. *Canadian Journal of School Psychology, 25*, 40–54.

Vossekuil, B., Reddy, M., & Fein, R. (2000). *USSS Safe School Initiative: An interim report on the prevention of targeted violence in schools.* Washington, DC: US Secret Service National Threat Assessment Center and US Dept. of Education with the support of the National Institute of Justice.

Walden, L. M., & Beran, T. N. (2010). Attachment quality and bullying behavior in school-aged youth. *Canadian Journal of School Psychology, 25*(1), 5–18.

Williams, K. D. (2002). *Ostracism: The power of silence.* New York, NY: Guilford Press.

Williams, K. D., Forgas, J. P., & Von Hippel, W. (Eds.). (2005). *The social outcast: Ostracism, social exclusion, rejection, and bullying.* New York, NY: Psychology Press.

Williams, K. D., & Nida, S. A. (2011). Ostracism. *Current Directions in Psychological Science, 20,* 71–75.

CHAPTER 6: "ANGRY WORDS ECHO IN MY BRAIN": HEALTH AND MENTAL HEALTH IMPACTS

Ahmed, E., & Braithwaite, V. (2004). "What, me ashamed?" Shame management and school bullying. *Journal of Research in Crime and delinquency, 41,* 269–294.

Alexander, P. C. (2009). Childhood trauma, attachment, and abuse by multiple partners. *Psychological Trauma: Theory, Research, Practice, and Policy, 1,* 78–88.

Allison, S., Roeger, L., & Reinfeld-Kirkman, N. (2009). Does school bullying affect adult health? Population survey of health-related quality of life and past victimization. *Australian and New Zealand Journal of Psychiatry, 43,* 1163–1170.

Almquist, Y. (2011). The school class as a social network and contextual effects on childhood and adult health: Findings from the Aberdeen Children of the 1950s cohort study. *Social Networks, 33,* 281–291.

Almquist, Y. B., & Brännström, L. (2014). Childhood peer status and the clustering of social, economic, and health-related circumstances in adulthood. *Social Science and Medicine, 105,* 67–75.

Andersen, S., Tomada, A., Vincow, E., Valente, E., Polcari, A., & Teicher, M. (2008). Preliminary evidence for sensitive periods in the effect of childhood sexual abuse on regional brain development. *Journal of Neuropsychiatry and Clinical Neurosciences, 20,* 292–301.

Anthony, B. J., Wessler, S. L., & Sebian, J. K. (2010). Commentary: Guiding a public health approach to bullying. *Journal of Pediatric Psychology, 35,* 1113–1115.

Arseneault, L., Bowes, L., & Shakoor, S. (2010). Bullying victimization in youths and mental health problems: "Much ado about nothing"? *Psychological Medicine, 40,* 717–729.

Arseneault, L., Cannon, M., Fisher, H. L., Polanczk, G., Moffitt, T. E., & Caspi, A. (2011). Childhood trauma and children's emerging psychotic symptoms: A genetically sensitive longitudinal cohort study. *American Journal of Psychiatry, 168,* 65–72.

Benedict, F. T., Vivier, P. M., & Gjelsvik, A. (2014). Mental health and bullying in the United States among children aged 6 to 17 years. *Journal of Interpersonal Violence, 30,* 782–795. doi:0886260514536279.

Bentall, R. P., Wickham, S., Shevlin, M., & Varese, F. (2012). Do specific early-life adversities lead to specific symptoms of psychosis? A study from the 2007 Adult Psychiatric Morbidity Survey. *Schizophrenia Bulletin, 38,* 734–740.

Biebl, S. J., DiLalla, L. F., Davis, E. K., Lynch, K. A., & Shinn, S. O. (2011). Longitudinal associations among peer victimization and physical and mental health problems. *Journal of Pediatric Psychology, 36,* 868–877.

Bogart, L. M., Elliott, M. N., Klein, D. J., Tortolero, S. R., Mrug, S., Peskin, M. F., . . . Schuster, M. A. (2014). Peer victimization in fifth grade and health in tenth grade. *Pediatrics, 133,* 440–447.

Boulton, M. J. (2013). Associations between adults' recalled childhood bullying victimization, current social anxiety, coping, and self-blame: Evidence for moderation and indirect effects. *Anxiety, Stress and Coping: An International Journal, 26,* 270–292.

Bowes, L., Joinson, C., Wolke, D., & Lewis, G. (2015). Peer victimisation during adolescence and its impact on depression in early adulthood: Prospective cohort study in the United Kingdom. *British Medical Journal, 350,* h2469.

Bowlby, J. (1969). *Attachment and Loss: Vol. 1. Attachment.* New York, NY: Basic Books.

Bowlby, J. (1973). *Attachment and Loss: Vol. 2. Separation*. New York, NY: Penguin Books.

Bowlby, J. (1980). *Attachment and Loss: Vol. 3. Loss*. New York, NY: Basic Books.

Bradshaw, C. P., Waasdorp, T. E., Goldweber, A., & Johnson, S. L. (2013). Bullies, gangs, drugs, and school: Understanding the overlap and the role of ethnicity and urbanicity. *Journal of Youth and Adolescence, 42*, 220–234.

Brent, B. K. (2011). Increased risk of psychotic symptoms at 12 years in children who have been maltreated by adults or bullied by peers. *Evidence Based Mental Health, 14*, 65. doi:10.1136/ebmental1176.

Burk, L. R., Armstrong, J. M., Park, J. H., Zahn-Waxler, C., Klein, M. H., & Essex, M. J. (2011). Stability of early identified aggressive victim status in elementary school and associations with later mental health problems and functional impairments. *Journal of Abnormal Child Psychology, 39*, 225–238.

Burton, K. A., Florell, D., & Wygant, D. B. (2013). The role of peer attachment and normative beliefs about aggression on traditional bullying and cyberbullying. *Psychology in the Schools, 50*, 103–115.

Cappadocia, M. C., Craig, W. M., & Pepler, D. (2013). Cyberbullying prevalence, stability, and risk factors during adolescence. *Canadian Journal of School Psychology, 28*, 171–192.

Carlisle, N., & Rofes, E. (2007). School bullying: Do adult survivors perceive long-term effects? *Traumatology, 13*, 16–26.

Cassidy, W., Faucher, C., & Jackson, M. (2013). Cyberbullying among youth: A comprehensive review of current international research and its implications and application to policy and practice. *School Psychology International, 34*, 575–612.

Centers for Disease Control and Prevention (CDC). (2013). *Adverse Childhood Experiences (ACE) Study*. Retrieved from http://www.cdc.gov/ace/index.htm.

Centers for Disease Control and Prevention (CDC).(2010). Youth Violence: Electric Aggression. Retrieved from http://www.cdc.gov/ViolencePrevention/youthviolence/electronicaggression/index.htm

Coan, J. A. (2010). Adult attachment and the brain. *Journal of Social and Personal Relationships, 27*, 210–217.

Copeland, W. E., Wolke, D., Angold, A., & Costello, E. J. (2013). Adult psychiatric outcomes of bullying and being bullied by peers in childhood and adolescence. *Journal of the American Medical Association Psychiatry, 70*, 419–426.

Copeland, W. E., Wolke, D., Lereya, S. T., Shanahan, L., Worthman, C., & Costello, E. J. (2014). Childhood bullying involvement predicts low-grade systemic inflammation into adulthood. *Proceedings of the National Academy of Sciences, 111*, 7570–7575.

Corrigan, F. M., Fisher, J. J., & Nutt, D. J. (2011). Autonomic dysregulation and the window of tolerance model of the effects of complex emotional trauma. *Journal of Psychopharmacology, 25*, 17–25.

Cronholm, P. F., Ismailji, T., & Mettner, J. (2013). Academy on violence and abuse: Highlights of proceedings from the 2011 conference, "Toward a New Understanding." *Trauma, Violence, and Abuse, 14*, 271–281.

Cyberbullying Research Center (n.a.). *What is cyberbullying?* Retreived from http://www.cyberbullying.us/anecdotes.

deLara, E. W. (2012). Why adolescents don't disclose incidents of bullying and harassment to adults. *Journal of School Violence, 11*, 288–305.

Diamond, L. M., & Fagundes, C. P. (2010). Psychobiological research on attachment. *Journal of Social and Personal Relationships, 27*, 218–225.

Duke, N. N., Pettingell, S. L., McMorris, B. J., & Borowsky, I. W. (2010). Adolescent violence perpetration: Associations with multiple types of adverse childhood experiences. *Pediatrics, 125,* e778–e786.

Eisenberg, M. E., Neumark-Sztainer, D., & Story, M. (2003). Associations of weight-based teasing and emotional well-being among adolescents. *Archives of Pediatrics and Adolescent Medicine, 157,* 733–738.

Espelage, D. L., & De La Rue, L. (2012). School bullying: Its nature and ecology. *International Journal of Adolescent Medicine and Health, 24,* 3–10.

Espelage, D. L., & Swearer, S. M. (2011). *Bullying in North American schools* (2nd ed.). New York, NY: Routledge.

Farrow, C. V., & Fox, C. L. (2011). Gender differences in the relationships between bullying at school and unhealthy eating and shape-related attitudes and behaviours. *British Journal of Educational Psychology, 81,* 409–420.

Fisher, H. L., Moffitt, T. E., Houts, R. M., Belsky, D. W., Arseneault, L., & Caspi, A. (2012). Bullying victimisation and risk of self harm in early adolescence: longitudinal cohort study. *British Medical Journal, 344*(7855), 1–9.

Fisher, H. L., Schreier, A., Zammit, S., Maughan, B., Munafò, M. R., Lewis, G., & Wolke, D. (2013). Pathways between childhood victimization and psychosis-like symptoms in the ALSPAC birth cohort. *Schizophrenia Bulletin, 39,* 111.

Fitzpatrick, S., & Bussey, K. (2011). The development of the social bullying involvement scales. *Aggressive Behavior, 37,* 177–192.

Fosse, G. K., & Holen, A. (2006). Childhood maltreatment in adult female psychiatric outpatients with eating disorders. *Eating Behaviors, 7,* 404–409.

Garbarino, J., & deLara, E. W. (2002). *And words can hurt forever: How to protect adolescents from bullying, harassment, and emotional violence.* New York, NY: Free Press.

Gladstone, G. L., Parker, G. B., & Malhi, G. S. (2006). Do bullied children become anxious and depressed adults?: A cross-sectional investigation of the correlates of bullying and anxious depression. *Journal of Nervous and Mental Disease, 194,* 201–208. doi:10.1097/01.nmd.0000202491.99719.c3.

Hatzenbuehler, M. L. (2011). The social environment and suicide attempts in lesbian, gay, and bisexual youth. *Pediatrics, 127,* 896–903.

Heikkilä, H. K., Väänänen, J., Helminen, M., Fröjd, S., Marttunen, M., & Kaltiala-Heino, R. (2013). Involvement in bullying and suicidal ideation in middle adolescence: a 2-year follow-up study. *European child & adolescent psychiatry, 22,* 95–102.

Herman, J. L. (1992). Complex PTSD: A syndrome in survivors of prolonged and repeated trauma. *Journal of Traumatic Stress, 5,* 377–391.

Hinduja, S., & Patchin, J. W. (2010). Bullying, cyberbullying, and suicide. *Archives of Suicide Research, 14,* 206–221.

Hoertel, N., Le Strat, Y., Lavaud, P., & Limosin, F. (2012). Gender effects in bullying: Results from a national sample. *Psychiatry Research, 200,* 921–927.

Holt, M. K., Vivolo-Kantor, A. M., Polanin, J. R., Holland, S. G., Matjasko, J. L., Wolfe, M., & Reid, G. (2015). Bullying and suicidal ideation and behaviors: A meta-analysis. *Pediatrics, 135,* 1–14. doi:10.1542/peds.2014-1864.

Hong, J., Kral, M., & Sterzing, P. (2014). Pathways from bullying perpetration, victimization, and bully victimization to suicidality among school-aged youth: A review of the potential mediators and a call for further investigation. *Trauma Violence Abuse, 6,* 1–12.

Interactive, H., Gay, L., & Network, S. E. (2005). *From teasing to torment: School climate in America.* New York: Gay, lesbian, and straight education network.

Jiang, Y., Perry, D. K., & Hesser, J. E. (2010). Suicide patterns and association with predictors among Rhode Island public high school students: A latent class analysis. *American Journal of Public Health, 100,* 1701.

Jokinen, J. (2015). Early antecedents of suicide: The role of prenatal and childhood risk factors. *Evidence Based Mental Health, 18,* 11.

Kashdan, T. B., & Collins, R. L. (2010). Social anxiety and the experience of positive emotion and anger in everyday life: An ecological momentary assessment approach. *Anxiety, Stress, and Coping, 23,* 259–272.

Kendrick, K., Jutengren, G., & Stattin, H. (2012). The protective role of supportive friends against bullying perpetration and victimization. *Journal of Adolescence, 35,* 1069–1080.

Kim, M. J., Catalano, R. F., Haggerty, K. P., & Abbott, R. D. (2011). Bullying at elementary school and problem behaviour in young adulthood: A study of bullying, violence and substance use from age 11 to age 21. *Criminal Behaviour and Mental Health, 21,* 136–144.

Klomek, A. B., Kleinman, M., Altschuler, E., Marrocco, F., Amakawa, L., & Gould, M. S. (2011). High school bullying as a risk for later depression and suicidality. *Suicide and Life Threatening Behavior, 41,* 501–516.

Landstedt, E., & Persson, S. (2014). Bullying, cyberbullying, and mental health in young people. *Scandinavian Journal of Public Health, 42,* 393–399.

Leone, D. R., Ray, S. L., & Evans, M. (2013). The lived experience of anxiety among late adolescents during high school an interpretive phenomenological inquiry. *Journal of Holistic Nursing, 3,* 188–197. 0898010113488243.

Lereya, S. T., Copeland, W. E., Costello, E. J., & Wolke, D. (2015). Adult mental health consequences of peer bullying and maltreatment in childhood: Two cohorts in two countries. *Lancet Psychiatry.* Retrieved from http://www.thelancet.com/pdfs/journals/lanpsy/PIIS2215-0366(15)00165-0.pdf

Longden, E., Madill, A., & Waterman, M. G. (2012). Dissociation, trauma, and the role of lived experience: Toward a new conceptualization of voice hearing. *Psychological Bulletin, 138,* 28–76.

McMahon, E. M., Reulbach, U., Keeley, H., Perry, I. J., & Arensman, E. (2012). Bullying victimisation, self harm and associated factors in Irish adolescent boys. *Social Science and Medicine, 74,* 490–497.

Menesini, E., & Camodeca, M. (2008). Shame and guilt as behaviour regulators: Relationships with bullying, victimization and prosocial behaviour. *British Journal of Developmental Psychology, 26,* 183–196.

Nansel, T. R., Overpeck, M., Pilla, R. S., Ruan, W. J., Simons-Morton, B., & Scheidt, P. (2001). Bullying behaviors among US youth: Prevalence and association with psychosocial adjustment. *JAMA, 285,* 2094–2100.

Niemelä, S., Brunstein-Klomek, A., Sillanmäki, L., Helenius, H., Piha, J., Kumpulainen, K., . . . Sourander, A. (2011). Childhood bullying behaviors at age eight and substance use at age 18 among males: A nationwide prospective study. *Addictive Behaviors, 36,* 256–260.

Ogden, C. L., Carroll, M. D., Kit, B. K., & Flegal, K. M. (2014). Prevalence of childhood and adult obesity in the United States, 2011–2012. *Journal of the American Medical Association, 311,* 806–814.

Ouellet-Morin, I., Danese, A., Bowes, L., Shakoor, S., Ambler, A., Pariante, C. M., . . . Arseneault, L. (2011). A discordant monozygotic twin design shows blunted cortisol reactivity among bullied children. *Journal of the American Academy of Child and Adolescent Psychiatry, 50,* 574–582.

Peguero, A. A., & Kahle, L. (2014). Gender, weight, and the inequality associated with school bullying. In J. Hawdon, J. Ryan, & M. Lucht (Eds.), *The causes and consequences of group violence: From bullies to terrorists* (pp. 143–164). Blue Ridge Summit, PA: Rowman & Littlefield.

Pietromonaco, P. R., DeBuse, C. J., & Powers, S. I. (2013). Does attachment get under the skin? Adult romantic attachment and cortisol responses to stress. *Current Directions in Psychological Science, 22,* 63–68.

Quirin, M., Gillath, O., Pruessner, J. C., & Eggert, L. D. (2010). Adult attachment insecurity and hippocampal cell density. *Social Cognitive and Affective Neuroscience, 5,* 39–47.

Redmond, S. M. (2011). Peer victimization among students with specific language impairment, attention-deficit/hyperactivity disorder, and typical development. *Language, Speech, and Hearing Services in Schools, 42,* 520–535.

Renda, J., Vassallo, S., & Edwards, B. (2011). Bullying in early adolescence and its association with anti-social behaviour, criminality and violence 6 and 10 years later. *Criminal Behaviour and Mental Health, 21,* 117–127.

Rivers, I. (2004). Recollections of bullying at school and their long-term implications for lesbians, gay men, and bisexuals. *Crisis: The Journal of Crisis Intervention and Suicide Prevention, 25,* 169.

Roeger, L., Allison, S., Korossy-Horwood, R., Eckert, K. A., & Goldney, R. D. (2010). Is a history of school bullying victimization associated with adult suicidal ideation?: A South Australian population-based observational study. *Journal of Nervous and Mental Disease, 198,* 728–733.

Sansone, R. A., Leung, J. S., & Wiederman, M. W. (2013). Having been bullied in childhood: Relationship to aggressive behaviour in adulthood. *International Journal of Social Psychiatry, 59,* 824–826.

Sansone, R. A., & Sansone, L. A. (2008). Bully victims: Psychological and somatic aftermaths. *Psychiatry, 5,* 62–64.

Schneider, S. K., O'Donnell, L., Stueve, A., & Coulter, R. W. (2012). Cyberbullying, school bullying, and psychological distress: A regional census of high school students. *American Journal of Public Health, 102,* 171–177.

Simpson, J. A., & Rholes, W. S. (2010). Attachment and relationships: Milestones and future directions. *Journal of Social and Personal Relationships, 27,* 173–180.

Smith, P. K. (2011). Why interventions to reduce bullying and violence in schools may (or may not) succeed: Comments on this special section. *International Journal of Behavioral Development, 35,* 419–423. doi:0165025411407459.

Sourander, A., Jensen, P., Rönning, J. A., Niemelä, S., Helenius, H., Sillanmäki, L., . . . Almqvist, F. (2007). What is the early adulthood outcome of boys who bully or are bullied in childhood? The Finnish "From a Boy to a Man" study. *Pediatrics, 120,* 397–404.

Sourander, A., Ronning, J., Brunstein-Klomek, A., Gyllenberg, D., Kumpulainen, K., Niemelä, S., . . . Almqvist, F. (2009). Childhood bullying behavior and later psychiatric hospital and psychopharmacologic treatment: Findings from the Finnish 1981 birth cohort study. *Archives of General Psychiatry, 66,* 1005–1012.

Srabstein, J., & Piazza, T. (2012). Is there a syndrome of bullying? *International Journal of Adolescent Medical Health, 24,* 91–96.

Staubli, S., & Killias, M. (2011). Long-term outcomes of passive bullying during childhood: Suicide attempts, victimization and offending. *European Journal of Criminology, 8,* 377–385.

Swearer, S. M., Collins, A., Radcliff, K. H., & Wang, C. (2011). Externalizing problems in problems in students involved in bullying and victimization. In D. L. Espelage & S. M. Swearer (Eds.), *Bullying in North American schools* (2nd ed., pp. 45–61). New York, NY: Routledge.

Teicher, M. H., Samson, J. A., Sheu, Y. S., Polcari, A., & McGreenery, C. E. (2010). Hurtful words: Association of exposure to peer verbal abuse with elevated psychiatric symptom scores and corpus callosum abnormalities. *American Journal of Psychiatry, 167,* 1464–1471.

Timmermanis, V., & Wiener, J. (2011). Social correlates of bullying in adolescents with attention-deficit/hyperactivity disorder. *Canadian Journal of School Psychology, 26,* 301–318.

Tompkins County Mental Health Association. (2003). *States of mind.* Ithaca, NY: Author.

Ttofi, M. M., Farrington, D. P., Lösel, F., & Loeber, R. (2011a). Do the victims of school bullies tend to become depressed later in life? A systematic review and meta-analysis of longitudinal studies. *Journal of Aggression, Conflict and Peace Research, 3,* 63–73.

Ttofi, M. M., Farrington, D. P., Lösel, F., & Loeber, R. (2011b). The predictive efficiency of school bullying versus later offending: A systematic/meta-analytic review of longitudinal studies. *Criminal Behaviour and Mental Health, 21,* 80–89.

Wade, T. D., Keski-Rahkonen, A., & Hudson, J. (2011). Epidemiology of eating disorders. In M. Tsuang & M. Tohen (Eds.), *Textbook in psychiatric epidemiology* (3rd ed., pp. 343–360). New York, NY: Wiley.

Wang, J., Nansel, T. R., & Iannotti, R. J. (2011). Cyber and traditional bullying: Differential association with depression. *Journal of Adolescent Health, 48,* 415–417.

CHAPTER 7: "I AM SO SELF-CONSCIOUS": THE IMPACT OF SEXUAL HARASSMENT

American Association of University Women (AAUW). (2011). *Crossing the line: Sexual harassment at school.* Washington, DC: Author.

Arseneault, L., Cannon, M., Fisher, H. L., Polanczyk, G., Moffitt, T. E., & Caspi, A. (2011). Childhood trauma and children's emerging psychotic symptoms: A genetically sensitive longitudinal cohort study. *American Journal Psychiatry, 168,* 65–72.

Booren, L. M., Handy, D. J., & Power, T. G. (2011). Examining perceptions of school safety strategies, school climate, and violence. *Youth Violence and Juvenile Justice, 9,* 171–187.

Brunstein, K. A., Sourander, A., & Gould, M. (2012). The association of suicide and bullying in childhood to young adulthood: A review of cross-sectional and longitudinal research findings. *Canadian Journal of Psychiatry, 55,* 282–288.

Connolly, J., Josephson, W., Schnoll, J., Simkins-Strong, E., Pepler, D., MacPherson, A., . . . Jiang, D. (2015). Evaluation of a youth-led program for preventing bullying, sexual harassment, and dating aggression in middle schools. *Journal of Early Adolescence, 35,* 403–434.

Connolly, J., Pepler, D., Craig, W., & Taradash, A. (2000). Dating experiences of bullies in early adolescence. *Child Maltreatment, 5,* 299–310.

Cunningham, N. J., Taylor, M., Whitten, M. E., Hardesty, P. H., Eder, K., & DeLaney, N. (2010). The relationship between self-perception of physical attractiveness and sexual bullying in early adolescence. *Aggressive Behavior, 36,* 271–281.

D'Augelli, A. R., Pilkington, N. W., & Hershberger, S. L. (2002). Incidence and mental health impact of sexual orientation victimization of lesbian, gay, and bisexual youths in high school. *School Psychology Quarterly, 17,* 148–167. doi:10.1521/scpq.17.2.148.20854

deLara, E. W. (2008a). Bullying and aggression on the school bus: School bus drivers' observations and suggestions. *Journal of School Violence, 7,* 48–70.

deLara, E. W. (2008b). Developing a philosophy about bullying and sexual harassment: Cognitive coping strategies among high school students. *Journal of School Violence, 7,* 72–96.

Espelage, D. L., Aragon, S. R., Birkett, M., & Koenig, B. W. (2008). Homophobic teasing, psychological outcomes, and sexual orientation among high school students: What influence do parents and schools have?. *School Psychology Review,* (37), 202–216.

Espelage, D. L., & Holt, M. K. (2007). Dating violence and sexual harassment across the bully-victim continuum among middle and high school students. *Journal of Youth and Adolescence, 36,* 799–811.

Fineran, S. (2002). Sexual harassment between same-sex peers: Intersection of mental health, homophobia, and sexual violence in schools. *Social Work, 47,* 65–74.

Fineran, S., & Bennett, L. (1998). Teenage peer sexual harassment: Implications for social work practice in education. *Social Work, 43,* 55–64.

Fossey, R. (2010). Should a school district always be liable when a teacher sexually assaults a student? *Teachers College Record.* (2010, March 3). Retrieved from http://www.tcrecord.org/content.asp?contentid=15927

Gadin, K. G. (2012). Sexual harassment of girls in elementary school. *Journal of Interpersonal Violence, 27,* 1762–1779.

Garbarino, J., & deLara, E. W. (2002). *And words can hurt forever: How to protect adolescents from bullying, harassment, and emotional violence.* New York, NY: Simon & Schuster/The Free Press.

Gaughan, E., Cerio, J.D., & Myers, R.A. (2001). Lethal violence in schools: A national survey final report. Alfred, NY, Alfred University: 3-39.

Grossman, A. H., & Kerner, M. S. (1998). Support networks of gay male and lesbian youth. *International Journal of Sexuality and Gender Studies, 3,* 27–46.

Gruber, J., & Fineran, S. (2008). Comparing the impact of bullying and sexual harassment victimization on the mental and physical health of adolescents. *Sex Roles, 59*(1–2), 1–13.

Harris Interactive & Gay, Lesbian, and Straight Education Network (2005). *From teasing to torment: School climate in America.* New York: Gay, Lesbian, and Straight Education Network.

Hatzenbuehler, M. L. (2011). The social environment and suicide attempts in lesbian, gay, and bisexual youth. *Pediatrics, 127,* 896–903.

Hill, C., & Kearl, H. (2011). *Crossing the line: Sexual harassment at school.* American Association of University Women. 1111 Sixteenth Street NW, Washington, DC 20036.

Hlavka, H. R. (2014). Normalizing sexual violence young women account for harassment and abuse. *Gender and Society, 28,* 337–358. doi:10.1177/1524838014520637

Jordan, C. E., Combs, J. L., & Smith, G. T. (2014). An exploration of sexual victimization and academic performance among college women. *Trauma, Violence, and Abuse, 15,* 191–200. doi:1524838014520637

Josephson, W. L., & Pepler, D. (2012). Bullying: A stepping stone to dating aggression? *International Journal of Adolescent Medicine and Health, 24*, 37–47.

Keeshin, B. R., Cronholm, P. F., & Strawn, J. R. (2011). Physiologic changes associated with violence and abuse exposure: An examination of related medical conditions. *Trauma, Violence, and Abuse, 13*, 41–56.

Kristof, N. (2012, February 29). Born to not get bullied. *New York Times*. Retrieved from http://www.nytimes.com/2012/03/01/opinion/kristof-born-to-not-get-bullied.html?_r=1&src=me&ref=general

Landstedt, E., & Gådin, K. G. (2011). Deliberate self-harm and associated factors in 17-year-old Swedish students. *Scandinavian Journal of Public Health, 39*, 17–25.

Lehti, V., Sourander, A., Klomek, A., Niemelä, S., Sillanmäki, L., Piha, J., . . . Almqvist, F. (2011). Childhood bullying as a predictor for becoming a teenage mother in Finland. *European Child and Adolescent Psychiatry, 20*, 49–55.

Lichty, L. F., & Campbell, R. (2012). Targets and witnesses. *Journal of Early Adolescence, 32*(3), 414–430.

Marks, S., Mountjoy, M., & Marcus, M. (2012). Sexual harassment and abuse in sport: The role of the team doctor. *British Journal of Sports Medicine, 46*, 905–908.

Meraviglia, M. G., Becker, H., Rosenbluth, B., Sanchez, E., & Robertson, T. (2003). The expect respect project creating a positive elementary school climate. *Journal of Interpersonal Violence, 18*, 1347–1360.

Mishna, F., Newman, P. A., Daley, A., & Solomon, S. (2009). Bullying of lesbian and gay youth: A qualitative investigation. *British Journal of Social Work, 39*, 1598–1614.

Morgan, J. J., Mancl, D. B., Kaffar, B. J., & Ferreira, D. (2011). Creating safe environments for students with disabilities who identify as lesbian, gay, bisexual, or transgender. *Intervention in School and Clinic, 47*, 3–13.

Newman, B. M., & Newman, P. R. (2014). *Development through life: A psychosocial approach* (12th ed.). Belmont, CA: Wadsworth Cengage Learning.

Parker, I. (2012, February 6). The story of a suicide. *New Yorker*. Retrieved from http://www.newyorker.com/magazine/2012/02/06/the-story-of-a-suicide

Pepler, D. J., Craig, W. M., Connolly, J. A., Yuile, A., McMaster, L., & Jiang, D. (2006). A developmental perspective on bullying. *Aggressive Behavior, 32*, 376–384.

Petersen, J. L., & Hyde, J. S. (2009). A longitudinal investigation of peer sexual harassment victimization in adolescence. *Journal of Adolescence, 32*, 1173–1188.

Poteat, V. P., Kimmel, M. S., & Wilchins, R. (2011). The moderating effects of support for violence beliefs on masculine norms, aggression, and homophobic behavior during adolescence. *Journal of Research on Adolescence, 21*, 434–447.

Poteat, V. P., Mereish, E. H., DiGiovanni, C. D., & Koenig, B. W. (2011). The effects of general and homophobic victimization on adolescents' psychosocial and educational concerns: The importance of intersecting identities and parent support. *Journal of Counseling Psychology, 58*, 597.

Rivers, I. (2004). Recollections of bullying at school and their long-term implications for lesbians, gay men, and bisexuals. *Crisis: The Journal of Crisis Intervention and Suicide Prevention, 25*, 169–175.

Shakeshaft, C. (2004). *Educator sexual misconduct: A synthesis of existing literature*. PPSS 2004–09. (ED-02-PO-3281). US Department of Education.

Silverman, J. G., Raj, A., Mucci, L. A., & Hathaway, J. E. (2001). Dating violence against adolescent girls and associated substance use, unhealthy weight control, sexual risk behavior, pregnancy, and suicidality. *JAMA, 286*, 572–579.

Smith, P. K. (2014). *Understanding school bullying: Its nature and prevention strategies*. New York, NY: Sage.

Tompson, T., Benz, J., & Agiesta, J. (2013). *The digital abuse study: Experiences of teens and young adults*. Chicago, IL: Associated Press-NORC Center/MTV.

Wallace, K. (2013, December 11). 6-year-old suspended for kissing girl, accused of sexual harassment. *CNN*. Retrieved from http://www.cnn.com/2013/12/11/living/6-year-old-suspended-kissing-girl/index.html

Yoon, E., Funk, R. S., & Kropf, N. P. (2010). Sexual harassment experiences and their psychological correlates among a diverse sample of college women. *Affilia, 25*, 8–18.

York, K. M. (1989). Defining sexual harassment in workplaces: A policy-capturing approach. *Academy of Management Journal, 32*, 830–850.

CHAPTER 8: DOES BULLYING AFFECT DECISIONS?

Apel, R., & Burrow, J. D. (2011). Adolescent victimization and violent self-help. *Youth Violence and Juvenile Justice, 9*, 112–133.

Astor, R. A., & Behre, W. J. (1997). Violent and nonviolent children's and parents' reasoning about family and peer violence. *Behavioral Disorders, 22*, 231–45.

Baldry, A. C. (2003). Bullying in schools and exposure to domestic violence. *Child Abuse and Neglect, 27*, 713–732.

Baumeister, R. F., & Leary, M. R. (1995). The need to belong: Desire for interpersonal attachments as a fundamental human motivation. *Psychological Bulletin, 117*, 497–529.

Bechara, A., Damasio, H., & Damasio, A. R. (2000). Emotion, decision making and the orbitofrontal cortex. *Cerebral cortex, 10*(3), 295–307.

Bernstein, M. J., Sacco, D. F., Young, S. G., Hugenberg, K., & Cook, E. (2010). Being "in" with the in-crowd: The effects of social exclusion and inclusion are enhanced by the perceived essentialism of ingroups and outgroups. *Personality and Social Psychology Bulletin, 36*, 999–1009.

Bowlby, J. (1969). *Attachment and Loss* (Vol. 1). New York, NY: Basic Books.

Bowlby, J. (2008). *Attachment*. New York, NY: Basic Books.

Bradshaw, C. P., Waasdorp, T. E., Goldweber, A., & Johnson, S. L. (2013). Bullies, gangs, drugs, and school: Understanding the overlap and the role of ethnicity and urbanicity. *Journal of Youth and Adolescence, 42*, 220–234.

Bruine de Bruin, W., Parker, A. M., & Fischhoff, B. (2007). Individual differences in adult decision-making competence. *Journal of Personality and Social Psychology, 92*, 938–956.

Burton, K. A., Florell, D., & Wygant, D. B. (2013). The role of peer attachment and normative beliefs about aggression on traditional bullying and cyberbullying. *Psychology in the Schools, 50*, 103–115.

Cleary, S. D. (2000). Adolescent victimization and associated suicidal and violent behaviors. *Adolescence, 35*, 671–682.

Corvo, K., & deLara, E. W. (2010). Towards an integrated theory of relational violence: Is bullying a risk factor for domestic violence? *Aggression and Violent Behavior, 15*, 181–190.

Daniels, T., Quigley, D., Menard, L., & Spence, L. (2010). "My best friend always did and still does betray me constantly": Examining relational and physical victimization within a dyadic friendship context. *Canadian Journal of School Psychology, 25*, 70–83.

deLara, E. W. (2002). Peer predictability: An adolescent strategy for increasing a sense of personal safety at school. *Journal of School Violence, 1*, 31–56.

deLara, E. W. (2008). Bullying and aggression on the school bus: School bus drivers' observations and their suggestions. *Journal of School Violence, 7*, 48–70.

deLara, E. W. (2012). Why adolescents don't disclose incidents of bullying and harassment. *Journal of School Violence, 11*, 288–305.

DeWall, C. N., Twenge, J. M., Gitter, S. A., & Baumeister, R. F. (2009). It's the thought that counts: The role of hostile cognition in shaping aggressive responses to social exclusion. *Journal of Personality and Social Psychology, 96*, 45–59.

Dixon, R. (2007). Ostracism: One of the many causes of bullying in groups? *Journal of School Violence, 6*, 3–26.

Duke, N. N., Pettingell, S. L., McMorris, B. J., & Borowsky, I. W. (2010). Adolescent violence perpetration: Associations with multiple types of adverse childhood experiences. *Pediatrics, 125*, e778–e786.

Eliot, M., & Cornell, D. G. (2009). Bullying in middle school as a function of insecure attachment and aggressive attitudes. *School Psychology International, 30*, 201–214.

Falb, K. L., McCauley, H. L., Decker, M. R., Gupta, J., Raj, A., & Silverman, J. G. (2011). School bullying perpetration and other childhood risk factors as predictors of adult intimate partner violence perpetration. *Archives of Pediatric and Adolescent Medicine, 165*, 890–894.

Farrington, D. P. (1998). Predictors, causes, and correlates of male youth violence. In M. Tonry & M.H. Moore (Eds.), *Youth violence* (pp. 421–476). Chicago, IL: University of Chicago Press.

Farrington, D., & Ttofi, M. (2011). Bullying as a predictor of offending violence and later life outcomes. *Criminal Behavior and Mental Health, 21*, 90–98.

Fatum, W. R., & Hoyle, J. C. (1996). Is it violence? School violence from the student perspective: Trends and interventions. *School Counselor, 44*, 28–34.

Feinberg, M., Willer, R., & Schultz, M. (2014). Gossip and ostracism promote cooperation in groups. *Psychological Science, 25*, 656–664.

Fisher, H. L., Moffitt, T. E., Houts, R. M., Belsky, D. W., Arseneault, L., & Caspi, A. (2012). Bullying victimisation and risk of self harm in early adolescence: Longitudinal cohort study. *BMJ: British Medical Journal, 344*, e2683.

Garbarino, J., & deLara, E.W. (2002). *And words can hurt forever: How to protect adolescents from bullying, harassment, and emotional violence.* New York, NY: Simon & Schuster/Free Press.

Goldbaum, S., Craig, W. M., Pepler, D., & Connolly, J. (2003). Developmental trajectories of victimization: Identifying risk and protective factors. *Journal of Applied School Psychology, 19*, 139–156.

Gruter, M., & Masters, R. D. (1986). Ostracism as a social and biological phenomenon: An introduction. *Ethology and Sociobiology, 7*, 149–158.

Gupta, R., Koscik, T. R., Bechara, A., & Tranel, D. (2011). The amygdala and decision-making. *Neuropsychologia, 49*, 760–766.

Harel-Fisch, Y., Walsh, S. D., Fogel-Grinvald, H., Amitai, G., Pickett, W., Molcho, M., . . . Craig, W. (2011). Negative school perceptions and involvement in school bullying: A universal relationship across 40 countries. *Journal of Adolescence, 34*, 639–652.

Hay, C., & Meldrum, R. (2010). Bullying victimization and adolescent self-harm: Testing hypotheses from general strain theory. *Journal of Youth and Adolescence, 39*, 446–459.

Hinduja, S., & Patchin, J. W. (2010). Bullying, cyberbullying, and suicide. *Archives of Suicide Research, 14,* 206–221.

Holt, M. K., & Espelage, D. L. (2007). Perceived social support among bullies, victims, and bully-victims. *Journal of Youth and Adolescence, 36,* 984–994.

Ireland, J. L., & Power, C. L. (2004). Attachment, emotional loneliness, and bullying behaviour: A study of adult and young offenders. *Aggressive Behavior, 30,* 298–312.

Jiang, Y., Perry, D. K., & Hesser, J. E. (2010). Suicide patterns and association with predictors among Rhode Island public high school students: A latent class analysis. *American Journal of Public Health, 100,* 1701.

Jiang, D., Walsh, M., & Augimeri, L. K. (2011). The linkage between childhood bullying behaviour and future offending. *Criminal Behaviour and Mental Health, 21,* 128–135.

Johnson, S. (2006). Are you there for me? *Psychotherapy Networker, 30*(5), 40–53.

Jozefowicz-Simbeni, D. M. H. (2008). An ecological and developmental perspective on dropout risk factors in early adolescence: Role of school social workers in dropout prevention efforts. *Children and Schools, 30,* 49–62.

Kanetsuna, T., Smith, P. K., & Morita, Y. (2006). Coping with bullying at school: children's recommended strategies and attitudes to school-based interventions in England and Japan. *Aggressive Behavior, 32,* 570–580.

Klomek, A. B., Kleinman, M., Altschuler, E., Marrocco, F., Amakawa, L., & Gould, M. S. (2011). High school bullying as a risk for later depression and suicidality. *Suicide and Life-Threatening Behavior, 41,* 501–516.

Klomek, A. B., Sourander, A., Kumpulainen, K., Piha, J., Tamminen, T., Moilanen, I., ... Gould, M. S. (2008). Childhood bullying as a risk for later depression and suicidal ideation among Finnish males. *Journal of Affective Disorders, 109,* 47–55.

Kohlberg, L. (1991). *The philosophy of moral development: Moral stages and the idea of justice.* New York, NY: Harper Row.

Kohlberg, L. (2008). The development of children's orientations toward a moral order. *Human Development, 51,* 8–20.

Krieg, A., & Dickie, J. R. (2013). Attachment and hikikomori: A psychosocial developmental model. *International Journal of Social Psychiatry, 59,* 61–72.

Kurzban, R., & Leary, M. R. (2001). Evolutionary origins of stigmatization: The functions of social exclusion. *Psychological Bulletin, 127,* 187–208.

Leary, M. R. (1990). Responses to social exclusion: Social anxiety, jealousy, loneliness, depression, and low self-esteem. *Journal of Social and Clinical Psychology, 9,* 221–229.

MacDonald, G., & Leary, M. R. (2005). Why does social exclusion hurt? The relationship between social and physical pain. *Psychological Bulletin, 131,* 202–223.

Malti, T., Gasser, L., & Buchmann, M. (2009). Aggressive and prosocial children's emotion attributions and moral reasoning. *Aggressive Behavior, 35,* 90–102.

McMahon, E. M., Reulbach, U., Keeley, H., Perry, I. J., & Arensman, E. (2012). Reprint of: Bullying victimisation, self harm and associated factors in Irish adolescent boys. *Social Science and Medicine, 74,* 490–497.

Mishna, F., & Alaggia, R. (2005). Weighing the risks: A child's decision to disclose peer victimization. *Children and Schools, 27,* 217–226.

Mishna, F., Cook, C., Gadalla, T., Daciuk, J., & Solomon, S. (2010). Cyber bullying behaviors among middle and high school students. *American Journal of Orthopsychiatry, 80,* 362–374.

Nikiforou, M., Georgiou, S. N., & Stavrinides, P. (2013). Attachment to parents and peers as a parameter of bullying and victimization. *Journal of Criminology, 2013*, 1–9.

Nishida, T., Hosaka, K., Nakamura, M., & Hamai, M. (1995). A within-group gang attack on a young adult male chimpanzee: Ostracism of an ill-mannered member? *Primates, 36*, 207–211.

Pellegrini, A. D., & Bartini, M. (2000). A longitudinal study of bullying, victimization, and peer affiliation during the transition from primary school to middle school. *American Educational Research Journal, 37*, 699–725.

Perren, S., Ettekal, I., & Ladd, G. (2012). The impact of peer victimization on later maladjustment: Mediating and moderating effects of hostile and self-blaming attributions. *Journal of Child Psychology and Psychiatry, 54*, 46–55.

Piaget, J. (1997). *The moral judgement of the child.* New York, NY: Simon & Schuster.

Pronk, R. E., & Zimmer-Gembeck, M. J. (2010). It's "mean," but what does it mean to adolescents? Relational aggression described by victims, aggressors, and their peers. *Journal of Adolescent Research, 25*, 175–204.

Rawls, J. (1971, 2009). *A theory of justice.* Cambridge, MA: Harvard University Press.

Reimer, J., Paolitto, D. P., & Hersh, R. H. (1990). *Promoting moral growth: From Piaget to Kohlberg* (2nd Ed.). Long Grove, IL: Waveland.

Sansone, R. A., Leung, J. S., & Wiederman, M. W. (2013). Having been bullied in childhood: Relationship to aggressive behaviour in adulthood. *International Journal of Social Psychiatry, 59*, 824–826.

Smith, P. K. (2014). *Understanding school bullying: Its nature and prevention strategies.* Thousand Oakes, CA: Sage.

Smith, P. K., Cowie, H., Olafsson, R. F., & Liefooghe, A. P. (2002). Definitions of bullying: A comparison of terms used, and age and gender differences, in a fourteen-country international comparison. *Child Development, 73*, 1119–1133.

Sourander, A., Klomek, A. B., Kumpulainen, K., Puustjärvi, A., Elonheimo, H., Ristkari, T., . . . Ronning, J. A. (2011). Bullying at age eight and criminality in adulthood: Findings from the Finnish Nationwide 1981 Birth Cohort Study. *Social Psychiatry and Psychiatric Epidemiology, 46*, 1211–1219.

Sweetingham, R., & Waller, G. (2008). Childhood experiences of being bullied and teased in the eating disorders. *European Eating Disorders Review, 16*, 401–407.

Walden, L. M., & Beran, T. N. (2010). Attachment quality and bullying behavior in school-aged youth. *Canadian Journal of School Psychology, 25*, 5–18.

Wei, H. S., & Jonson-Reid. M. (2011). Friends can hurt you: Examining the coexistence of friendship and bullying among early adolescents. *School Psychology International, 32*, 244–262.

Wong, J. S., & Schonlau, M. (2013). Does bully victimization predict future delinquency? A propensity score matching approach. *Criminal Justice and Behavior, 40*, 1184–1208.

Yu, Y.-Z., & Shi, J.-X. (2009). Relationship between levels of testosterone and cortisol in saliva in aggressive behaviors of adolescents. *Biomedical and Environmental Sciences, 22*, 44–49.

CHAPTER 9: IT COMES HOME TO ROOST: BULLYING AND THE FAMILY

Balsam, K. F., Rothblum, E. D., & Beauchaine, T. P. (2005). Victimization over the life span: A comparison of lesbian, gay, bisexual, and heterosexual siblings. *Journal of Consulting and Clinical Psychology, 73*, 477.

Bowes, L., Maughan, B., Caspi, A., Moffitt, T. E., & Arseneault, L. (2010). Families promote emotional and behavioural resilience to bullying: Evidence of an environmental effect. *Journal of Child Psychology and Psychiatry, 51*, 809–817.

Caffaro, J. V. (2013). *Sibling abuse trauma: Assessment and intervention strategies for children, families, and adults*. New York, NY: Routledge.

Centers for Disease Control and Prevention (CDC). (2010). *Understanding teen dating violence*. http://www.cdc.gov/ViolencePrevention/intimatepartnerviolence/teen_dating_violence.html. Accessed 5-5-10

Centers for Disease Control and Prevention (CDC). (2011). Bullying among middle school and high school students—Massachusetts, 2009. *MMWR Morbidity and Mortality Weekly Report, 60*, 465–71.

Corvo, K., & deLara, E. W. (2010). Towards an integrated theory of relational violence: Is bullying a risk factor for domestic violence? *Aggression and Violent Behavior, 15*, 181–190.

deLara, E. W. (2012). Why adolescents don't disclose incidents of bullying and harassment. *Journal of School Violence, 11*, 288–305.

de Waal, F. B. (2005). A century of getting to know the chimpanzee. *Nature, 437*(7055), 56–59.

Diamond, G. M., Diamond, G. S., Levy, S., Closs, C., Ladipo, T., & Siqueland, L. (2012). Attachment-based family therapy for suicidal lesbian, gay, and bisexual adolescents: A treatment development study and open trial with preliminary findings. *Psychotherapy, 49*, 62–71.

Doumas, D., Margolin, G., & John, R. S. (1994). The intergenerational transmission of aggression across three generations. *Journal of Family Violence, 9*, 157–175.

Duncan, R. D. (1999). Peer and sibling aggression: An investigation of intra-and extra-familial bullying. *Journal of Interpersonal Violence, 14*, 871–886.

Duncan, R. D. (2004). The impact of family relationships on school bullies and victims. In Espelage, D. L., & Swearer, S. M. (Eds.), *Bullying in American schools: A social-ecological perspective on prevention and intervention* (pp. 227–244). New York, NY: Routledge.

Hoetger, L. A., Hazen, K. P., & Brank, E. M. (2015). All in the family: A retrospective study comparing sibling bullying and peer bullying. *Journal of Family Violence, 30*, 103–111.

Hong, J. S., & Espelage, D. L. (2012). A review of research on bullying and peer victimization in school: An ecological system analysis. *Aggression and Violent Behavior, 17*, 311–322.

Hildyard, K. L., & Wolf, D. A. (2002). Child neglect: Developmental issues and outcomes. *Child Abuse and Neglect, 26*, 679–695.

Khan, R., & Rogers, P. (2015). The normalization of sibling violence does gender and personal experience of violence influence perceptions of physical assault against siblings? *Journal of Interpersonal Violence, 30*, 437–458.

Lamont, A. (2010). *Effects of child abuse and neglect for children and adolescents*. Australian Institute of Family Studies. National Child Protection Clearinghouse Published by the Australian Institute of Family Studies ISSN 1448–9112 (Online) http://www.aifs.gov.au/nch/pubs/sheets/rs17/rs17.html

Levin, A. (2011). Victims find little escape from cyber bullies. *Psychiatric News, 46*, 22.

Mackey, A. L., Fromuth, M. E., & Kelly, D. B. (2010). The association of sibling relationship and abuse with later psychological adjustment. *Journal of Interpersonal Violence, 25*, 955–968.

Maxim, P. E. (1978). Quantitative analysis of small group interaction in rhesus monkeys. *American Journal of Physical Anthropology, 48*, 283–295.

Maxim, P. E. (1982). Contexts and messages in macaque social communication. *American Journal of Primatology, 2*, 63–85.

Mishna, F., & Alaggia, R. (2005). Weighing the risks: A child's decision to disclose peer victimization. *Children and Schools, 27*, 217–226.

Resnick, M. D., Bearman, P. S., Blum, R. W., Bauman, K. E., Harris, K. M., Jones, J., . . . Udry, J. R. (1997). Protecting adolescents from harm: Findings from the National Longitudinal Study on Adolescent Health. *JAMA, 278*, 823–832.

Ryan, C., Russell, S. T., Huebner, D., Diaz, R., & Sanchez, J. (2010). Family acceptance in adolescence and the health of LGBT young adults. *Journal of Child and Adolescent Psychiatric Nursing, 23*, 205–213.

Sapouna, M., & Wolke, D. (2013). Resilience to bullying victimization: The role of individual, family and peer characteristics. *Child Abuse and Neglect, 37*, 997–1006.

Straus, M. A., & Field, C. J. (2003). Psychological aggression by American parents: National data on prevalence, chronicity, and severity. *Journal of Marriage and Family, 65*, 795–808.

Tanrikulu, I., & Campbell, M. A. (2014). Sibling bullying perpetration associations with gender, grade, peer perpetration, trait anger, and moral disengagement. *Journal of Interpersonal Violence, 30*, 1010–1024. 0886260514539763.

Tomoda, A., Sheu, Y. S., Rabi, K., Suzuki, H., Navalta, C. P., Polcari, A., & Teicher, M. H. (2011). Exposure to parental verbal abuse is associated with increased gray matter volume in superior temporal gyrus. *Neuroimage, 54*, S280–S286.

Tucker, C. J., Finkelhor, D., Turner, H., & Shattuck, A. (2013). Association of sibling aggression with child and adolescent mental health. *Pediatrics, 132*, 79–84.

Vissing, Y. M., Straus, M. A., Gelles, R. J., & Harrop, J. W. (1991). Verbal aggression by parents and psychosocial problems of children. *Child Abuse and Neglect, 15*, 223–238.

Walsh, C. A., Ploeg, J., Lohfeld, L., Horne, J., MacMillan, H., & Lai, D. (2007). Violence across the lifespan: Interconnections among forms of abuse as described by marginalized Canadian elders and their care-givers. *British Journal of Social Work, 37*, 491–514.

CHAPTER 10: IS THERE ANYTHING POSITIVE?: UNEXPECTED OUTCOMES OF BULLYING AND HARASSMENT

Alfred University. (2001). *Lethal violence in schools*. Alfred, NY: Author.

Aisenberg, E., & Herrenkohl, T. (2008). Community violence in context risk and resilience in children and families. *Journal of Interpersonal Violence, 23*, 296–315.

Barrett, M. J. (2010). Therapy in the danger zone. *Psychotherapy Networker, 34*, 28.

Beaver, K. M., Mancini, C., DeLisi, M., & Vaughn, M. G. (2011). Resiliency to victimization: The role of genetic factors. *Journal of Interpersonal Violence, 26*, 874–898.

Bentall, R. P., Wickham, S., Shevlin, M., & Varese, F. (2012). Do specific early-life adversities lead to specific symptoms of psychosis? A study from the 2007 the Adult Psychiatric Morbidity Survey. *Schizophrenia Bulletin, 38*, 734–740.

Bonanno, G. A., Galea, S., Bucciarelli, A., & Vlahov, D. (2007). What predicts psychological resilience after disaster? The role of demographics, resources, and life stress. *Journal of Consulting and Clinical Psychology, 75*, 671–682.

Bowes, L., Maughan, B., Caspi, A., Moffitt, T. E., & Arseneault, L. (2010). Families promote emotional and behavioural resilience to bullying: evidence of an environmental effect. *Journal of Child Psychology and Psychiatry, 51*, 809–817.

Bronfenbrenner, U. (1979). *The ecology of human development: Experiments by design and nature.* Cambridge, MA: Harvard University Press.

Casel.org (Collaborative for Academic, Social, and Emotional Learning). (n.d.)

Clinton, B. (2004). *My life.* New York, NY: Knopf.

Cohen, P. (2011). Abuse in childhood and the risk for psychotic symptoms in later life. *American Journal of Psychiatry, 168*, 7–8.

deLara, E. W. (2008). Developing a philosophy about bullying and sexual harassment: Cognitive coping strategies among secondary school students. *Journal of School Violence, 7*, 72–96.

DeWall, C. N., Twenge, J. M., Gitter, S. A., & Baumeister, R. F. (2009). It's the thought that counts: The role of hostile cognition in shaping aggressive responses to social exclusion. *Journal of Personality and Social Psychology, 96*, 45–59.

Feder, A., Nestler, E. J., & Charney, D. S. (2009). Psychobiology and molecular genetics of resilience. *Nature Reviews Neuroscience, 10*, 446–457.

Gini, G., Pozzoli, T., & Hauser, M. (2011). Bullies have enhanced moral competence to judge relative to victims, but lack moral compassion. *Personality and Individual Differences, 50*, 603–608.

Greeff, A. P., & Van den Berg, E. (2013). Resilience in families in which a child is bullied. *British Journal of Guidance and Counselling, 41*, 504–517.

James, D. J., Lawlor, M., Courtney, P., Flynn, A., Henry, B., & Murphy, N. (2008). Bullying behaviour in secondary schools: What roles do teachers play? *Child Abuse Review, 17*, 160–173.

McEvoy, A. (2005, September). Teachers who bully students: Patterns and policy implications. In *Teachers who bully students.* Presentation to the Conference on Persistently Safe Schools–Philadelphia (September 11–14. 2005).

McMahon, E. M., Reulbach, U., Keeley, H., Perry, I. J., & Arensman, E. (2010). Bullying victimisation, self harm and associated factors in Irish adolescent boys. *Social Science Medicine, 71*, 1300–1307.

Mizell, V. (2006). Tom Cruise talks about his father. *CBS News.* http://www.cbsnews.com/news/tom-cruise-talks-about-his-father/

Newman, B. M., & Newman, P. R. (2014). *Development through life: A psychosocial approach* (12th ed.). Stamford, CT: Cengage Learning.

Nilsson, D. K., Gustafsson, P. E., & Svedin, C. G. (2012). Lifetime polytraumatization in adolescence and being a victim of bullying. *Journal of Nervous and Mental Disease, 200*, 954–961.

Perren, S., & Gutzwiller-Helfenfinger, E. (2012). Cyberbullying and traditional bullying in adolescence: Differential roles of moral disengagement, moral emotions, and moral values. *European Journal of Developmental Psychology, 9*, 195–209.

Reimer, J., & Paolitto, D. (1990). *Promoting moral growth: From Piaget to Kohlberg* (2nd ed.). Prospect Heights, IL: Waveland Press.

Seligman, M. (2007). *The optimistic child: A proven program to safeguard children against depression and build lifelong resilience.* New York, NY: Mariner Books.

Shakeshaft, C. (2004). *Educator sexual misconduct: A synthesis of existing literature.* PPSS 2004–09. US Department of Education.

Tedeschi, R. G., & Calhoun, L. G. (2004). Posttraumatic growth: Conceptual foundations and empirical evidence. *Psychological Inquiry, 15*, 1–18.

Twemlow, S. W., Fonagy, P., Sacco, F. C., & Brethour, J. R. (2006). Teachers who bully students: A hidden trauma. *International Journal of Social Psychiatry, 52,* 187–198.

Volk, A. A., Camilleri, J. A., Dane, A. V., & Marini, Z. A. (2012). Is adolescent bullying an evolutionary adaptation? *Aggressive Behavior, 38,* 222–238.

Vossekuil, B., Reddy, M., & Fein, R. (2000). *USSS Safe School Initiative: An interim report on the prevention of targeted violence in schools.* Washington, DC: US Secret Service National Threat Assessment Center and US Dept. of Education with the support of the National Institute of Justice.

Warren, A. (2011, August 15). Barack Obama bullied: Big ears, fat, curly hair. *The Post Chronicle.* Retrieved May 13, 2015, from http://www.postchronicle.com/ cgi-bin/artman/exec/view.cgi?archive=270&num=380189

CONCLUSION

Agelink, M. W., Sanner, D., Eich, H., Pach, J., Bertling, R., Lemmer, W., . . . Lehmann, E. (2003). Does acupuncture influence the cardiac autonomic nervous system in patients with minor depression or anxiety disorders? *European PubMed Central, Fortschritte der Neurologie-Psychiatrie, 71,* 141–149.

Ahmed, E., & Braithwaite, V. (2012). Learning to manage shame in school bullying: Lessons for restorative justice interventions. *Critical Criminology, 20,* 79–97.

Allison, S., Roeger, L., & Reinfeld-Kirkman, N. (2009). Does school bullying affect adult health? Population survey of health-related quality of life and past victimization. *Australian and New Zealand Journal of Psychiatry, 43,* 1163–1170.

Almquist, Y. B., & Brännström, L. (2014). Childhood peer status and the clustering of social, economic, and health-related circumstances in adulthood. *Social Science and Medicine, 105,* 67–75.

Apel, R., & Burrow, J. D. (2011). Adolescent victimization and violent self-help. *Youth Violence and Juvenile Justice, 9,* 112–133.

Barrett, M. J., & Stone Fish, L. (2014). *Treating complex trauma: A relational blueprint for collaboration and change.* New York, NY: Routledge.

Bebbington, P., Jonas, S., Kuipers, E., King, M., Cooper, C., Brugha, T., . . . Jenkins, R. (2011). Childhood sexual abuse and psychosis: Data from a cross-sectional national psychiatric survey in England. *British Journal of Psychiatry, 199,* 29–37.

Beck, A. T. (1979). *Cognitive therapy and the emotional disorders.* New York, NY: Penguin.

Beck, A. T., Rush, A. J., Shaw, B. F., & Emery, G. (1979). *Cognitive therapy of depression.* New York, NY: Guilford.

Biebl, S. J., DiLalla, L. F., Davis, E. K., Lynch, K. A., & Shinn, S. O. (2011). Longitudinal associations among peer victimization and physical and mental health problems. *Journal of Pediatric Psychology, 36,* 868–877.

Bonanno, G. A., Galea, S., Bucciarelli, A., & Vlahov, D. (2007). What predicts psychological resilience after disaster? The role of demographics, resources, and life stress. *Journal of Consulting and Clinical Psychology, 75,* 671–682.

Boss, P. (2006). *Loss, trauma, and resilience: Therapeutic work with ambiguous loss.* New York, NY: Norton.

Boulton, M. J. (2013). Associations between adults' recalled childhood bullying victimization, current social anxiety, coping, and self-blame: Evidence for moderation and indirect effects. *Anxiety, Stress and Coping, 26,* 270–292.

Brown, E. C., Low, S., Smith, B. H., & Haggerty, K. P. (2011). Outcomes from a school-randomized controlled trial of Steps to Respect: A bullying prevention program. *School Psychology Review, 40,* 423–443.

Calhoun, L. G., & Tedeschi, R. G. (1998). Beyond recovery from trauma: Implications for clinical practice and research. *Journal of Social Issues, 54,* 357–371.

Calhoun, L. G., & Tedeschi, R. G. (Eds.). (2014). *Handbook of posttraumatic growth: Research and practice.* New York, NY: Routledge.

Carbone-Lopez, K., Esbensen, F. A., & Brick, B. T. (2010). Correlates and consequences of peer victimization: Gender differences in direct and indirect forms of bullying. *Youth Violence and Juvenile Justice, 8,* 332–350.

Carr, A. (2000). Evidence-based practice in family therapy and systemic consultation. *Journal of Family Therapy, 22,* 29–60.

Carr, A. (2009). The effectiveness of family therapy and systemic interventions for child-focused problems. *Journal of Family Therapy, 31,* 3–45.

Carter, S. (2012). The bully at school: An interdisciplinary approach. *Issues in Comprehensive Pediatric Nursing, 35,* 153–162.

CASEL (Collaborative for Academic, Social, and Emotional Learning). Website. http:www.casel.org

Cheng, Y. Y., Chen, L. M., Ho, H. C., & Cheng, C. L. (2011). Definitions of school bullying in Taiwan: A comparison of multiple perspectives. *School Psychology International, 32,* 227–243.

Cicchetti, D., & Rogosch, F. A. (2001). Diverse patterns of neuroendocrine activity in maltreated children. *Development and Psychopathology, 13,* 677–693.

Cloitre, M., Courtois, C. A., Charuvastra, A., Carapezza, R., Stolbach, B. C., & Green, B. L. (2011). Treatment of complex PTSD: Results of the ISTSS expert clinician survey on best practices. *Journal of Traumatic Stress, 24,* 615–627.

Cohen, P. (2011). Abuse in childhood and the risk for psychotic symptoms in later life. *American Journal of Psychiatry, 168,* 7–8.

Committee for Children. (2015). *Steps to Respect: Bullying prevention for elementary school.* Retrieved from http://www.cfchildren.org/steps-to-respect.aspx

Copeland, W. E., Wolke, D., Lereya, S. T., Shanahan, L., Worthman, C., & Costello, E. J. (2014). Childhood bullying involvement predicts low-grade systemic inflammation into adulthood. *Proceedings of the National Academy of Sciences, 111,* 7570–7575.

Copeland, W. E., Wolke, D., Angold, A., & Costello, E. J. (2013). Adult psychiatric outcomes of bullying and being bullied by peers in childhood and adolescence. *JAMA Psychiatry, 70,* 419–426.

Courtois, C. A., & Ford, J. D. (Eds.). (2009). *Treating complex traumatic stress disorders: An evidence-based guide.* New York, NY: Guilford Press.

Cuadrado-Gordillo, I. (2011). Repetition, power imbalance, and intentionality: Do these criteria conform to teenagers' perception of bullying? A role-based analysis. *Journal of Interpersonal Violence, 27,* 1889–1910. 0886260511431436.

Davidson, R. J., Kabat-Zinn, J., Schumacher, J., Rosenkranz, M., Muller, D., Santorelli, S. F., . . . Sheridan, J. F. (2003). Alterations in brain and immune function produced by mindfulness meditation. *Psychosomatic Medicine, 65,* 564–570.

DeJong, W. (1993). *Building the peace: The resolving conflict creatively program (RCCP).* Washington, DC: Department of Justice, National Inst. of Justice.

deLara, E. W. (2008). Developing a philosophy about bullying and sexual harassment: Cognitive coping strategies among secondary school students. *Journal of School Violence, 7,* 72–96.

deLara, E. W. (2012). Why adolescents don't disclose incidents of bullying and harassment to adults. *Journal of School Violence, 11,* 288–305.

Diego, M. A., & Field, T. (2009). Moderate pressure massage elicits a parasympathetic nervous system response. *International Journal of Neuroscience, 119,* 630–638. doi:10.1080/00207450802329605

Edmiston, E. E., Wang, F., Mazure, C. M., Guiney, J., Sinha, R., Mayes, L. C., & Blumberg, H. P. (2011). Corticostriatal-limbic gray matter morphology in adolescents with self-reported exposure to childhood maltreatment. *Archives of Pediatrics and Adolescent Medicine, 165,* 1069–1077.

Espelage, D. L. (2013). Why are bully prevention programs failing in the U.S.? *Journal of Curriculum and Pedagogy, 10,* 1–4.

Evans, S., Ferrando, S., Findler, M., Stowell, C., Smart, C., & Haglin, D. (2008). Mindfulness-based cognitive therapy for generalized anxiety disorder. *Journal of Anxiety Disorders, 22,* 716–721.

Feder, A., Nestler, E. J., & Charney, D. S. (2009). Psychobiology and molecular genetics of resilience. *Nature Reviews and Neuroscience, 10,* 446–457.

Foa, E. B., Keane, T. M., Friedman, M. J., & Cohen, J. A. (Eds.). (2008). *Effective treatments for PTSD: Practice guidelines from the International Society for Traumatic Stress Studies.* New York, NY: Guilford Press.

Forbes, D., Creamer, M., Phelps, A., Bryant, R., McFarlane, A., Devilly, G. J., . . . Newton, S. (2007). Australian guidelines for the treatment of adults with acute stress disorder and post-traumatic stress disorder. *Australasian Psychiatry, 41,* 637–648.

Garbarino, J., & deLara, E. W. (2002). *And words can hurt forever: How to protect adolescents from bullying, harassment, and emotional violence.* New York, NY: Free Press.

Gladstone, G. L., Parker, G. B., & Malhi, G. S. (2006). Do bullied children become anxious and depressed adults? A cross-sectional investigation of the correlates of bullying and anxious depression. *Journal of Nervous and Mental Disease, 194,* 201–208.

Goleman, D. (1996). Emotional intelligence: Why it can matter more than IQ. *Learning, 24,* 49–50.

Goleman, D. (2006). *Emotional intelligence.* New York, NY: Bantam.

Gruber, J. E., & Fineran, S. (2008). Comparing the impact of bullying and sexual harassment victimization on the mental and physical health of adolescents. *Sex Roles, 59,* 1–13.

Hauner, K. K., Howard, J. D., Zelano, C., & Gottfried, J. A. (2013). Stimulus-specific enhancement of fear extinction during slow-wave sleep. *Nature Neuroscience, 16,* 1553–1555.

Healy, D. (2004). Shaping the intimate: Influences on the experience of everyday nerves. *Social Studies of Science, 34,* 219–245.

Hill, C., & Kearl, H. (2011). *Crossing the line: Sexual harassment at school.* American Association of University Women. 1111 Sixteenth Street NW, Washington, DC 20036.

Jantzer, A. M., Hoover, J. H., & Narloch, R. (2006). The relationship between school-aged bullying and trust, shyness and quality of friendships in young adulthood a preliminary research note. *School Psychology International, 27,* 146–156.

Johnson, S. (2011). An ecological model of workplace bullying: A guide for intervention and research. *Nursing Forum, 46,* 55–63.

Jozefowicz-Simbeni, D. M. H. (2008). An ecological and developmental perspective on dropout risk factors in early adolescence: Role of school social workers in dropout prevention. *Children and Schools*, *30*, 49–62.

Kabat-Zinn, J., & Hanh, T. N. (2009). *Full catastrophe living: Using the wisdom of your body and mind to face stress, pain, and illness*. McHenry, IL: Delta.

Keeshin, B. R., Cronholm, P. F., & Strawn, J. R. (2012). Physiologic changes associated with violence and abuse exposure: An examination of related medical conditions. *Trauma, Violence, and Abuse*, *13*, 41–56. doi:10.1177/1524838011426152

Kim, M. J., Catalano, R. F., Haggerty, K. P., & Abbott, R. D. (2011). Bullying at elementary school and problem behaviour in young adulthood: A study of bullying, violence and substance use from age 11 to age 21. *Criminal Behaviour and Mental Health*, *21*, 136–144.

Leenarts, L. E., Diehle, J., Doreleijers, T. A., Jansma, E. P., & Lindauer, R. J. (2013). Evidence-based treatments for children with trauma-related psychopathology as a result of childhood maltreatment: A systematic review. *European Child and Adolescent Psychiatry*, *22*, 269–283.

Levine, P. A. (2010). *In an unspoken voice: How the body releases trauma and restores goodness*. Berkeley, CA: North Atlantic Books.

Liddle, H. (2010). Treating adolescent substance abuse using multidimensional family therapy. In E. Weisz & J.R. Kazdin (Eds.), *Evidence-based psychotherapies for children and adolescents* (2nd ed., pp. 416–432). New York, NY: Guilford Press.

Mannarino, A. P., Cohen, J. A., & Deblinger, E. (2014). Trauma-focused cognitive-behavioral therapy. In S. Timmer & A. Urquiza (Eds.), *Evidence-based approaches for the treatment of maltreated children* (pp. 165–185). Netherlands: Springer.

Matthiesen, S. B., & Einarsen, S. (2007). Perpetrators and targets of bullying at work: Role stress and individual differences. *Violence and Victims*, *22*, 735–753.

Mishna, F., & Alaggia, R. (2005). Weighing the risks: A child's decision to disclose peer victimization. *Children and Schools*, *27*, 217–226.

Monsvold, T., Bendixen, M., Hagen, R., & Helvik, A. S. (2011). Exposure to teacher bullying in schools: A study of patients with personality disorders. *Nordic Journal of Psychiatry*, *65*, 323–329.

Olweus, D. (2003). A profile of bullying at school. *Educational Leadership*, *60*, 12–17.

Olweus, D. (2004). Bullying at school: Prevalence estimation, a useful evaluation design, and a new national initiative in Norway. *Association for Child Psychology and Psychiatry Occasional Papers*, *23*, 5–17.

Olweus, D. (2007). *Bullying Prevention Program Kit*. Hazelden, MN.

Olweus, D., & Limber, S. P. (2010). Bullying in school: Evaluation and dissemination of the Olweus Bullying Prevention Program. *American Journal of Orthopsychiatry*, *80*, 124–134.

Perry, B. D. (2001). The neurodevelopmental impact of violence in childhood. In D. Schetky & E. P. Benedek (Eds.), *Textbook of child and adolescent forensic psychiatry* (pp. 221–238). Washington, DC: American Psychiatric Press.

Perry, B. D. (2009). Examining child maltreatment through a neurodevelopmental lens: Clinical applications of the neurosequential model of therapeutics. *Journal of Loss and Trauma*, *14*, 240–255.

Renda, J., Vassallo, S., & Edwards, B. (2011). Bullying in early adolescence and its association with anti-social behaviour, criminality and violence 6 and 10 years later. *Criminal Behaviour and Mental Health*, *21*, 117–127.

Resick, P. A., Suvak, M. K., Johnides, B. D., Mitchell, K. S., & Iverson, K. M. (2012). The impact of dissociation on PTSD treatment with cognitive processing therapy. *Depression and Anxiety, 29*, 718–730.

Rohner, R. (1975). *They love me, they love me not: A worldwide study of the effects of parental acceptance and rejection.* New Haven, CT: Human Relations Area Files Press.

Rohner, R. (1986). *The warmth dimension: Foundations of parental acceptance/rejection theory.* Thousand Oaks, CA: Sage.

Rowe, C. L., & Liddle, H. A. (2008). When the levee breaks: Treating adolescents and families in the aftermath of Hurricane Katrina. *Journal of Marital and Family Therapy, 34*, 132–148.

Salmivalli, C., Kärnä, A., & Poskiparta, E. (2011). Counteracting bullying in Finland: The KiVa program and its effects on different forms of being bullied. *International Journal of Behavioral Development, 35*, 405–411.

Schäfer, M., Korn, S., Smith, P. K., Hunter, S. C., Mora-Merchán, J. A., Singer, M. M., & Meulen, K. (2004). Lonely in the crowd: Recollections of bullying. *British Journal of Developmental Psychology, 22*, 379–394.

Schonert-Reichl, K. A., Smith, V., Zaidman-Zait, A., & Hertzman, C. (2012). Promoting children's prosocial behaviors in school: Impact of the 'Roots of Empathy' program on the social and emotional competence of school-aged children. *School Mental Health, 4*, 1–21.

Schor, A. N. (2003). Early relational trauma, disorganized attachment, and the development of a predisposition to violence. In M. Solomon & D. J. Siegel (Eds.), *Healing trauma: Attachment, mind, body and brain* (pp. 107–167). New York, NY: Norton.

Scott, W. (1995). *Institutions and organizations.* Thousand Oaks, CA: Sage.

Segal, Z. V., Williams, J. M. G., & Teasdale, J. D. (2012). *Mindfulness-based cognitive therapy for depression.* New York, NY: Guilford Press.

Selfridge, J. (2004). The resolving conflict creatively program: How we know it works. *Theory into Practice, 43*, 59–67.

Shapiro, F. (1998). *EMDR: The breakthrough "eye movement" therapy for overcoming anxiety, stress, and trauma.* New York, NY: Basic Books.

Shapiro, F. (2013). *Getting past your past: Take control of your life with self-help techniques from EMDR therapy.* New York, NY: Rodale.

Silverman, W. K., Ortiz, C. D., Viswesvaran, C., Burns, B. J., Kolko, D. J., Putnam, F. W., & Amaya-Jackson, L. (2008). Evidence-based psychosocial treatments for children and adolescents exposed to traumatic events. *Journal of Clinical Child and Adolescent Psychology, 37*, 156–183.

Sourander, A., Jensen, P., Rönning, J. A., Niemelä, S., Helenius, H., Sillanmäki, L., . . . Almqvist, F. (2007). What is the early adulthood outcome of boys who bully or are bullied in childhood? The Finnish "From a Boy to a Man" study. *Pediatrics, 120*, 397–404.

Sourander, A., Ronning, J., Brunstein-Klomek, A., Gyllenberg, D., Kumpulainen, K., Niemelä, S., . . . Almqvist, F. (2009). Childhood bullying behavior and later psychiatric hospital and psychopharmacologic treatment: Findings from the Finnish 1981 birth cohort study. *Archives of General Psychiatry, 66*, 1005–1012.

Stratton, P. (2011). *The evidence base of systemic family and couples therapies.* Warrington, United Kingdom: Association for Family Therapy.

Streeter, C. C., Gerbarg, P. L., Saper, R. B., Ciraulo, D. A., & Brown, R. P. (2012). Effects of yoga on the autonomic nervous system, gamma-aminobutyric-acid, and allostasis in epilepsy, depression, and post-traumatic stress disorder. *Medical Hypotheses, 78*, 571–579.

Swearer, S. M., Turner, R. K., Givens, J. E., & Pollack, W. S. (2008). "You're So Gay!": Do different forms of bullying matter for adolescent males? *School Psychology Review, 37*, 160.

Tedeschi, R. G., & Calhoun, L. G. (1995). *Trauma and transformation: Growing in the aftermath of suffering.* Thousand Oaks, CA: Sage.

Tedeschi, R. G., & Calhoun, L. G. (2004). Posttraumatic growth: Conceptual foundations and empirical evidence. *Psychological Inquiry, 15*, 1–18.

Teicher, M. H., Samson, J. A., Sheu, Y. S., Polcari, A., & McGreenery, C. E. (2010). Hurtful words: Association of exposure to peer verbal abuse with elevated psychiatric symptom scores and corpus callosum abnormalities. *American Journal of Psychiatry, 167*, 1464–1471.

The Association for Family Therapy and Systemic Practice. (2010). *The evidence base of systemic family and couples therapy.* Warrington, United Kingdom: Author.

Twemlow, S. W., Fonagy, P., Sacco, F. C., & Brethour, J. R. (2006). Teachers who bully students: A hidden trauma. *International Journal of Social Psychiatry, 52*, 187–198.

Twemlow, S. W., Biggs, B. K., Nelson, T. D., Vernberg, E. M., Fonagy, P., & Twemlow, S. W. (2008). Effects of participation in a martial arts–based antibullying program in elementary schools. *Psychology in the Schools, 45*, 947–959.

Vaillancourt, T., Duku, E., Decatanzaro, D., Macmillan, H., Muir, C., & Schmidt, L. A. (2008). Variation in hypothalamic-pituitary-adrenal axis activity among bullied and non-bullied children. *Aggressive Behavior, 34*, 294–305.

Van der Kolk, B. A. (2005). Developmental trauma disorder: Toward a rational diagnosis for children with complex trauma histories. *Psychiatric Annals, 35*, 401–408.

Vazsonyi, A. T., Belliston, L. M., & Flannery, D. J. (2004). Evaluation of a school-based universal violence prevention program low-, medium-, and high-risk children. *Youth Violence and Juvenile Justice, 2*, 185–206.

Vissing, Y. M., Straus, M. A., Gelles, R. J., & Harrop, J. W. (1991). Verbal aggression by parents and psychosocial problems of children. *Child Abuse and Neglect, 15*, 223–238.

Von Bertalanffy, L. (1973). *General system theory: Foundations, development, applications* (Rev. ed.). New York, NY: George Braziller.

Weathers, F. W., Litz, B. T., Herman, D. S., Huska, J. A., & Keane, T. M. (1991). *The PTSD Checklist—Civilian Version (PCL-C).* Available from FW Weathers National Center for PTSD, Boston Veterans Affairs Medical Center 150 S. Huntington Avenue.

White, B., Driver, S., & Warren, A. M. (2008). Considering resilience in the rehabilitation of people with traumatic disabilities. *Rehabilitation Psychology, 53*, 9–17.

Wolke, D., Copeland, W. E., Angold, A., & Costello, E. J. (2013). Impact of bullying in childhood on adult health, wealth, crime, and social outcomes. *Psychological Science, 24*, 1958–1970.

Wong, D. S., Cheng, C. H., Ngan, R. M., & Ma, S. K. (2011). Program effectiveness of a restorative whole-school approach for tackling school bullying in Hong Kong. *International Journal of Offender Therapy and Comparative Criminology, 55*, 846–862.

Young, A. S., Klap, R., Sherbourne, C. D., & Wells, K. B. (2001). The quality of care for depressive and anxiety disorders in the United States. *Archives of General Psychiatry, 58*, 55–61.

Zapf, D., & Einarsen, S. (2011). Individual antecedents of bullying: Victims and perpetrators. In S. Einarsen, H. Hoel, D. Zapf, & C. Cooper (Eds.), *Bullying and harassment in the workplace: Developments in theory, research, and practice* (pp. 177–200). Boca Raton, FL: CRC Press.

INDEX

love and, 108–109
to school
    bullying effects on, 135
attachment anxiety
    in relationships
        hippocampus in, 109
attachment issues
    trust and, 108–109
attachment pattern
    bullying and decisions related to,
        134–135
attachment theory
    infidelity and, 89–90
attention-deficit/hyperactivity
        disorder (ADHD)
    bullying related to, 97
attributional theory
    in rejection-related counseling, 72
attribution bias
    hostile, 183
authenticity
    sense of
        finding, 55–56
authentic voice
    finding, 55–56
autonomy
    psychological needs for, 71
avoidance
PTSD and, 20

Babbi J., 92
balance
    interpersonal
        finding, 55–56
Barbie dolls
    body image issues related to, 37,
        125–126
    sexual harassment issues related to,
        125–126
behavior(s). see also specific types, e.g.,
        aggressive behavior
    aggressive (see aggressive behavior)
    criminal
        violent behavior precipitating,
            144–146
    promiscuous
        of gay teenagers in heterosexual
            relationships, 120
    shunning
        decision-making related to, 149–151

trauma-related, 17
violent
    bullying resulting in, 102–103
    criminal behavior related to,
        144–146
behavioral immune system
    being different and, 50–51
Behre, W., 132
being different, 30–51
    academic prowess and, 39–40
    behavioral immune system
        and, 50–51
    body image and, 36–39
    bullying related to, 197–198, xx–xxi
    disabilities, 41–42
    economic status and, 42–43
    examples of, 30–31
    racial, 40–41
    sexual orientation–related, 44–50
        case example, 45–49
    shame and, 31–36 (see also shame)
    small differences and, 43–44
    as threat, 30
belonging
    psychological needs for, 71
Bennett, L., 115
Bentall, R.P., 105
Berchtold, A., 41
Berlan, E.D., 45
bias(es)
    hostile attribution, 183
    hostile cognitive, 146
biological reactions
    stress and trauma and, 210–211
body(is)
    children ostracized about, 36–39
body image
    APBS and, 25
    Barbie dolls effects on, 37,
        125–126
    being different and, 36–39
        case examples, 37–39
    sexual harassment effects on, 115
Bonanno, G.A., 209
Boulton, M.J., 98
Bowes, L., 166, 162
Bowlby, J., 74, 108
boy(s)
    physical bullying by, 198–199
    physical violence among, 3

brain
  angry words echoing in, 92–111,
      xxi–xxii (*see also* "angry words
      echo in my brain")
  of bullies, 18–19
  bullying effects on
    biological changes, xx
  fear of danger experienced by, 17
  hypothalamic-pituitary-
      adrenocortical axis of
    activation of, 109
  stress and trauma effects on,
      210–211
  verbal abuse imprint on, 18
brain development
  trauma effects on, 17–18
Braithwaite, J., 34
Brethour, J.R., 187
Bronfenbrenner, U., 180–181
brother(s)
  bullying by, 164–165
Bucciarelli, A., 209
Buck, P.S., 30
bully(ies)
  anxiety of, 97–99
  athletes not targeted by, 137–138
  brain of, 18–19
  deficits in moral compassion in, 186
  guilt of, 42
  lack of insight or of taking personal
      responsibility in, 100–101
  parents as, 159–161 (*see also*
      parent(s), as bullies)
  proving them wrong, 182–184
  siblings as, 161–166
  suicidal ideation of, 103–104
  workplace
    recognizing, 13
bullying. *see also* adult post-bullying
      syndrome (APBS); childhood
      bullying
  ACEs related to, 93–95 (*see also*
      adverse childhood experiences
      (ACEs))
  ADHD and, 97
  adult effects of, 16–29 (*see also* adult
      post-bullying syndrome (APBS))
  by adults, 159–161, 102–103
  adults coping with aftermath of,
      207–209, 172–173

alcoholism related to, 139
among adolescents, 36
"angry words echo in my brain,"
      xxi–xxii (*see also* "angry words
      echo in my brain")
APBS (*see* adult post-bullying syn-
      drome (APBS))
by athletes, 10
  impact on intimate partner
      relationships, 86–88
athletes not targeted by, 137–138
attachment at school related to, 135
attachment issues related to,
      108–109
attachment pattern effects on,
      134–135
being different and, 30–51, 197–198,
      xx–xxi (*see also* being different)
being parent after being, 173–175
biological changes brain undergoes
      related to, xx
causes of, 197–198
  parents as bullies, 159–161
cerebral changes related to, 96–97
circular nature of, 97
consequences in adulthood,
      198, 14–15
  detrimental outcomes, 196
  infidelity-related, 89–91
  lifelong negative consequences, 95,
      109–111
  positive, 181–182
  post-traumatic growth, 209–210
  relationship-related, 200
  resiliency, 209–210
C-reactive protein levels related to, 96
criminal behavior related to, 144–146
cyberbullying (*see* cyberbullying)
dating violence and, 68–69
decisions affected by, 132–157, xxii
      (*see also* decision-making,
      bullying effects on)
decisions and decision-making effects
      of, 201
definitions of, 187, 4–8, xx
depression related to, 61,
      105, 99–100
described, 196
developmental effects of, 52–65
disabilities, 41–42

bullying (*cont.*)
case example, 86–88
teachers' perception of, 187
self-esteem effects of, 143
self-harm resulting from, 57, 143, 103–104
self-medicating after, 57
self-talk related to, 143
sense of self after, 55–56
sexual harassment, 201, 111–113 (*see also* sexual harassment)
sexual orientation–related, 44–50
shame related to, 31–33, 100–101
sibling, 202, 161–166 (*see also* sibling bullying)
small differences and, 43–44
social anxiety after, 97–99, 56–57
statistics on, 2–4
strategies for coping through, 204–209
alternative treatments, 210–211
CBT, 207–208
CCM, 209
EMDR therapy, 208–209
mindfulness-based CBT, 208
multidimensional family therapy, 209
multisystemic family therapy, 209
PCL-C, 208
programs, 205–207
TF-CBT, 208
study on
importance of, xix–xx
methods in, xvii–xix
questionnaire for, xvii–xix
reasons for participation in, xvii
retrospective, xix
suicide related to, 103–104
systemic responses to, 96–97
in systems, 135, 158, 9–14 (*see also* system(s))
trauma related to, 17–19, 35–36, 93–95, 124–125, 210–211, xx (*see also* trauma)
trust issues related to, 108–109 (*see also* trust; trust issues; trust issues in adulthood)
types of, 2
unexpected outcomes of, 203, 177–195, xxiii

cognitive growth, 179–181
educators can contribute to problem, 187–191
independence, 193–194
morality issues, 185–187
positive consequences, 181–182
positives in relationships, 193
post-traumatic growth, 179–181
proving the bullier wrong, 182–184
self-acceptance and self-worth, 194–195
strength, 191–192
success, 184–185
US Department of Education on, 5
verbal
imprint on brain, 18
at workplace, 14
victims of (*see* victim(s))
shame among, 31
well-being effects of, 92–111
of well-known people, 184–185
White House Press Conference on by Obama, 184–185
witnesses of
effects on, 3, 81
workplace, 12–14 (*see also* workplace bullying)
Bullying: A Guide to Research, Intervention, and Prevention, 42
bus
school
sexual harassment on, 118–119
Butterfield, F., 34–35

Calhoun, L.G., 210, 179
Campbell, M.A., 161
CASEL (Collaborative for Academic, Social, and Emotional Learning), 207, 206
Caspi, A., 162
Catalano, R.F., 103
CBT. *see* cognitive-behavioral therapy (CBT)
CCM. *see* collaborative change model (CCM)
CDC. *see* Centers for Disease Control and Prevention (CDC)
Centers for Disease Control and Prevention (CDC)
on ACEs effects on adults, 93–95

name-calling, 2
Nansel, T.R., 105
National Basketball Association
    on bullying, 13
National Football League (NFL)
    bullying and harassment in, 13
National Institute of Health study
    on bullying, 2–3
National Longitudinal Survey of Youth
        (NLSY97), 145
need(s)
    psychological, 71
negative changes in thinking and mood
    PTSD and, 20
neurodevelopment
    ACEs effects on, 95
Newman, B.M., 115
Newman, P.R., 115
Newsweek, 72
NFL. *see* National Football
        League (NFL)
NLSY97. *see* National Longitudinal
        Survey of Youth (NLSY97)
Northwestern University
    shock study at, 211
"not seeing it," 11

Obama, B., Pres., 184–185, xxiii
    White House Press Conference on
        bullying by, 184–185
obesity
    bullying related to, 36–39
Olweus, D., 6, 4, 145
"optimistic child," 183–184
ostracism, 72, 135
    body shape– and size–related, 36–39
    cyber-, 72
    feelings resulting from, 73
    purposes of, 72
    types of, 72
Ostracism: The Power of Silence, 73
Ouellet-Morin, I., 96
overweight
    mental health effects of being,
        101–102

parent(s)
    being
        after being bullied, 173–175
        as bullies, 159–161

impact of, 159–161
    of LGBTQ youth, 160–161
    getting help from, 172–173
parental bullying, 159–161
parenting
    childhood bullying victimization
        effects on, 168–176
    on getting help from parent,
        172–173
    intergenerational effects, 170–172
    parents handling emotional effects
        of bullying, 175–176
Park, J.H., 50–51
partnership(s)
    intimate
        rejection effects on, 74
passive incomprehension, 87
PCL–C. *see* PTSD Checklist–Civilian
        Version (PCL–C)
PeaceBuilders, 205
peer bullying
    sibling bullying as, 202
peer relationships
    bullying and betrayal in
        trust issues in adulthood related
            to, 75–81
Peony, 30
people-pleasing
    APBS and, 23
    described, 54–55
    revenge *vs.*, 52–65, xxi
"permission"
    to bully, 10–11
Perren, S., 185
personality
    bullying effects on decisions related
        to, 141–143
physical abuse, 2
    at school
        "games" played related
            to, 152–153
physical bullying
    by boys, 198–199
physical violence
    among boys, 3
Piaget, J., 138
Pinto-Gouveia, J., 35–36
Pittet, I., 41
playground
    bullying on, 52–53

shame and, 35–36
trauma-focused cognitive-behavioral
    therapy (TF-CBT)
    in bullying-related treatment, 208
Trauma Symptom Checklist for Children
    victims of bullying scoring on, 177
trust
    attachment issues and, 108–109
    relationship impact of, 66–67
trust issues
    in adulthood (*see* trust issues in
        adulthood)
    APBS and, 22–23
trust issues in adulthood
    bullying and betrayal experienced
        in youthful friendships or peer
        relationships related to, 75–81
    case example, 76–81
T.S. v. the Rapides Parish School Board,
    122–123
Ttofi, M., 206, 145
Tucker, C.J., 162
Turner, H., 162
Twemlow, S.W., 187
twin(s)
    identical
        resiliency to bullying at school, 180

*Understanding School Bullying: Its Nature
    and Prevention Strategies*, 206
unexpected outcomes
    of bullying and harassment, 203,
        177–195 (*see also* bullying;
        harassment)
US Department of Education
    on bullying, 5
US Education Amendments of 1972
    Title IX of, 114

value(s)
    moral
        cyberbullying related to lack
            of, 185
Van der Kolk, B., 203
Varese, F., 105
verbal abuse, 2
    cerebral changes related to, 96–97
    imprint on brain, 18
    sexual harassment–related, 120
Verbal Abuse Questionnaire, 18

verbal bullying
    imprint on brain, 18
    at workplace, 14
victim(s)
    of bullying
        scoring on Trauma Symptom
            Checklist for Children, 177
        shame among, 31–33
        workplace-related, 12
Vincenza, 82–84, ix
violence
    dating
        bullying and, 68–69
        CDC on, 166
        sexual harassment and, 117
    domestic
        bullying and, 146
    physical
        among boys, 3
    relational
        among girls, 3
    shame-related
        absence of guilt and, 35
    sibling
        prevalence of, 161–162
    social exclusion and, 183
violent behavior
    bullying resulting in, 102–103
    criminal behavior related
        to, 144–146
Virginia Tech
    massacre at
        revenge related to, 60
Vivolo-Kantor, A.M., 5
Vlahov, D., 209
voice
    authentic
        finding, 55–56

Wang, J., 105
Warren, 1
Washington Post, 9
weight
    bullying related to, 36
    as last acceptable prejudice, 101
Wei, M., 121
Weiner, J., 97
well-being
    bullying effects on, 92–111 (*see also*
        "angry words echo in my brain")